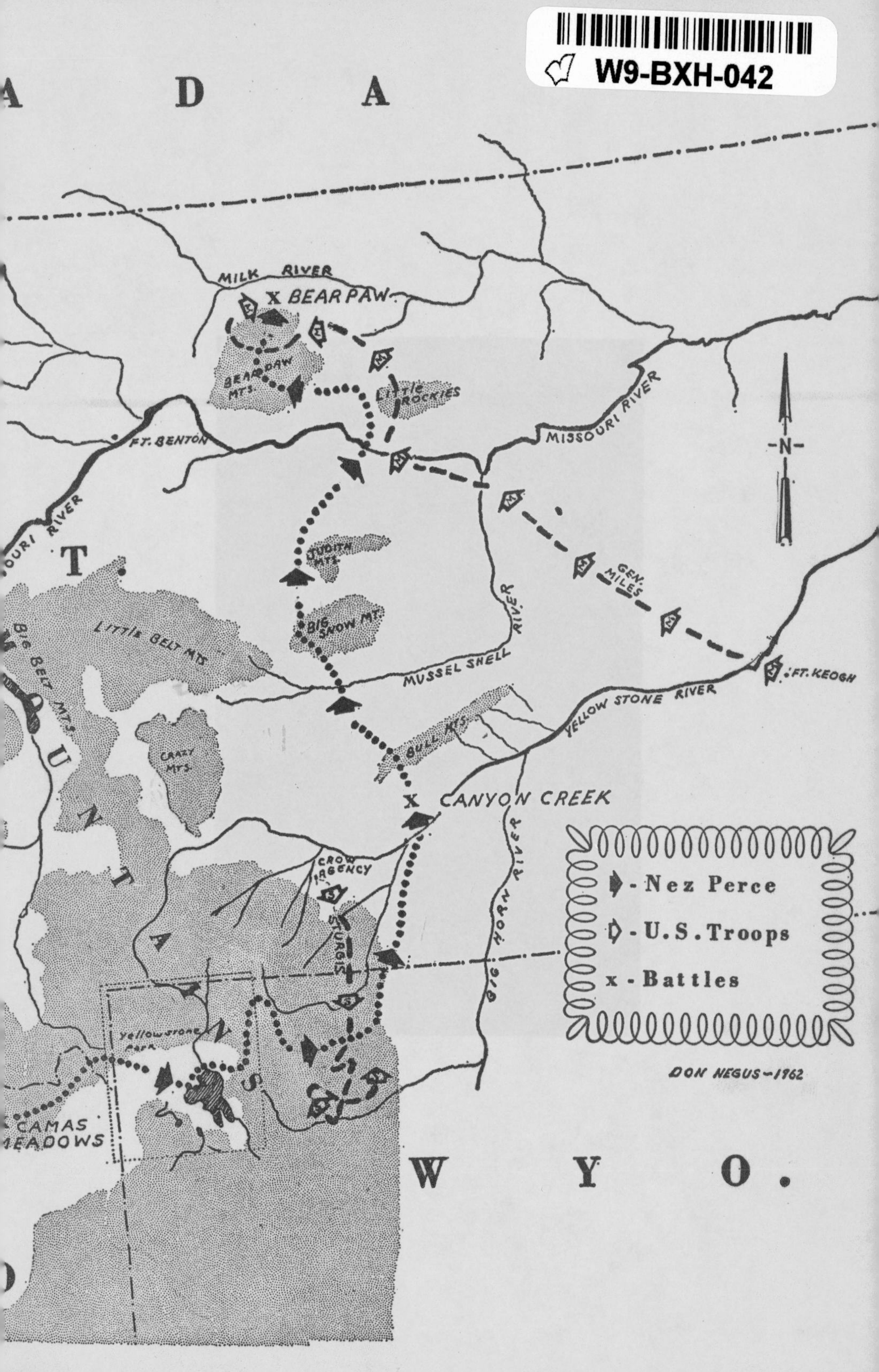

A D A
MILK RIVER
X BEAR PAW
BEARPAW MTS.
Little ROCKIES
FT. BENTON
MISSOURI RIVER
OURI RIVER
T
JUDITH MTS
BIG SNOW MT.
LITTLE BELT MTS
BIG BELT MTS.
CRAZY MTS.
MUSSEL SHELL RIVER
GEN. MILES
FT. KEOGH
YELLOW STONE RIVER
BULL MTS.
X CANYON CREEK
CROW AGENCY
STURGIS
BIG HORN RIVER
Yellowstone Park
CAMAS MEADOWS
W Y O.
- Nez Perce
- U.S. Troops
x - Battles
DON NEGUS–1962

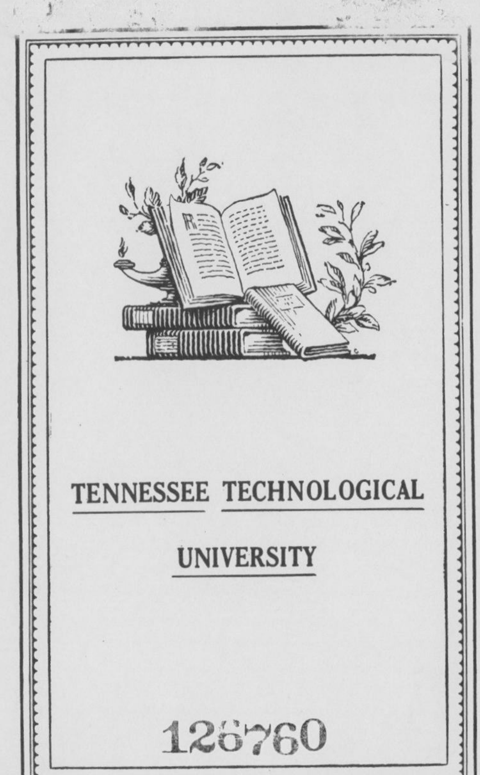
TENNESSEE TECHNOLOGICAL
UNIVERSITY
126760

THE LAST STAND OF THE NEZ PERCE

Destruction of a People

OTHER BOOKS BY HARVEY CHALMERS II

West to the Setting Sun, 1943

Drums Against Frontenac, 1949

Joseph Brandt: Mohawk, 1955

The Birth of the Erie Canal, 1960

THE LAST STAND OF THE NEZ PERCE

DESTRUCTION OF A PEOPLE

by HARVEY CHALMERS II

TWAYNE PUBLISHERS
NEW YORK

Library of Congress Catalog Card Number 62–19356

END PAPERS BY DON NEGUS

TYPE SET BY BARDU LINOTYPING SERVICE INC.

PRINTED BY PROFILE PRESS

For

SHIRLEY,

my blue-eyed Grass Flower

ACKNOWLEDGMENTS

To Alvin M. Josephy, Jr. for permission to use photographs from the files of American Heritage Publishing Co., Inc.

To Eve Rockwell Little for assembling a number of the photographs.

To Commander Theodore Little for suggestions, advice, and a true copy of Chief Joseph's speech at the surrender.

For research in photography: Mrs. Emmett Avery
Mrs. Emmett B. Moore
Mrs. James A. Raymer
Mary Ann Sheldon

To Washington State University for the privilege of using photographs from their archives.

To the Memory of L. V. McWhorter who secured the Yellow Wolf story.

To Don Negus for drawing the endpaper maps.

To National Park Service and its representative, Jack R. Williams at Big Hole Battlefield for photographs.

CONTENTS

LIST OF ILLUSTRATIONS

Following page 160

FOREWORD

THE TITLE OF THIS BOOK DERIVES FROM THE BELIEF THAT TO DESTROY the spirit of a people is to destroy the people. Individuals of the race may linger on, but they soon become insignificant and are absorbed by their conquerors, just as the glory that was Greece merged into the grandeur that was Rome.

During the latter half of the Nineteenth Century the path of progress in the United States became the course of destruction. The vast forests of the northeast were destroyed to make room for farms. The soil, being thin, was soon exhausted. The farms were abandoned. The farmers moved westward. Stunted hardwood trees inadequately replaced the towering pines and hemlocks which had graced the northeastern hills.

Then the armies of the North destroyed the South. After that many of the veterans were sent to the far west to hold the Indians in check while buffalo hunters wantonly destroyed the buffaloes. Meanwhile gold had been discovered in the northwest. In the stampede of placer miners, Indian rights were brushed aside.

The culture of the Indians living in the basin drained by the Columbia River (Oregon, Washington and eastern Idaho) somewhat resembled that of the Cro-Magnon during the late Stone Age of Europe. They were a sturdy, hardy people, well fed and happy and living within the abundant supporting power of their environment. They lived in widely separated groups according to the distribution of game, and although they were of one tribe (Nez Perce), they had no central authority or government. In this they differed from the Iroquois of the northeast and were therefore more easily subdued. Indeed the Iroquois were never completely subdued, for the Mohawks at Oshweken in Ontario rebelled against constituted authority even within the past decade.

Most of the Nez Perce bands, when commanded by order

from Washington, tamely went on reservation at Lapwai and endeavored to adjust to farm life and church worship. But the Wallamwatkins led by Chief Joseph, living in the Wallowa Valley in eastern Oregon, and the bands of Chief White Bird and Chief Looking Glass refused to settle on a designated portion of the Lapwai Reservation.

According to the record, the Nez Perce, more than any other tribe, had been friendly to the white people. They occasionally fought with their hereditary enemies, the Sioux, in southern Montana, but although they endured plenty of provocations from white settlers, they avoided any sort of armed clash, mainly because the Nez Perce didn't have a sufficiency of arms. The best of archers have no chance against mountain and field artillery, gatling guns and mortar fire.

As pioneer ranchers, cowboys and gold miners increased their aggravations and depredations, the warlike bands grimly set their teeth and turned the other cheek. They were a proud people but they endured undeserved humiliations without complaining, choking back their offended dignity because they had no choice. However, when an irascible, ill-natured cowboy and a rancher, assuming that a Wallamwatkin had stolen their horses, heedlessly shot and killed a prominent warrior at the edge of the Indian village, Chief Joseph's young men could no longer restrain their resentment.

When the white men returned to their ranch they found the horses quietly grazing in the front yard. Only an hour or two had elapsed, but it was too late for explanations and apologies. The Earth Mother had drunk the blood of one of her children almost before his very door. The young men took matters in their own hands. Within twenty-four hours a war had started which did not end until War Chief Joseph, retreating but still undefeated, surrendered the remnant of his band practically within sight of the border between Montana and Canada. Despite abundant equipment and overwhelming numbers, only the silver-starred genius of Captain Nelson Miles saved American arms from disgrace. Nothing saved them from ridicule.

The sort of vengeance which was visited upon the Confederate States after the Civil War then descended upon the Wallamwatkins. They were sent to malarial Indian Territory, a warm climate unfavorable for hardy northern people. Eight years later 268 survivors were sent north, 118 to Lapwai Reservation in northern Idaho, the rest, including Chief Joseph, to the Colville Reservation in the State of Washington.

In this narrative, the chain of events leading up to the outbreak of war is related step by step according to the records. Then Yellow Wolf, a nephew of Chief Joseph, gives his account of the same events, as told by him in a personal interview (through an interpreter) to L. V. McWhorter, a rancher and a man of education and refinement. The first battle, the flight of the Indians, the succeeding battles, the surrender, captivity and the final return are told in the same manner: first according to the record and then as Yellow Wolf remembered them. Thus there are two voices, one of the Twentieth Century, the other a North American primitive speaking from a level somewhat higher than that of late Stone Age. Alternating, a chapter at a time, each tells the story from his own viewpoint and in his own way.

Portions of the text marked □ are quoted from "War Chief Joseph" by Helen Howard and Dan McGrath, by permission of the owners of the copyright, Caxton Printers, Ltd., Caldwell, Idaho.

Portions of the text marked ○ are quoted from "Nez Perce Joseph" by General O. O. Howard, published by Lee & Shepard. According to the letter received from the successors to Lee & Shepard the book is now in public domain.

Portions of the text marked † are quoted from "Chief Joseph, the Biography of a Great Indian," by C. A. Fee, published by Wilson-Erickson.

CAST OF INDIAN CHARACTERS:

MEN, WOMEN, CHILDREN OF THE WALLOWA VALLEY

NON-CHRISTIAN NEZ PERCE—the Wallamwatkins and militarily allied bands, roaming the territory adjoining the Snake and Salmon Rivers, who acknowledged Chief Joseph as their leader.

Aihits Palojami (Fair Land)—Wife of Alokut. Died at Camas Meadows.

Alokut—Chief Joseph's younger brother, a man of peace, but a natural military leader.

Atsipeeten—A twelve-year-old girl of the Wallamwatkins who, with her grandmother, Intetah, was killed by a bursting shell during the last battle near Bearpaw Mountains.

Auskewush—Also called Espowyes (Light in the Mountain)—In White Bird Battle and all succeeding engagements; escaped to Canada; later returned to Lapwai, where he died.

Chelooyeen (Bow and Arrow Case), alias Philip Evans.—Chronicler.

Chuslum Hahlap Kanoot (Naked-footed Bull)—Nez Perce scout. Killed R. Dietrich, German music teacher, at Mammoth Springs, Yellowstone Park.

Chuslum Mox Mox (Yellow Bull)—Nez Perce sentinel at White Bird Canyon.

Dakoopin (Broken Leg)—Nez Perce woman killed by a white man while she was chasing his horse out of her garden in Imnaha Valley.

Dookiyoon (Smoker)—An old warrior who carried a flintlock.

Eeahlokoon—Received a leg wound in Canyon Creek skirmish.

Elaskolatat (Animal Entering a Hole), alias Joe Albert—A Christian Nez Perce who deserted from General Howard to Chief Joseph after Clearwater Battle. Wounded at Canyon Creek.

Espowyes—See "Auskewush."

Hatya Takonnin—A medicine man. He was the father of Speaking Thunder, one of Chief Joseph's warriors. He wanted his son to go with him on reservation but his son chose to continue with the Wallamwatkins. Hatya predicted accurately that all of the Wallamwatkins would be killed or put in bondage.

Heinmot Ilppilp (Red Thunder)—Killed at Clearwater Battle.

Heinmot Tooyalakekt (Thunder Traveling to Loftier Mountain Heights)—Alias Chief Joseph of the Wallamwatkin Band of the Lower Nez Perce.

Hekkik Takkawkaakon (Charging Hawk)—Rear guard scout and game hunter for Nez Perce during flight to Canada.

Henawit (Going Fast)
Jyeloo } Committed depredations upon the white people which contributed to hostilities.

Heyoom Iklakit (Grizzly Bear Lying Down)—Participated in Bear Paw Battle. Talked in sign language with Cheyenne scout. Received gesture of peace; treacherously murdered by the Cheyennes.

Heyoom Pishkish (Lame John)—Survived a stabbing by Itsiyiyi Opseen.

Hohots Elotoht (Bad Boy Grizzly Bear)—At Big Hole Battle he was thrown by a seven-foot tall soldier.

Howallits (Mean Man)—Wounded at Clearwater Battle.

Husis Owyeen, alias Wettustolalumtikt—Participated in Salmon River outbreak. Fought at White Bird, Big Hole and Bearpaw, escaped to Canada. Became a chronicler.

Intetah—See "Atsipeeten."

Iskatpoo Tismooktismook (Black Trail)—Yellow Wolf's uncle. Wounded at Big Hole.

Itsiyiyi Opseen (Coyote with Flints)—While drunk he stabbed Lame John.

Itskimze Kin (Feet and Hands Cut Off)
Wettiwetti Houlis (Vicious Weasel) } Sentinels posted by Chief Joseph on the rim of White Bird Canyon the night before the battle, Itskimze carried the message of warning.

Jeekunkun (John Dog)—Wounded at Big Hole.

Jyeloo—See "Henawit."

Ketalkpoosmin (Stripes Turned Down)—A Flathead name. Helped in capture of Gibbon's cannon at Big Hole.

Kipkip Owyeen (Wounded Breast)—Wounded at Clearwater Battle.

Kosooyeen (Going Alone)—Together with Red Star he executed a successful turning movement on Captain Norwood's detachment at the Camas Meadows skirmish.

Kowtoliks—A warrior who thundered out orders during the confusion of battle at the Big Hole.

Kowwaspo
Koyehkown } Shot by mistake by Hush-hush-cute at Bear Paw.

Lahpeealoot (Two Flocks on Water)—At Salmon River outbreak and narrator of Cottonwood skirmish.

Lakochets Kunnin (Rattle on Blanket)—Fought at Camas Meadows.

Lazzykoon—Killed at Big Hole.

Lepeet Hessemdooks (Two Moons)—Nez Perce chronicler.

Many Wounds—Nez Perce interpreter. Son of Wottolen.

Mimpow Owyeen, alias Weesculatat (Wounded Mouth)—Killed at Cottonwood.

Moositsa (Four Blankets)—Boy onlooker at White Bird Canyon Battle.

Moses, Charley—Chief of a band on the Columbia River.

Natalekin—An old warrior of the Wallamwatkins. He bore responsibility for the pony herd.

Nosnakuhet Moxmox (Yellow Long Nose)—Scouted in Yellowstone Park.

Old Man Burning Coals—A Wallamwatkin who owned some fine, swift horses, but would not lend them to Yellow Wolf and his friends for scouting the back trail after reaching the Big Hole.

Old Yellow Wolf—Uncle of Yellow Wolf. He received head wounds at Clearwater Battle.

Ooyekun
Tomamo
Tahmiteahkun } Nez Perce who returned from the Sioux camp in Canada to the States

Otskai (Going Out)—Prominent warrior in the raid on General Howard at Camas Meadows.

Otstotpoo (Fire Body)—Fought at White Bird Canyon.

Owhi—Member of the Yakima Band. Joined Chief Joseph in the Bitterroot Valley.

Pahka Alyanakt (Five Snows)—While drunk he mortally wounded Stripes Turned Down. Five Snows was later killed in battle.

Pahka Pahtahank (Five Fogs)—Shot at Big Hole while shooting arrows.

Pahkatos Owyeen (Five Wounds)
Wahchumyus (Rainbow)
} Two Nez Perce buffalo hunters and leaders in battle, always together, and known by reputation throughout the western tribes. They had vowed that both would die in battle and on the same day. They achieved this at Big Hole.

Pahkatos Watyekit (Five Times Looking Up)—Involved in preliminary hostilities.

Pauh Wahyakt—An old Wallamwatkin who seemed to be able to create a dense fog by smoking his pipe.

Peetomyanon Teemenah (Hawk Heart)
Teeto Hoonod
} Single-handed they held back Col. Sturgis and 7th Cavalry at mouth of Canyon Creek while Wallamwatkins escaped.

Peopeo Ipsewahk (Lone Bird)—At Big Hole Camp he loudly predicted disaster and urged the Indians to break camp right away and move on. His prophecy was ignored. Shot by Hush-hush-cute at Bear Paw by mistake.

Putim Soklahtomah (Ten Owl)—Nez Perce scout in Yellowstone Park.

Quiloishkish—A Lower Nez Perce who deserted to the Flatheads.

Seeyakoon Ilppilp (Red Scout)—Fought in Cottonwood skirmish.

Tabador, Henry—Half-blood interpreter, considered untrustworthy.

Tahmiteahkun—*See* "Ooyekun."

Tahomchits Humkon—Medicine man.

Tahwis Tokaitat (Bighorn Bow)—At Big Hole he recovered body of Red Moccasin Tops.

Teeto Hoonod—*See* "Peetomyanon Teemenah."

Teeweawea—Active in scouting before the Nez Perce assembled in White Bird Canyon.

Teeweeyownah (Over Point of Hill)—Fought at Clearwater, Camas Meadows; killed at Canyon Creek.

Teminisiki (No Heart)—Yellow Wolf's cousin. He permitted a Nez Perce woman to sleep beside him and paid the penalty. He was killed in the next battle.

Tenahtalkah Weyun (Dropping from a Cliff)
Pitpellooheen (Calf of Leg)
} Captured Colonel Gibbon's cannon.

Tewit Toitoi–Killed at Big Hole.

Tipyahlanah Siskon (Eagle Robe)–Father of the redoubtable Wahlitits. Tipyehlanah was killed near the Salmon River by Larry Ott, who promptly fled to Florence Mines and hid by dressing like a Chinese.

Tiskusia Kowiakowia–Nez Perce scout in Yellowstone.

Tissaikpee (Granite Crystal)–Killed at Big Hole.

Toma Alwawinmi (Springtime)–One of Joseph's wives. She had just had a new baby.

Tomamo–*See* "Ooyekun."

Tomyunmene–Warrior in front line at Clearwater Battle.

Tookleiks (Fish Trap)
Wetyetmas Hapima (Surrounded Goose) } Old Nez Perce killed by Crow Tribe while looking for horses.

Towassis (Bowstring)–Onlooker at Big Hole Battle.

Tuekakas–Father of Chief Joseph. During his life recognized by all bands of Lower Nez Perce for his tenacious clinging to his homeland and the faith of his people.

Wahchumyus (Rainbow)–*See* "Pahkatos Owyeen."

Wahnistas Aswetesk–During Big Hole massacre he sat before his tepee smoking a pipe. He was shot twenty times, and Yellow Wolf saw steam come out of the wounds. Yet he survived to die years later of malaria in Indian Territory.

Wattes Kunnin (Earth Blanket)–Scout at Canyon Creek.

Watyochakoon (Passing Overhead)–Warrior.

Wayakat (Going Across)–Killed at Clearwater Battle.

Weesculatat–Killed at Cottonwood.

Wemastaktus–Warrior at Clearwater Battle.

Wettiwetti Houlis (Vicious Weasel)–*See* "Itskimze Kin."

Wetyetmas Hapima (Surrounded Goose)–*See* "Tookleiks."

Wetyetmas Likleinen (Circling Swan)–He and his wife were both killed in front of their tepee at Big Hole.

Wetyetmas Wahyakt (Swan Necklace), alias John Minthon–About the same age as his intimate friend, Yellow Wolf.

Wetyettamaweyun (I Give No Orders)–One of Chief Joseph's scouts.

Weweatsa (Log)–Wounded at Big Hole. Later killed by the Flatheads.

Weyatanatoo Latpat (Sun Tied)–His wife, who had just given birth, the baby, and her other two children and her old nurse, Granite

Crystal, were killed in their tepee by soldiers, who beat them with rifle butts.

White Bird—Leader of a band allied to Chief Joseph.

White Bull—Led one wing of Nez Perce raid on Howard at Camas Meadows.

Wookawkaw (Woodpecker)—Killed at Big Hole.

Wottolen (Hair Combed Over Eyes)—Chronicler.

Yellow Wolf—Nephew of Chief Joseph, warrior and historian.

Yettahlapnat Alwun (Shooting Thunder)—Shot a white man in Yellowstone Park.

Yoomtis Kunnin (Grizzly Bear Blanket)—Killed at Clearwater.

Reservation Indians (Lapwai unless otherwise stated), also called Christian Indians:

Brooks, Abraham
Sheared Wolf (John Levi) } Both Christian Nez Perce and scouts for Howard. Both ambushed on Lolo Trail by Joseph's warriors and mortally wounded.

Chojykies (Lazy)—Christian Indian, acted as a peace envoy for General Howard at final surrender.

Jason—Delegate at a treaty meeting.

Kip Kip Elwhekin—Lapwai Reservation Indian policeman.

Lawyer, Chief—Said to have protected Governor Stevens after Peopeo Mox Mox, a hostage, had been murdered by the Army. Regarded as traitor and grafter by other Indians.

Reuben, James—Interpreter for Nez Perce Commission. Scout for Howard.

Paloos Band, a subdivision of the Yakimas which was closely allied with the Nez Perce. *Hush-hush-cute* (alias Bald Head) was a subchief of the band. *Hatalekin* (Red Echo) was followed by some Asotin Indians. The whole group was opposed to war, but when they reached Kamiah and found that their horses and cattle had been stolen, reportedly by white men, they joined Chief Joseph.

Tulhulhutsut—Nez Perce Chief, appointed in fall of 1876 to be spokesman for all of the Lower Nez Perce bands. His own band roamed between the Salmon and Snake Rivers. He was arrested and imprisoned at the Lapwai Council by order of General Howard. After release from prison he joined Chief Joseph. Included in his small band were:

Sarpsis Ilppilp (Red Moccasin Tops)—Killed at Big Hole. He was one of the "Three Red Coats."

Tipyahlahnah Kapskaps (Strong Eagle)—Fought at White Bird Canyon, Cottonwood Skirmish, Clearwater and Big Hole. Nearing the Canadian Border, Chief Joseph sent him ahead to negotiate with Sitting Bull for an unmolested entry into Canada. On the way he stopped overnight with some Assiniboines. They murdered him for his rifle. He was one of the "Three Red Coats."

WAHWOOKYA WASAAW (Kiniknik Hototo), alias Lean Elk, alias Poker Joe—A half-blood Nez Perce buffalo hunter; a short, sturdy man, who, by rotation of leadership, was head chief of the bands on the last leg of their journey from Big Hole to the northern tip of the Bearpaw Mountains. Among his followers was:

Tom Hill (Delaware Tom)—His father was a half-blood Delaware, his mother a full-blood Nez Perce. Warrior and interpreter, go-between representing Joseph at the surrender.

CHIEF LOOKING GLASS (Alalimya Takanin) included among his band of warriors the following:

Temme Ilppilp (Red Heart)—A veteran warrior. He argued very strongly for peace up to the moment of Captain Whipple's unprovoked attack on his village. He was mortally wounded at Big Hole.

Lelooskin—Shot out of a pine tree where he was functioning as a sharpshooter at Clearwater Battle.

Peopeo Tholekt (Bird Alighting)—Chronicler.

Tommimo—Yellow Wolf's stepfather. He was arrested and jailed to keep him from joining Chief Joseph.

Wahlitits (Shore Crossing)—A warrior of magnificent physique and great courage. Instigator of the war by an overt act. Killed at Big Hole. He was one of the "Three Red Coats."

SIOUX INDIANS:

Hawk—Yellow Wolf was his guest in the Sioux camp in Canada during the winter 1877–1878.

Sitting Bull—Sioux Chief with over 2,000 Sioux in sancutary in Canada.

1 THE COUNCIL

In small bands, each following a chosen leader whom they could depose and replace at any time, the Nez Perce tribe had roamed for centuries the plateaus, valleys and canyons of the Rocky Mountains in southeastern Washington, northern Idaho and northeastern Oregon. As an ethnic group of primitives they were hunters similar in some ways to the prehistoric Cro-Magnon. Soon after the advent of the white man the Nez Perce acquired horses. Through survival of the hardiest they developed a small durable animal which came to be known as the Indian pony. Their ponies thrived on bunch grass, bushes and similar browse. Acclimated to the Rocky Mountain habitat they became inured to the rigors of winter. The ponies learned through trial and error how to walk along narrow ledges at dizzy heights. This was necessary because twice a year the Nez Perce migrated across the Bitterroot Mountains to hunt buffalo on the plains of eastern Montana.

By 1870 the Nez Perce had evolved into nomads. They had many thousands of ponies which they sold to ranchers, miners and to the Army. With the proceeds they bought Winchester rifles and abundant ammunition. Because there was always need of fresh meat in their encampments the warriors, young and old, spent much of their time in the hills stalking deer and antelope and improving their marksmanship.

The boys were in charge of the vast pony herds. The old men kept an eye on the boys, although mostly the old men sat around the fire smoking their pipes and cracking jokes, like the nice old men in any well-ordered community.

None of the Nez Perce went hungry. They had all of the salmon, venison, buffalo, wild carrots and onions that they could eat. Perhaps that explains why they were so tall, strong and good-natured.

Although bunch grass, sage and various bushes and scrub grew moderately in the valleys, and to a lesser extent on the hillsides, the soil was too alkaline, and the climate too arid, for agriculture. The mountains were a dreary gray waste of steeply sloping rock and broken slabs and boulders. Snow capped many of the peaks the year round. For the white man the scene spelled isolation and desolation, but to the Nez Perce it was perfection; it was home.

In 1840 Tuekakas, the son of a Cayuse chief and a Nez Perce mother, was the leader of the Wallamwatkin band of the "Lower Nez Perce." He became the father of Joseph, whose Indian name meant Thunder Rolling in the Mountains. Afterward Tuekakas had another son whom he named Alokut. Tuekakas' creed was □ "No man owns any part of the earth. No man can sell what he does not own." □

According to General O. O. Howard, the Cayuse were a turbulent, unstable people with a penchant for the wholesale slaughtering of white people, such as the massacre of the Whitman Mission. Indeed it was the opinion of practically every jury in the far west, during the latter half of the Nineteenth Century, that the shooting of Indians under any circumstances, especially by exhibitionistic cowboys, should be condoned. But if an Indian, even in self-defense, killed a white man he became guilty of a crime.

The favorite camping ground of the Wallamwatkins was the flat land in northeastern Oregon at the confluence of the Grande Ronde River and Wallowa Creek in the Wallowa Valley. The combined waters flow into the Snake River.

The Wallamwatkins were not molested until 1847 when troops supplemented by volunteer companies arrived to punish the Cayuse for killing people of the Whitman Mission. Guilty members of the Cayuse took off for the hills, and not any particular place in the hills.

By nature cowboys are suspicious of everything, except whiskey. Many of the volunteers were cowboys, suspicious and vindictive. Naturally they suspected the Nez Perce of having assisted the Cayuse in escaping and wanted them to be held guilty until proven innocent. A conference was called. Tuekakas, followed by two hundred and fifty warriors, appeared with an American flag in one hand, and a New Testament in the other. General Palmer, Indian Agent for Oregon, having seen cowboys with pistols and whiskey bottles, but never an American flag or a Bible, was favorably impressed with the Nez Perce and dismissed the case.

Incidentally Tuekakas was very much of a family man. He had four wives and seven children. The Nez Perce did not believe in divorce. When a husband saw someone he liked better he invited her in and told the others to move over. Naturally there was a little competition around the hearth, which kept each wife on her toes and the husband deeply contented. It was an ideal arrangement. Domestic difficulties were unknown to the Nez Perce.

The Oregon Trail crossed the Grande Ronde River at a ford about twenty miles west of Wallowa Valley. When the horses which had hauled the immigrants' covered wagons reached that ford, they were just about through. Tuekakas was usually there with a small herd of fat, frisky ponies and a big grin. He would trade one pony for two big horses, or perhaps hold out for three horses if they lay down on the bank when they saw the swift waters of the ford. Sometimes out of the greatness of his heart Tuekakas would accept two horses, which when halted had to lean together to stand up, and a serviceable rifle and ammunition in exchange for a pony.

Inevitably a few of the immigrants, instead of crossing the ford, elected to remain in the Wallowa Valley and go into the horsetrading business. They proved to be sharp and greedy. They were also smart horse thieves. They soon acquired herds of their own at Tuekakas' expense. Then they gave him some hard competition.

Yearly increasing numbers of immigrants rolled into the Columbia Basin and settled themselves on Indian lands. To provide those potential voters with land titles Major Isaac Stevens, appointed Governor of the Washington Territory, asked Congress for appropriations and authority to negotiate treaties with all the tribes of the Northwest, for the purpose of placing all Indians in that part of the country on reservations.

Governor Stevens' reasoning was that if all northwestern Indians could be confined to restricted areas, even though they be large ones, the project would keep the Indians off of the white immigrants and settlers, and each other. But the western Indian was a roamer. It was against his nature to stay put. When an Indian camp ground became unsanitary, they packed up and moved to another. Consequently the Indian primitives were free from zymotic and endemic diseases. On reservations they would be more or less in contact with disease-ridden white people. Like the white people they would be unable to move their camp sites because of the restraints of agriculture. Naturally the Indians did not take kindly to the Governor's sudden demand that they change their way of life. On the other hand, Stevens, believing that the white man's culture was superior to the Indian's, rationalized that he was doing the Indians a good turn. The government would provide for each reservation an Indian agent who would teach them agriculture, animal husbandry, how to build frame houses and barns and how to be provident. Also there would be present a teacher and a preacher.

None of the Indian tribes agreed with Stevens' view, but under threat of military compulsion the weaker tribes accepted reservation existence. The warlike Sioux and several other tribes including certain bands of the Nez Perce resisted.

In May of 1855 Governor Stevens, in pursuance of his purpose, summoned representatives from the bands of all northwestern tribes to a council at Walla Walla. They came, and continued to arrive, until there was assembled along the banks of Mill Creek a city of tepees. Negotiations were protracted and disputatious, but by June 11th a rather compulsive treaty had been written and was duly signed. Heads of the various tribes received salaries and annuities. For the Nez Perce, the treaty guaranteed to their reservation exemption from settlement by white men. The provisions were clearly expressed, but no arrangement was made to enforce them. Naturally white settlers squatted all over the reservations. The Indian agents were powerless. The Indians couldn't enforce the treaty without violating it. Scattered ranch shanties were augmented by bigger and better shanties until the aggregations became settlements with names, names which characterized the residents: Boring, Drain, Amity, and Bonanza, for instance.

The Indians could have destroyed at any time the white settlements, as easily as crushing ants. But forts were being built and garrisoned. Always there was a mounting threat of armed retaliation. The only justice in the land was the white man's justice. As the years went by Tuekakas regretted more and more having signed that treaty.

Governor Stevens' treaty kept peace in the Columbia Basin for a few months. Then miners and prospectors popped up here and there like poison ivy. They made their own rules in defiance of the government and treaties and changed those rules whenever they pleased. They were rude, desperate men capable of using passing Indians for target practice. Hostilities soon broke out in what came to be known as the Yakima War.

In the fall of 1861 gold in quantity was discovered along Orofino Creek, a tributary of Clearwater River. This was on the Lapwai Reservation in northern Idaho, the home of the "Upper Nez Perce." The treaty, by then ratified by the Senate and proclaimed by President Buchanan, was ignored by the miners. Without property right or justification, about ten thousand of them invaded the Lapwai Reservation and carried off all of the gold that they could find.

Not all of the agents who were entrusted with the welfare

of Indians on reservations were rascals, but some were certainly dishonest. Superintendent Kendall's report about the Nez Perce on the Lapwai Reservation in 1862 stated:

□ "Not far from sixty thousand dollars have been expended by the agent heretofore in charge of this tribe. I regret to say that the visible results of this liberal expenditure are meagre indeed.

The buildings erected by Mr. Cain for the agency were mere shells hardly fit for human habitation. The want of comfort displayed can only be accounted for on the ground that the agent did not make the reservation his headquarters and consequently felt little if any interest in the matter.

I sought in vain to find the first foot of land fenced or broken (to plough) by him or his employees. The only product that I could discover consisted of three tons of oats in the straw piled up within a rude uncovered enclosure of rails to raise which must have cost the government more than seven thousand dollars. Even this property was barely saved from the hands of departing employees who claimed it as the result of their private labor.

As I witnessed the withdrawal from this meagre pile of the rations for my horse, I could hardly fail to sigh from the thought that every chomp of his jaws devoured at least a dollar's worth of government bounty." □

As for government bounty, there were Southerners among the miners who assured the Indians that the Federal Government couldn't meet its obligations because it was about to collapse.

In 1863, on June 7th, the federation of the Nez Perce split. The Upper Nez Perce signed another treaty, selling to the United States Government the Wallowa Valley, the home of the Lower Nez Perce. The Lower Nez Perce would not sign. Tuekakas maintained that his signing of the treaty of 1855 did not constitute a sale to the Government of the Wallowa Valley (winding water). He stated that his people, the Wallamwatkins, had never accepted anything at all from the Government, and since there had been no payment there could be no sale. Indeed the Upper

Nez Perce were not bound to fulfill their treaty obligations, if any, because the Government had made only a few of the payments which it had promised to them and was therefore in violation of its own agreement.

Joseph, now old enough to partake in councils, described the attempt of the Upper Nez Perce to sell the Wallowa Valley, ancestral home of the Wallamwatkins of the Lower Nez Perce:

□ "If we ever owned the land, we own it still for we never sold it. In the treaty councils the commissioners have claimed that our country had been sold to the Government. Suppose a white man should come to me and say, 'Joseph, I like your horses. I want to buy them.'

"If we sold our lands to the Government, this is the way they were bought." □

In 1868 the Secretary of the Interior ordered the Lapwai agents to inform Tuekakas that his non-treaty band should be given to understand that the Government expected them to leave the Wallowa Valley and settle permanently on what was left of the Lapwai Reservation. The Indian Bureau in Washington held that because the Upper Nez Perce had signed the Treaty of 1863, as the head of the Nez Perce Confederacy, all of the Nez Perce bands, including those who had not signed, were subject to the provisions of that treaty. The Indians called it the Thief Treaty.

For such high-handed procedure in Washington there was only one possible explanation for the Indians—a Bad Spirit. Just as the Great Spirit loved his Indian children, so there was a Bad Spirit who hated them and plotted to destroy them.

The Indians reasoned that there had been a Bad Spirit in some great man* in Washington who had directed the murderer of President Lincoln. If that great man had now been removed from office, perhaps the Bad Spirit would have moved into some great general.

---

* Secretary of War Stanton has been suspected of being the man behind John Wilkes Booth, the actor who murdered Lincoln.

Observing the shabby treatment accorded the Upper Nez Perce on the Lapwai Reservation, it occurred to Tuekakas that instead of submitting to such humiliations perhaps it would be as well to fight. Consequently he ignored the orders of the ever changing agents. Why place the welfare of his people in the hands of agents who failed to keep their word, either through their own dishonesty, or the unwillingness of the Government to meet its obligations? Indeed when Tuekakas was told of the decision of the Indian Bureau, he tore up the Wallamwatkins' copy of the Treaty of 1863 for the worthless scrap of paper it had been, and burned bit by bit his New Testament. By these acts he signified that he had cut himself and his people off from the white men. His son Joseph watched him do it.

In 1871 Joseph's father, Tuekakas, was dying. Joseph described their parting: □ "My father sent for me. I saw he was dying. I took his hand in mine. He said, 'My son, my body is returning to my mother earth and my spirit is going very soon to see the Great Spirit Chief. When I am gone think of your country. You are the chief of these people. They look to you to guide them.

"'Always remember that your father never sold his country. You must stop your ears whenever you are asked to sign a treaty selling your home. A few years more and white men will be all around you. They have their eyes on this land.

"'My son, never forget my dying words. This country holds your father's body. Never sell the bones of your father and your mother.'

"I pressed my father's hand and told him I would protect his grave with my life. My father smiled and passed away to the spirit-land.

"I buried him in that beautiful valley of winding waters. I love that land more than all the rest of the world. A man who would not love his father's grave is worse than a wild animal." □

In conformity with his father's wishes Joseph refused all annuities for the Wallamwatkins. According to the report of the Nez Perce agent in 1872, the Wallamwatkins lived beyond the reservation along the Snake River, never asked for assistance and never accepted anything except a little tobacco.

Some of the Nez Perce had submitted to an agricultural life and had gone on reservation at Lapwai, but Joseph and his followers clung to their old way of living.

A sportsman who visited Wallowa Lake in 1875 wrote in a letter that there were only a dozen settlers there at that time. Their sole occupation was cattle raising, as the land was unfit for anything else.

Captain Whipple, who was stationed with troops in Wallowa Valley in 1875, wrote the Secretary of War that no one seemed anxious to locate in the Wallowa Valley. † "The white population is less than a year ago. Three families have disposed of their improvements for a trifle. Not a man has taken a claim in the valley since that time. People were disappointed to learn that it was not to be taken for an Indian reservation. One man regretted because it would have given him a chance to sell his land to the government. The valley is only fit for stock raising and because of the long winters not desirable for that, but the Indians' horse herds live where white men's cattle would perish.

"This band of Indians (the Wallamwatkins) are proud-spirited, self-supporting and intelligent. I know of no Indians who give better promise of rising in the cultural scale. They have not been hostile to the whites nor do I believe that they can easily be made hostile." †

However this report made little impression upon the Commissioner of Indian Affairs. He wrote:

† "The settlement made in Wallowa Valley which has for years been the pasture of a large herd of horses owned by Joseph's band will occasion more or less trouble between that band and the whites until Joseph is induced or compelled to settle on a reservation." †

In 1873 the superintendent of Indian Affairs for Oregon, acting on instructions from the Secretary of the Interior, held a council on March 27th at Lapwai with Joseph. They told him that the President had ordered the Nez Perce to go on the Lapwai

Reservation. If they obeyed, the government would help them. Joseph replied:

□ "I did not want to come to this council, but I came hoping that we could save blood. The white man has no right to come here and take our country. We have never accepted any presents from the Government. Neither Lawyer,* nor any other chief, had authority to sell this land. It has always belonged to my people. It came unclouded to them from our fathers. And we will defend this land as long as a drop of Indian blood warms the hearts of our men." □

When the superintendent declared that whether Joseph liked it or not he and his people must go on reservation, Joseph replied:

□ "I will not. I do not need your help. We have plenty. We are contented and happy, if the white man will let us alone. The Lapwai reservation is too small for so many people with all their stock. You can keep your presents. We can go to your towns and pay for all we need. We have plenty of horses and cattle to sell. We won't have any help from you. We are free. We can go where we please. Our fathers were born here. Here they lived. Here they died. Here are their graves. We will never leave them." □

The Superintendent then suggested the possibility of converting the Wallowa Valley into a reservation for the Nez Perce. Annuities were offered to induce the Nez Perce to become civilized. The Superintendent asked Joseph if he would like schools on the reservation if one were established in the Wallowa Valley. Joseph replied in the negative. When the Superintendent asked why, Joseph answered: □ "Because schools will teach us to have churches." □

The astonished Superintendent asked Joseph why he didn't want churches. Joseph said: □ "They will teach us to quarrel about God as the Catholics and Protestants do on the Nez Perce reservation (at Lapwai) and other places. We do not want to

* A chief of the Upper Nez Perce.

learn that. We may quarrel with men sometimes about things on this earth, but we never quarrel about God. We do not want to learn that." □

The Superintendent and the agent were so impressed by Joseph's speech that they recommended to Washington that the Wallowa Valley be withdrawn from settlement and made a public domain. Grant issued such an executive order, but did not include all of the land that Joseph had claimed for his people, nor all that the commissioners had recommended. Miners and ranchers continued pouring in.

The white people who had squatted on the Lapwai reservation along the Salmon River (White Bird's territory) complained continuously about the Indians in letters which they wrote to Agent Monteith. Monteith was a man with blankly staring, fanatical eyes. Reasoning from fanaticism rather than judgment, Monteith stupidly believed that if he were to have one of those letters translated into the Nez Perce language and should show it to White Bird and other non-treaty Nez Perce, they would be convinced that they would not be subject to such complaints in the future. Acting on impulse Monteith did this. Joseph's reaction to that letter was that white squatters on Indian land with the effrontery to complain about the Indians who owned it could no longer be tolerated. Monteith's reasoning had not been normal. Indian reaction was. The incident aroused a resentment among the non-treaty Nez Perce which smoldered until it flamed into the overt acts of some of White Bird's young warriors, which in turn sparked military retaliation by General Howard's cavalry.

To retain the good will (and the votes) of the white men who had squatted on Indian lands, and to compensate them for the shacks they had built but would have to abandon, the Department of the Interior included in the executive order a provision for purchasing from the squatters. Whether the schedule of purchase prices for squatters' claims was fair or excessive mattered little. By offering to buy, the government had recognized squatter ownership of Indian lands. That little provision became eventually the base upon which the politicians built their arguments for evicting the Indians from nearly all of their ancestral lands.

As soon as the executive order was made public the squatters ceased building and waited for their money. But the days passed and no indemnity came from the Department of the Interior. Naturally the more stupid became impatient. The less stupid soon perceived that the money which the government might pay them was of no consequence. For them the battle had been won when the government recognized their ownership. The real money would be in retention of Indian land, extension of claims and selling small parcels of land to immigrants.

At that point the scheming and clever squatters began a sequence of propaganda. They called attention to the fact that Joseph and his band wanted to continue in their wild way of life. Until they could be persuaded to a civilized life there was no hope of making them stay put on a reservation. The Nez Perce lived in Oregon, but they loved to go buffalo hunting in Montana. The Sioux lived there. In one of his reports the Indian agent wrote:

□ "Some measures ought to be adopted whereby the Indians can be prevented from going to the buffalo country. A party has just come in with great stories of how they whipped a party of Sioux and captured mules, horses, etc. creating quite a desire on the part of many who had remained at home to go next spring and try their hand at it."□

But mostly it was the improvements made in the Oregon-land claimed by Joseph as his homeland that brought on a crisis. The Wallowa Road and Bridge Co. and the Prairie Creek Ditch Co. and various individual ranchers had constructed roads and bridges and had erected buildings assessed all together at nearly $68,000 by the Department of the Interior. These moneyed interests put pressure on Governor Grover of Oregon to protest Grant's order closing the Wallowa Valley to public settlement and occupation. In his letter of complaint Governor Grover said in part:

□" I learn that Joseph does not object to going on the reservation at this time, but that certain leading spirits of his band do object for the reason that by so doing they would have to abandon some of their nomadic habits and haunts. The very objection which they make is a strong reason why they should be required to do so. No beneficial influence can be exerted by agents and missionaries among the Indians while they maintain their aboriginal habits."□

Grover further stated that by treaty the Nez Perce had relinquished to the United States all of their territorial rights in the Wallowa Valley. It was afterward proved that Grover was in error in these statements. He was also wrong when he said that Joseph had no objection to going on reservation. The commissioners of the Indian Department in Washington accepted Governor Grover's letter and a similar recommendation by the Congressman from Oregon at face value. Acting on their recommendations the Department of the Interior recommended a revocation of the executive order of 1873 closing the Wallowa Valley to the public. On June 10, 1875, the President issued a new proclamation opening the Wallowa Valley to settlement by white people. Until that moment the Nez Perce had held in respect the Great White Chief in Washington. Thenceforth they spoke of him as the Great White Chief with a forked tongue.

In that same year General O. O. Howard assumed command of the Department of Columbia with headquarters at Vancouver. Howard was an experienced officer, a devout man and in civilian matters kindly. As part of a brilliant career in the Civil War he planned the Federal strategy before the Battle of Gettysburg. He first met Joseph at the Umatilla Agency in northeastern Oregon. They shook hands and as Howard afterward described the meeting:

○ "Joseph put his large black eyes on my face and maintained a fixed look for some time. It did not appear to me as an audacious stare but I thought he was trying to open the windows of his heart to me and at the same time endeavoring to read my disposition and character. I think that Joseph and I became then quite good friends. There was at the time little appearance of that distrust and deceit which some time afterward very strongly marked his face, especially while listening to white men in council." ○

Apparently Joseph sized up Howard pretty accurately, as subsequent events proved. For in the battles, and during the long pursuit, Joseph seemed to be able to forecast Howard's reactions and to anticipate Howard's famed strategy so unerringly that Howard appeared to behave like a boy. Inferentially Howard profited but little from their meeting, for he ever afterward underestimated Joseph's intelligence.

In his first report to the Secretary of War Howard uncovered the injustice that had been done the Indians when he wrote: □ "The troubles at Wallowa Valley have not thus far resulted in bloodshed, but it has been prevented only by great carefulness on the part of government agents—I think it a great mistake, to take from Joseph and his band of Nez Perce that valley. The white people really do not want it. They wished to be bought out. Possibly Congress can be induced to let these really peaceable Indians have this poor valley for their own." □

Actually it was a poor valley for the raising of crops by cultivating the soil. A river wound through it. There were bushes where Indians' ponies or a shepherd's sheep could find plenty of browse. Other than that the valley had only one value. By the addition of a few roads, bridges and ditches it became a first class sucker trap. Pioneers from the east who by their fortitude and hardihood had crossed the plains and mountains and had finally reached Oregon were not in a mood to be choosy about the soil. Having travelled thousands of miles without seeing a road, the ditched roads in the Wallowa Valley would naturally look to them like civilization at last. The vested interests back of the land improvement companies stood to make a large profit in the settling of the Wallowa Valley. Governor Grover may not have been identified with the "Interests," but possibly some of his friends were. When Indians came between vested interests and their expected profits, the Indians had to go.

The attitude of the white settlers in Wallowa Valley was exemplified in February, 1876, when they telegraphed the governor of Oregon that Joseph's band was stealing and killing cattle and threatening to kill them. At that very time and for several preceding weeks Joseph and most of his band had been at the agency celebrating Christmas and attending feasts. As for stealing cattle, Joseph's people had driven back into the hills settlers' cattle which had followed their herds of ponies.

That sneak attempt against the peaceful and honest character of the members of Joseph's band having failed, McNall and Findley, two settlers in the Wallowa Valley, attempted a different approach. On June 23, 1876, they entered the cluster of tepees which sheltered Joseph's band and accused the first warriors they met of having stolen their horses. The Indians had not stolen their horses and resented the accusation. The Indians were unarmed. McNall and Findley had their rifles. Findley shot and killed one of the unarmed Indians. Then they both ran. Upon arriving home Findley found his horses grazing near his ranch. That they had wantonly killed a fine Nez Perce warrior meant nothing to them.

There were other attempts by the Wallowa settlers to deliberately provoke the Nez Perce into some act of reprisal to furnish an excuse for calling in the soldiers to remove the Indians by force. Joseph spoke feelingly of those settlers:

☐ "They stole a great many horses from us and we could not get them back because we were Indians. The white men told lies for each other. They drove off a great many of our cattle. Some white men branded our young cattle so that they could claim them. We had no friends who would plead our cause before the law councils. It seemed to me that some of the white men in Wallowa were doing these things on purpose to get up a war. They knew we were not strong enough to fight them. I labored hard to avoid trouble and bloodshed. When the white men were few and we were strong we could have killed them off, but the Nez Perce wished to live at peace.

"We have had a few good friends among white men and they

have always advised my people to bear these taunts without fighting. Our young men are quick-tempered. I have had great trouble in keeping them from doing rash things. I have carried a heavy load on my back ever since I was a boy." □

Among all races the young men have inclined to be hot-tempered and to settle grievances by war rather than by negotiation. Indians were no exception, but among them the Indian mothers and the wise old councillors exercised a restraining influence.*

At the indignation meeting of Joseph's band after the murder of one of their warriors by two white settlers, the young men were all for war. Resentment mounted until it looked as if an Indian attack upon the white settlements in the Wallowa Valley would be inevitable. Then the daughter of the murdered warrior arose and said: □ "We do not wish other people to be killed for the killing of one person. So let us drop the matter." □

Because Indians hold their women in high esteem an Indian mother's word spoken in council was not to be taken lightly. An immediate attack upon the settlers was averted, but Joseph sent an ultimatum demanding surrender of the two guilty men within seven days.

The settlers appealed to the army post at Walla Walla for protection. A troop of cavalry came to Wallowa. The lieutenant in command met Joseph and his warriors. They were in battle array, but by promising to keep the settlers on the north side of Hurricane Creek, if the Nez Perce would remain on the south side, and by agreeing to use his influence to bring the guilty white men to trial before the civil authorities, the lieutenant persuaded Joseph to withdraw his ultimatum. However, the withdrawal did not settle the Indians' grievance. It was merely a truce.

---

* Before a military action the chiefs and sub-chiefs of the Lower Nez Perce bands met in council. Various tactics and stratagems would be offered and discussed. A vote might be taken, or selection might be left to the decision of presiding chief of the moment. Joseph never had dictatorial power, nor did he desire it, but his judgments carried great weight with all of his people.

Of course the two white men were not brought to trial right away. Had they been, they would probably have been discharged with a reprimand, something like "if you must shoot casual Indians, don't do it where a lot of Indians are standing around." Instead a group of army officers, not including General Howard, held a conference with Joseph at Umatilla on July 23, 1876. Joseph declaimed that among the Indians the chiefs controlled the members of their bands and had power to prevent ill-intentioned Indians from committing outrages. He therefore reasoned that those in authority should have similar control over white men and were accordingly responsible for the killing of that warrior. To Joseph the warrior's life was worth more than the Wallowa Valley, or the country, or the whole world. Indeed the value of his life could not be estimated. But since the warrior's life had been taken in the Wallowa Valley, the earth mother had drunk the warrior's blood and his body had been buried there, the Wallowa Valley was more sacred than ever. Joseph therefore claimed the Valley for the life taken, to be held by himself and his people and their descendants forever. All white people must be removed from the valley.

To the group of army officers Joseph had made it clear, although he hadn't said it in so many words, that if the government were to withdraw the settlers and renounce their claim to the Wallowa Valley, any future murders of Indians or raids by the settlers would at once become the responsibility of government representatives.

Major Wood pacified Joseph by assuring him that the two white murderers would be tried and that Indians would be summoned to the trial as witnesses.

The trial was held at Union, Oregon. A jury of ranchers acquitted the defendants. The Indians went home angry and sent a demand that the murderers be surrendered to them to be tried according to tribal custom. Naturally the settlers refused and Indian resentment mounted higher.

Because no actual agreement had been reached the Department of the Interior appointed a commission of distinguished men to meet with Joseph and his councillors to make a supreme effort to persuade him to settle on the Lapwai Reservation and to accept the civilized way of life, also to adjust the difficulties between the Indians and the settlers. The adjusting would have to be done entirely by the Indians, but of course that wouldn't develop until later.

The council was held in the mission church at Lapwai. The commissioners tried a new angle. They said that if Joseph with his band continued to roam, he would be almost sure to clash with white settlers. If he did, the President of the United States might not be able to justify or even defend Joseph. As for creating a reservation in Wallowa Valley, a portion of the Valley had been surveyed and opened to settlement. Therefore the State of Oregon wouldn't turn it over to the federal government for an Indian reservation. Even if the State of Oregon did and the federal government bought off the white settlers who were there, other white settlers would come and settle on the vacated land. Furthermore the climate was so cold that Wallowa Valley wouldn't be a healthy place for Joseph's band, although the Nez Perce had lived in that valley for generations.

Such nonsense spoken in council could have only one effect. The Indians felt insulted and became angered. Probably Joseph looked cross-eyed at the other chiefs. Then controlling his temper he replied with great dignity:

□ "The Great Spirit, when he made the earth, made no lines of division or separation on it. He meant that it should be allowed to remain as made. The earth was my mother. I was made of the earth and grew up on its bosom. The earth, my mother and nurse is sacred to my affections, too sacred to be valued by gold or sold for silver. I could not consent to sever my affections from the land which bore me. I ask nothing of the President. I am able to take care of myself. I do not desire the Wallowa Valley as a reservation, for that would subject me to the will of another and make me dependent on him and subject to laws not of our own making. I am disposed to live peaceably. Our band has suffered wrong rather than do wrong. One of our warriors was wantonly murdered by a white man last summer, but I will not avenge his death." □

Joseph did not let the quiet dignity of his speech descend to the level of incrimination, such as reminding the commissioners that the Lapwai Reservation, upon which the Department of the Interior wished to locate the Wallamwatkins, had already been invaded by ten thousand miners and settlers in complete disregard of treaty stipulations. The government was aware of this, but seemed to be powerless to do anything about it. The government had also agreed in a treaty to have the Lapwai Reservation surveyed so that, knowing where their property lines were, the Indians could invoke the law for the removal of white people who had encroached on Indian lands.

All of the logic seemed to be on Joseph's side. Believing that he had won the argument Joseph returned to Wallowa.

In January, 1877, the Department of the Interior acting upon the commission's report (adverse to Joseph) decided to move Joseph and his band on reservation and sent an order to that effect to the Indian agent. Some of the Nez Perce had gone on the Lapwai reservation years previously when the government first requested it. Among them were Joseph's father-in-law and brother-in-law. These, together with a Nez Perce scout, were persuaded by the agent to go to Joseph and tell him that reservation life was preferable in many ways to the roving way of living. They called upon Joseph and presented the case as best they could. Joseph listened attentively but did not reply until the next morning. Then he said:

□ "I have been talking to the white men many years about the land in question. It is strange that they cannot understand me. The country which they claim belonged to my father. Before he died he gave it to me and my people. I will not leave it until I am compelled to do so." □

When the Indian agent had received the report he notified Joseph that he would be given until April 1, 1877, to come on the reservation peaceably. Joseph was astonished. He believed that throughout the negotiations he had held the better of the argument, as indeed he had, if it had been an argument. Joseph had failed to realize that in the minds of the white men there had never been any argument. They had been telling him, in what they considered a polite way, to get out of the Wallowa Valley and go on the Lapwai reservation. Now they were ordering him to do it.

Suspecting that there might be a misapprehension due to bungling by the interpreters Joseph requested an interview with General Howard. First there was a preliminary meeting between Howard's aide-de-camp, Lieutenant Boyle, and Joseph's younger brother Alokut. As a result Howard travelled by steamer up the Columbia River and by train to Fort Walla Walla, arriving on April 18. Joseph was ill. The actual meeting took place twelve days later at Lapwai. Present besides Joseph were Alokut, leader of the young men and very enthusiastic, and White Bird, the most war-like spirit of all the Nez Perce. There was Looking Glass who spent most of his time leading his band on buffalo hunts in Montana. Also present were Hush-hush-cute, leader of a band and noted for his cunning, and Tulhulhutsut, a medicine man, very dynamic and the leader of another small band. Joseph was not the leader in council, but he stood first in military matters.

Because some of the chiefs had not arrived the council was protracted, although Howard discussed the problem daily with Joseph explaining again that because it was an order of the Department of the Interior the only thing Joseph could do was to comply. So there was no point in waiting for chiefs who might not appear anyway. But Joseph said that he would wait. This made Howard very impatient. Nevertheless Joseph would not give a final answer until all of the chiefs had arrived.

Monteith, the Indian agent, was a Department man who followed instructions to the letter. It was not in his nature to request authority to compromise, or even to make recommendations to his superiors. When the council reconvened on May 7 with General Howard and officers present, Monteith said that a medicine man who counselled disobedience of the clear instructions of the government would certainly have to be punished.

Tulhulhutsut, at whom this remark was aimed, arose and

retorted against the violence that would separate Indians from land that was theirs by inheritance. He then explained about the chieftainship of the earth.

Howard replied that the government had no wish to interfere with Indian religion † "Twenty times over you repeat that the earth is your mother and about the chieftainship from the earth. Let us hear no more about it but come to business at once." †

Tulhulhutsut retorted † "What you talk about isn't true law at all. You white people get together, measure the earth and then divide it." † Monteith interjected † "The law says 'You must come to the reservation.' The law is made in Washington. We don't make it." † Tulhulhutsut struck back. † "The earth is part of my body. I never gave up the earth." †

Howard said sternly † "You know very well that the government has set apart a reservation and that the Indians must go on it. If an Indian becomes a citizen he can have land outside like any other citizen, but he has to leave his tribe and take land precisely as a white man does." †

Tulhulhutsut demanded † "What person pretends to divide the land and put me on it." †

Howard answered † "I am the man. I stand here for the President. There is no spirit good or bad that will hinder me. My orders are plain and will be executed. I hoped that the Indians had good sense enough to make me their friend and not their enemy." †

At this point Joseph tried to check a mounting quarrel. He said: □ "I am ready to talk today. I have been in a great many councils, but I am no wiser. We are all sprung from a woman although we are unlike in many things. We cannot be made over again. You are as you were made and so you can remain. We are as we were made by the Great Spirit and you cannot change us. Then why should children of one mother and one father quarrel? Why should one try to cheat the other? I do not believe that the Great Spirit gave one kind of men the right to tell another kind of men what they must do." □

Tulhulhutsut endorsed Joseph's speech with: □ "The Great

Spirit made the world as it is and as He wanted it. And He made a part of it for us to live upon. I do not see where you get your authority to say that we shall not live where He placed us." □

Unable to come up with a rational reply to so forceful an argument Howard simply told Tulhulhutsut that his words were getting the Indians excited. Then, losing his temper, Howard threatened to put him in the guardhouse.

Tulhulhutsut retorted: □ "Who are you that you ask us to talk and then tell me that I shan't talk? Are you the Great Spirit? Did you make the world? Did you make the sun? Did you make the rivers to run for us to drink? Did you make the grass to grow? Did you make all these things that you talk to us as though we were boys? If you did, then you have the right to talk to us as you do." □

The Indians looked at each other and stirred uneasily. Howard sensed that any weakness on his part might invite a massacre by the Indians. To intimidate them Howard nodded to Captain Perry. Together they grabbed Tulhulhutsut by the arms and rushed him into the guardhouse. That act in itself was equivalent to a declaration of war. Howard probably never realized that he and every white man present would have been stabbed to death on the spot if it hadn't been for Joseph. Joseph saw them drawing their knives beneath their blankets. Long afterward Joseph said:

□ "My men whispered among themselves whether they should let this thing be done. I counseled them to submit. I knew that if we resisted, all of the white men present, including General Howard, would be killed in a moment and the chiefs would be blamed. If I had said nothing, General Howard would never have given another unjust order against my men. I saw the danger and while they dragged Tulhulhutsut to prison, I arose and said 'I am going to talk now. I don't care whether you arrest me or not.' I turned to my people and said 'The arrest of Tulhulhutsut was wrong but we will not resent the insult. We were invited to this council to express our hearts and we have done so.'" □

Before the council had dispersed, Joseph, Looking Glass and White Bird told Howard that they wanted him to ride with them to Kamiah to look at the land before deciding on the portion they would want for their farms.

After riding for several days with Howard the chiefs selected locations on the Lapwai which suited them. Joseph wanted to settle above Kamiah on the Clearwater. Howard offered Joseph a paper as a sort of land title and protection certificate. Joseph refused it. White Bird accepted one. Then Howard gave them thirty days to round up their stock and move. The Indians asked for a longer time because they would have to swim their stock across the turbulent Snake River swollen with spring rains. Their request was denied. They begged Howard to release Tulhulhutsut. Again they were denied.

Acting on instructions from the Department of the Interior, Howard ordered a number of soldiers to occupy the Wallowa Valley. He refused to give Hush-hush-cute a protection paper. On May 19th, before leaving for Portland, Howard ordered Tulhulhutsut to be released from the guardhouse. Unaware of having done anything which deserved punishment, but having paid his debt to society, Tulhulhutsut departed from the guardhouse resolving that society would now pay its debt to him.

Joseph immediately recognized that it was up to him to restrain the young men in his band. He knew that with only the rifles and such ammunition as they had been able to buy they would be no match for federal soldiers equipped with artillery and gatling guns. Of course they might capture some ammunition from army supply wagons and pack mules, but even that would be quickly expended. Thereafter his band would have to depend on bows and arrows. Arrows could never match artillery. Furthermore, there was so much jealousy between Indian tribes that Joseph's band could not count on support from other encampments of the Nez Perce except the small ones which had already joined him. Indeed Joseph could count himself lucky if scouts from the Crows, the Blackfeet or Sioux didn't actively join General Howard against the Nez Perce. In the event of war the Nez Perce women and children and the aged people would be the ones who would suffer most. One of Joseph's wives was about to have a baby. Therefore to Joseph it seemed better to obey General Howard and to endure the insults and murders perpetrated by the settlers until the women and children could be located in a place where they would be safe and well fed before the warriors matched their strength against Federal troops.

Joseph afterward gave his side of the story following the release of Tulhulhutsut: □ "When I returned to Wallowa, I found my people very much excited upon discovering that the soldiers were already in the Wallowa Valley. We held a council and decided to move immediately to avoid bloodshed.

Tulhulhutsut felt outraged by his imprisonment. He talked for war. He made many of our young men willing to fight rather than be driven like dogs from the land where they were born. He declared that blood alone would wash out the disgrace which General Howard had put upon him. It required a strong heart to stand up against such talk, but I urged my people to be quiet and not to begin a war. I said in my heart that rather than have war I would give up my country. I would give up my father's grave. I would give up everything rather than have the blood of white men upon the hands of my people." □

Joseph sent the teen-age boys among the hills to round up the wandering horses and cattle. The young men would not go. They knew that Joseph was about to lead his band out of the Wallowa Valley. In defiance of his authority they refused to leave. An army officer under such circumstances would have threatened his mutinous soldiers with pistols. Joseph merely strode to each one in turn, put a hand on his shoulder and looked him in the eye until the young man, yielding to a superior will, lowered his eyes. They all followed when Joseph left the valley. As to their emotions, they had them although they did not show them. Over the next months permanent lines of deep sadness settled in their faces. No one who does not have Indian blood can ever know what leaving his home land does to an Indian's heart.

At the Snake River Joseph's band crossed the one-quarter mile of swift deep current on rafts of buffalo hides stretched over frames made of willow saplings. Each raft was propelled by a pony, with a rider swimming at each corner. After the women, children and household goods were safely over in Idaho the warriors drove a lot of the ponies and cattle into the river expecting them to swim across. But a sudden cloudburst made the current much stronger. A few animals made it across, but a large number were swept away. Joseph told the warriors not to drive any more cattle into the river until it had subsided. While the warriors were waiting on the Oregon side a collection of thirty cowboys suddenly appeared, overpowered the guards and drove away the cattle. Because the women and children were across the river and unprotected Joseph dared not leave the spot to pursue the cowboys. None of the ponies was stolen. They were more important to Joseph's people than the cattle.

A few hours later Joseph followed his warriors and horses across the receding river. Afterward they all crossed the Salmon River and went on to Rocky Canyon where White Bird's band and Tulhulhutsut's people awaited. They were then eight miles west of Grangeville, and fairly near the southwest boundary of the Lapwai Reservation. Reunited they held a ten day council. Everyone with a grievance against the white men was given the opportunity to stand up and tell about it. Feeling ran high, but Joseph backed by Looking Glass spoke firmly against war. Joseph maintained that, admitting the truth of all that had been said, there was still nothing to be gained by declaring war on white people.

On the tenth day of council a young warrior named Wahlitits whose father had been murdered by a settler in an unprovoked quarrel over some land made a fiery speech. Joseph replied, pointing out that because there was no place for their women and children where food and fuel could be found which would be out of reach of the army's artillery, the Nez Perce would have to run away while they were fighting. This contention was something which had not occurred to the council. Observing the telling effect of his argument, Joseph believed that he had won his point. He therefore left the council and went up in the hills to catch some of their cattle and butcher some meat for his family. Unfortunately Joseph didn't know that the young warriors had a hidden supply of whiskey which they had bought from settlers.

Wahlitits and Red Moccasin Top, the son of Yellow Bull, and a third youth left the council and proceeded to get themselves intoxicated by drinking a lot of whiskey. Then they rode through the camp shouting defiance of white men. An old man with a distorted sense of humor asked them why they didn't do something about it. That left them no choice. They galloped off to a small settlement on Slate Creek, twenty miles from Fort Lapwai. Yellow Bull rode after his son arguing and pleading, but it was useless. The boy was drunk. During the afternoon of June 13th and the morning of the 14th they killed four white men and seriously wounded a fifth. Securing their victims' guns and ammunition they returned to camp boasting of their exploits and exhibiting the horses and guns of the murdered settlers.

Big Dawn, a brother of Yellow Bull and an angry man, one who caught fire easily, leaped astride one of the captured horses and rode through the camp shouting: □ "Now you will have to go to war. Wahlitits has killed white men and stolen their horses. Now the soldiers will be coming after us. Prepare for war!" □

The impact of Big Dawn's frenzy at first shocked Joseph's people into a state of unreality. While they were trying to adjust their emotions to a condition which they had dreaded but had not feared, some of the young warriors rode off and attacked a small settlement. The more prudent of the Wallamwatkins fled to the Lapwai Reservation. Most of the others moved their tepees to Looking Glass' camp on Cottonwood Creek.

When Joseph returned from butchering meat there were only five warriors left in camp. One was Joseph's brother-in-law. He said: □ "We must go back to Lapwai. There is no reason why we should have trouble. We were not here when the white men were killed." □

Three Eagles agreed to this but Joseph shook his head: □ "I

can hardly go back. The white people will blame me, telling me that my young men have killed white men. And the blame will come on me." □

Joseph's brother Alokut said nothing. The young men who had killed the settlers did not belong to Joseph's band, but to White Bird's. Afterward Joseph said:

□ "I was deeply grieved. I knew that their acts would involve all my people. I saw the war could not then be prevented. The time had passed. I counseled peace from the beginning. I knew that we were too weak to fight the United States. We had many grievances but I knew that war would bring more. I would have given my own life, if I could have undone the killing of white men by my people.

"I know that my young men did a great wrong, but I ask 'Who was first to blame?' They had been insulted a thousand times. Their fathers and brothers had been killed. Their mothers and wives had been disgraced. They had been driven to madness by the whiskey sold to them by the white men. They had been told by General Howard that all of their horses and cattle which they had been unable to drive out of Wallowa were to fall into the hands of the white men. Added to this they were homeless and desperate.

"I blame my young men and the white men and I blame General Howard for not giving my people time to get their stock away from Wallowa. I do not acknowledge that he had the right to order me to leave Wallowa at any time. I deny that either my father or myself ever sold that land. It may never again be our home but my father sleeps there. And I love it as I love my mother. I left there hoping to avoid bloodshed." After a moment's reflection Joseph added "I knew that I must lead my people in the fight for the white people would not believe my story." □

YELLOW WOLF'S[*] STORY

OF

THE COUNCIL

Under the sympathetic questioning, through an interpreter, of L. V. McWhorter, a white man of fine character, Yellow Wolf related the story of the persecution, pursuit and capture of his people in the spring, summer and fall of 1877. On further questioning he described the tragic breaking of their spirit and their near extinction during the succeeding seven years.

General Howard "Shows the Rifle"

It was our custom for the old people to instruct the children. That was not like the learning of today, but was what we needed for living in this world.

I paid attention to what the old people said. I have always told the truth. I am telling the truth now.

We had a good country until the white people came and crowded us. Now they have us to the bush. My fathers had property in lands, horses, and goods. Just as you have what belongs to you in town or in country. My ancestors were glad to see the white strangers come. My people made no trouble. Never thought about making trouble. Never held anything about the white race. I am telling you, my people made no trouble, although the whites killed many of them! Only when they wanted to put us in one small place, taking from us our home country, trouble started.

We were raising horses and cattle—fast race horses and many

---

[*] Yellow Wolf was a nephew of Chief Joseph.

cattle. We had fine lodges, good clothes, plenty to eat, enough of everything. We were living well. Then General Howard and Agent Monteith came to bother us.

I had seen twenty-one snows when they came. They told us we had to give up our homes and move to another part of the reservation. That we had to give up our part of the reservation[1] to the white people. Told us we must move in with the Nez Perce turned Christians, called Upper Nez Perce[2] by the whites. All of same tribe, but it would be hard to live together. Our religions different, it would be hard. To leave our homes would be hard. It was these Christian Nez Perce who made with the Government a *thief* treaty (1863). Sold to the Government all this land. Sold what did not belong to them. We got nothing for our country. None of *our* chiefs signed that land-stealing treaty. None was at that lie-talk council. Only Christian Indians and Government men.

Trouble began in the councils. First was a council at Umatilla. Alokut[3] and others went there to meet General Howard. But General Howard was not there. He sent a boy (Lieutenant Boyle) in his place. Alokut did not like this. He, a chief, could not talk[4] to a boy. Nothing was done. No agreement made.

Next council was at Walla Walla. All chiefs were instructed to be there. A call went out for Heinmot Tooyalakekt (Thunder Traveling to Loftier Mountain Heights),[5] known as Joseph; also for Alokut; for Peopeo Hihhih (White Bird); for Tulhulhutsut; for Looking Glass; and for Hahtalekin.

Joseph was my uncle (first cousin to Yellow Wolf's mother). He did not go to Walla Walla. Alokut said to him, "You stay here. I will go see what is wanted."

---

1 Yellow Wolf or the interpreter used the wrong word. He meant to say "homeland."

2 As distinguished from the Lower Nez Perce, the Wallamwatkins led by Tuekakas and later Chief Joseph.

3 He was Chief Joseph's brother.

4 Nearly all Indian tribes were particular about rank and protocol.

5 Also translated Thunder Rolling in the Mountains, Chief Joseph.

"All right! You go," Joseph told him.

I was surprised, my uncle saying that. But he was not feeling well, was why Alokut spoke to go.

Alokut was gone nearly one week. When it was morning, we heard a horse running, and soon Alokut came into the tepee. After eating and smoking, he said to Joseph:

"Government wants all Indians put in one place. If you say 'Yes' I will bring in the stock[6] and we will go there. If the white officers ask what you will do, you answer, 'Nothing to talk about. Alokut has settled everything.'"

Soon after this came report that General Howard and soldiers had come to Lapwai.[7] Our camp-village was on Asotain (Eel Creek) about where Asotin now stands. Not many miles from Lapwai. We wondered why they were at the fort. Then followed word for all the chiefs to meet General Howard and Agent Monteith there in council. The chiefs who could go went with their followers, and I, Yellow Wolf, went with Chief Joseph's band. But Peopeo Hihhih (Chief White Bird) and Tulhulhutsut of Salmon River country were not there. Slippery trails and mountain snowbanks held them back. They arrived later.

The soldier guardhouse was close to the council place. Indians stood all around—a lot of Indians. A soldier was there with only one good arm. Right arm mostly gone. Left arm sound. This soldier was General Howard. After they had a prayer-talk, he asked, "Where is Chief Joseph?"

"There he is," the interpreter said, pointing to my uncle. General Howard asked Joseph if he had anything to say. Joseph answered, "I will hear what you have to tell the chiefs. My brother and I came to listen. You must not hurry. White Bird and Tulhulhutsut will be here tomorrow."

But General Howard would not wait. He talked short. Said the Indians would have to do as ordered. Agent Monteith read

---

6 Indian ponies and cows.

7 Lapwai was the name of the reservation to which the Upper Nez Perce had removed.

a paper and said we had to go on a small reservation. (Lapwai Reservation).

Alokut made a short talk. He wanted to wait for the Salmon River chiefs before anything was done.

General Howard now said, "If you do not come on the reservation, my soldiers will put you there!"

This hurt the Indians. They said no more in that sun's council. But there was talk in camp that night. Many wondered what would happen.

With morning came Chiefs White Bird and Tulhulhutsut. The council met. General Howard had one Christian Nez Perce speak a prayer. Agent Monteith made his same talk, telling us we had to move to the small reservation. General Howard told us again if we refused orders, soldiers would drive us on that reservation. He asked for Tulhulhutsut and was told, "He is here." This chief was our speaker. General Howard shook hands with him, but would let him talk only a little. They quarreled some, then agreed to rest, to finish the talk three suns later.

During this delay, more Indians came in and more soldiers were seen to arrive. It was Sapalwit (Sunday) evening when this announcement was made all through the camp. "Tomorrow morning everybody be at the soldier council camp."

All went. I, Yellow Wolf, went. I wanted to hear what was talked. I did hear what was said. I saw what was done. In after snows I listened to my boy read in white people's history things not true about that council. The Indians were *not* armed! General Howard broke friendship. The council was held in front of the guardhouse, maybe 150 steps away.

Agent Monteith made his same talk again. How we must obey orders or soldiers would be sent against us. General Howard got up and shook hands with the chiefs. He told them they could talk, but they had to come on the reservation.

Chief Tulhulhutsut stood up to talk for the Indians. He told how the land always belonged to the Indians, how it came down to us from our fathers. How the earth was a great law, how everything must remain as fixed by the Earth-Chief. How the land must not be sold! That we came from the earth, and our bodies must go back to earth, our mother. General Howard stopped the chief.

He ordered, "I do not want to hear you say anything more like that. I am telling you! Thirty days you have to get on the reservation."

"You ask me to talk, then tell me to say no more," Tulhulhutsut replied. "I am chief! I ask no man to come and tell me anything what I must do. I am chief here!"

General Howard answered sharp. "Yes, you are chief. I am telling you! Thirty days you have to move in!"

"Yes, picking your own count!" our chief said. "Go back to your own country! Tell them you are chief there. I am chief here."

General Howard was showing mad. He spoke sharply. "If you do not mind me, if you say, 'No,' soldiers will come to your place. You will be tied up and your stock taken from you."

Tulhulhutsut answered, "I am telling you! I am a chief! Who can tell me what I must do in my own country?"

General Howard was now strong mad. He spoke in loud voice, "*I* am the man to tell you what you must do! You will come on the reservation within time I tell you. If not, soldiers will put you there or shoot you down!"

Chief Tulhulhutsut did not become afraid. His words were strong as he replied, "I hear you! I have *simiakia,* that which belongs to a man! I am a man, and will not go! I will not leave my home, and land where I grew up!"

General Howard now called a soldier to come forward. He pointed to Tulhulhutsut and ordered, "Take him to the guardhouse."

The chief turned around, and the soldier thought he was coming with him, but he was not. The soldier then shoved him over some Indians sitting on the ground close together. They called out, "Come get him."

The soldier did not come, and the other chiefs advised Tulhulhutsut, "Go! We do not think they will do much to you."

The chief then stepped forward to the soldier. General Howard went with them to the jail, and there he again asked Tulhulhutsut, "Have you decided to go on the reservation?"

The chief, a prisoner, made quick reply. "Have you no ears? I said NO! I am a chief! Raised here by my father! No one tells me anything what I am to do!"

"No more talk here now," General Howard said. "You study and decide if you come in or not."

To all of us General Howard now spoke. "If you do not mind me, I will take my soldiers and *drive* you on the reservation."

Again, Agent Monteith told us, "You must understand from this day you are going on the reservation. If you do not do as told, soldiers will put you there."

All that hurt us. In peace councils, force must not be talked. It was the same as showing us the rifle. General Howard was just pricking with needles. That was not suited for the Indians.

Tulhulhutsut was kept in the guardhouse several suns, like a thief.

That was what brought war, the arrest of this chief and showing us the rifle!

Some young men talked secretly among themselves. To one another they said, "General Howard has shown us the rifle. We answer 'Yes.' We will stir up a fight for him. We will start his war!"

The chiefs were not talking war. After the Lapwai council they gave orders, "Everyone get ready to move to our new home. Round up horses and cattle, as many as can be found."

That was done. Cattle were rounded up and herded south of Salmon River. Water was too high and swift for their crossing. All the young calves—there were many—would be drowned. So would the old cows. While this was being done the people assembled at Tepahlewam, our old camping grounds at Tolo Lake. There were about six hundred people in camp. Many old men, many women and children. The women dug camas[8] which

[8] A lilyaceus plant indigenous to the northwest. The bulb is edible if properly cooked.

grew thick on the prairie, while men and boys had good times gambling and racing horses. I was with Chief Joseph. I slept in his lodge.

None of the chiefs wanted war. They held many councils to hear what the older warriors had to say. Some of these said, "We will wait for those returning from buffalo hunting in Montana. Then will be decided what to do if war breaks."

There were six leading chiefs. Joseph, Alokut, White Bird, Tulhulhutsut, Looking Glass, and Hahtalekin. This last chief had the smallest band, the Paloos.[8] He did not want war. No chief talked or wanted war. Looking Glass was strong against fighting. I am telling you about three times, no chief wanted war.

McWhorter's Comment:

When informed that the Nez Perce are accused in history of having cavalry drills, and of training for the war before fighting broke out, Yellow Wolf replied earnestly:

Not true! There was no training with horses, no practicing with rifles for that war. True, we rode concealed on side of horses as did all buffalo-hunting Indians. There was always likely to be fighting with enemy tribes. We had learned, had done that riding from child days. We did it in Wallowa Valley for sport. Some of us would ride by where friends were standing or sitting and fire at them under our horse's neck, but not hit them. I have done that myself in play.

We were not expecting war with the whites. But when we did get into war, we used those tactics in battle. We did this at White Bird Canyon, Cottonwood, and Clearwater fights. It was our privilege, our right to do so.

Of men to fight should war come, there were less than 120. This was counting full-aged men, not too old, and young men of war age. No boys under seventeen snows did fighting. And those who proved actual fighters numbered less than fifty. I can give you names of all.

---

[9] A subdivision of the Lower Nez Perce.

To Chief Joseph's wife a baby was to come. It was because of this that Joseph, Alokut, and a few men and two women crossed Mahsamyetteen (Buzzard Mountain) to the White Bird (Canyon) for beef. As I have said, all our cattle were south of Salmon River, which Joseph and party boated.

It was then, while they were gone, that war started.

Many of our people had been killed by white men on our reservation.[10] But at no time was anything done to punish them. The discovery of gold on our reservation (1860) brought thousands of white men. That was the beginning of our trouble. Those white killers were never bothered from living on our lands. They were still there. Still robbing and shooting or hanging Indians.

One of those who had been killed was Chief Tipyahlanah Siskon (Eagle Robe). His home had been at the same place on Salmon River for many snows. A white man came to him who wanted land. The chief gave him some land. The man built a house and raised crops. Then he took more land, a part of Eagle Robe's garden. When the chief tried to stop him from plowing, he drew his six-shooter and shot Tipyahlanah, who was unarmed. He lived only a short time. When dying, he spoke to his son, Wahlitits, a boy, but almost grown.

He said, "Do not bother the white man for what he has done to me. Let him live his life!"

That was about two snows before the war. Now (1877) Wahlitits was grown strong of body, sound and quick of mind. He had two near-brothers (first cousins) Sarpsis Ilppilp (Red Moccasin Tops), and Wetyetmas Wahyakt (Swan Necklace). Wetyetmas was youngest of the three. The two older men made their minds to kill that white man. They talked this way, "General Howard spoke the rifle in a peace council. He made prisoner our speaker, Chief Tulhulhutsut. We will stir up a fight for him. We will kill the white man who killed Tipyahlanah Siskon!"

The three went to the Salmon, but could not find the killer

---

[10] Wallowa Valley was never a reservation.

of Tipyahlanah. Becoming scared, he had run away to Florence mines. He put on Chinamen clothes and worked with the Chinamen, washing gold.

The young men now killed another man who had badly treated the Indians. They took a good horse belonging to him and returned home. They arrived at camp late at night."

"With Joseph and Alokut away killing beef, four chiefs were at Tolo Lake. These four and some old men were holding council in one tepee. Not wanting war, they talked what to do about General Howard's orders.

Someone called to them from a nearby tepee, "You poor people are talking for nothing! Three boys have already started war! They killed a white man on Salmon River and brought his horse here to this camp. It is already war!"

That stopped the council. There was lots of excitement.

Next morning Lepeet Hessemdooks (Two Moons) rode out to meet Chief Joseph and Alokut. He told them what had been done. Leaving the women to bring the pack horses loaded with meat, the men rode fast to camp. They found most tepees already down, the people moving from there. They tried to stop them, but no use. All left but Joseph and his band and about thirty-five other men. These stayed to guard against any enemy surprise, but some were afraid Joseph and Alokut might desert the other Indians. The bands that moved away went to Sapachesap (Drive In), a cave on Cottonwood Creek.

This same sun the three young men—Wahlitits and his near-brothers—returned to the Salmon River. With them went several warriors. They killed a few more whites, all bad men. One of these, a mean man, liked by nobody, had killed Dakoopin, who was lame. Hungry, he had gone to this white man's house to ask for food. The man had shot him. Now this sun, the two sons of Dakoopin went to the white man and asked, "What you mean, killing our father?"

The man drew his six-shooter and fired at them, but missed. Then the older boy jumped off his horse and with one rifleshot killed the man.

The war now came on fast.

That night I was in Chief Joseph's tepee. We had no timepieces in those days, but it must have been about two hours before midnight when I heard the sound of horses approaching and a white man's voice. Then a gun sounded. A bullet came through the tepee, but hit nobody.

I grabbed a magazine rifle and stepped through the doorway. Out a way I could see shadow forms of mounted men.

Chuslum Lapitkif Hotswal (Bull Second Boy) called in our tongue, "Shoot him!"

The men must have seen as I drew up my rifle. They whirled and galloped swiftly away. I fired, but missed.

From that time, the Nez Perce had no more rest. No more soft pillows for the head.

As the sun was dawning, I heard a gun report. Its sound was like a two-mile distance. Shortly, full sunlight came, and Chief Joseph said, "We must pack and go to Sapachesap, where the other chiefs are."

We packed quickly and started. We had gone about a mile and a half when I heard someone say, "They have killed one white man. They have taken two wagons from some white men." I learned later there was whiskey in those wagons.

Before the capture of these wagons, General Howard said, "I do not want war. If the chiefs will give up the three Indians who did the killing, I will hang them and let the others go."

But Ad Chapman, a white man living on White Bird Creek with a Umatilla wife, declared, "I can whip the Injuns alone. They are cowardly."

That was what we were told.

It was during these first suns of trouble that an Indian and a white man were killed near Mount Idaho. Three Indians traveled from White Bird Canyon. They were Pahka Alyanakt (Five Winters), Henawit (Going Fast), and Jyeloo, also named Pykat.

They came to three buildings, the home of a white man. These buildings must have been a dwelling and outhouses. It was early morning, about breakfast time, when they arrived. Nobody was there. I understood the three were drinking, or had been drinking. Tired, they rested in the house. They slept a short while. When ready to leave, Henawit took a swift chestnut-colored racer belonging to Jyeloo and went to bring the other two horses. Pretty quick he came running the horses and called, "We are attacked!"

Pahka Alyanakt jumped on his horse. The white men, a bunch of them, were coming fast. The two mounted Indians could not wait for Jyeloo. He had a lame leg, and his back was weak from an old wound. He moved slowly. Maybe was part drunk. The horse left by Henawit walked away, and he had to run after it. Because they left him, the two Indians gave him the only gun among them, an old 45–70 with but one cartridge. They forgot to give him the belt of ammunition.

Jyeloo finally got on the horse, a poor runner. His partners were now some distance away, the white men fast gaining on him. Coming to a fence, Jyeloo had to dismount. He was no longer young, and had gone through many hardships. Slow moving, he was soon cornered and killed.

The whites did not try to catch Pahka Alyanakt and Henawit. The two came to our camp at Sapachesap and told what had happened.

Thirty of us quickly mounted and hurried with them to where the attack was made, where Jyeloo had been killed. We spread out, searching the tall grass for Jyeloo. We found him. I saw his body myself, all covered with blood. He had many gunshot wounds on his body and legs—eleven in all. His head, crushed, was all over blood. Blood on the ground. I saw he had drawn his sheath knife. It was in the grass not far from him—must have been shot from his hand. We did not find the rifle.

With only one cartridge and side knife in a running fight, Jyeloo could do nothing against so many enemies. But he was hard to kill.

His body was taken back over the trail while fifteen of us

went to the house where the three had been attacked. We wanted to see, and remained there for a time. Then one of us saw a white man approaching. He seemed coming to the house, so we lay concealed. We wondered why he was coming, but he had no chance to explain. When he got close, we made for him. We chased him toward a steep hill.

Pahkatos Watyekit (Five Times Looking Up) had a bow and arrows. He rode close to the man's side and drew an arrow on the bow. The man grabbed the arrow and nearly jerked Pahkatos from his horse. Six of us overtook him. Kosooyeen (Going Alone) was ahead. He shot the man from his horse while fast running; but he got up. He was then shot and brought down for good.

Nothing more happened, and we went no farther. The man killed was young. He had a six-shooter, but did not fire it. We thought maybe he owned the house and was returning for something left there.

We now rode back to camp where was great excitement. All knew trouble was ahead. The chiefs held council what to do. It was a short council. Soon they made announcement: "We will move to Lahmotta!"

Chief Looking Glass and his band, the Asotains, felt differently. They left for their old home on Clearwater River. The women had gardens planted there. The Asotains wanted no war. Looking Glass, strong against war, went with his people.

This left five chiefs, five bands, if fighting broke.

We packed up and started. Going about three miles, we saw a troop of soldiers (probably citizen scouts). They stopped when they saw us, and we crossed Buzzard Mountain to Lahmotta.

After supper three men went back on the trail to watch if soldiers followed. One went to the top of the mountain, two stopped on the side of the canyon. One of these two had been a bad Indian, a thief. He was not a Nez Perce. Before coming to us, he was a slave. For stealing, his master put steel traps on his wrists and ankles, then placed him outside the tepee in a winter night. He must have been left out too long. Both feet and one hand died and came off. We called him Seeskoomkee (No Feet).

In after part of night I heard Seeskoomkee shouting, "Soldiers coming this way! Soldiers coming this way!"

The people heard and ran out of the tepees. When I got out I saw Seeskoomkee sitting on his horse still calling, "Soldiers coming this way! Soldiers coming this way!"

No more sleep that night. All five chiefs gave orders to bring horses in close. When that was done, we caught and tied best ones up. The others were herded.

Sunlight breaking, the other two scouts galloped in and reported, "Soldiers coming close! Big bunch of them!"

At this announcement, warriors quickly stripped and armed for war. I saw them going out, one by one, to meet the soldiers. Most of them kept to the left (west), back of buttes near base of the mountain.

Four of us went up the creek, along edge of brush and timber. We wanted to get on other side of the soldiers. I had only hunting bow and arrows. My rifle was with my mother in Chief Looking Glass's camp at their gardens. We stopped at nearest of the two Cemetery Buttes, where some great Nez Perce chiefs are buried. We lay down on a low swell on south side of the butte. A young fellow took our horses back of the upper butte to hold for us, there hidden from our enemies.

Soon came lighter sun. I raised up and looked north. Something seemed moving away up country. I watched closely. Yes, there came the soldiers a good distance off. We all lay flat and watched.

2 THE CONFLICT

For the next few days while Joseph remained quietly at Cottonwood Creek, the young warriors throwing off all restraint shot settlers and their families and, after setting fire to their buildings, drove off their stock. As word spread from farm to ranch, settlers hitched horses to their wagons and, abandoning everything, drove at a gallop toward the nearest fort or village. Many of the fugitives were captured by small roving bands of Indians and nearly all exterminated. A few women and children badly wounded crawled into the brush and eventually reached safety. Joseph knew what was going on. He highly disapproved, but was powerless to stop it.

He knew that in a few days mounted soldiers would arrive. More would follow. Behind them the walking soldiers, the infantry, would march tirelessly. In their midst many mule teams would haul great howitzers, the thunder birds. There would be wagons and carts creaking under the weight of iron shells, which after being fired would explode wherever the artillery officer wished, at about the height of a man on horseback, and kill everyone within the radius of an arrow flight. There would also be gatling guns, the guns with many barrels which could be revolved and fired quickly while they swung on a pivot. Three of those guns could stop a charge of hundreds of mounted Indians, mowing them down in a horrible tangle.

Joseph thought of the precious ammunition which the young warriors were wasting on settler families when they should be saving it until the soldiers had arrived. They would need it and as much more as they could buy or capture.

Most of all Joseph thought of how he could protect the old

people, the women and children of his band. Obviously there was no place where Indian mothers and their children could be held in concealment for any length of time. The Wallamwatkin warriors would require time to defeat the white soldiers.

Joseph knew that his warriors were good shots and good fighters, far better than General Howard suspected, but they were woefully lacking in any sort of ammunition, and now that the war had begun, the trading posts wouldn't sell ammunition to Indians at any price. To meet the soldiers on equal terms, Joseph would have to retreat like a wounded grizzly bear into the mountain ravines and passes drawing the soldiers farther and farther from their supply base and even supply wagons. He would have to wear them down. Then, when they were slow and stupid from fatigue, he could strike and perhaps defeat them. After that he might lead his people to a new country where game would be plentiful and where white people would leave the Wallamwatkins alone. They had no enmity for the white people. They just wanted to be left alone.

In all of Joseph's plans there was a persistently recurring question. Could the Indian families endure the hardships and hazards of a rapid retreat for the length of time necessary to exhaust the United States Cavalry?

Joseph was still pondering this question when one of his scouts brought word that Captain David Perry had led ninety cavalry men out of Fort Lapwai at sunset on the middle day of the strawberry moon (June 15th) and that they were riding in the direction of Cottonwood Creek. Joseph's expectant wife still hadn't delivered. Reluctantly he gave the order to strike his tepee, pack up and remove to White Bird Canyon. There was neither law nor rule which compelled the rest of his band to follow him, but they did so without question.

From safely distant concealment a few mounted settlers who had been watching Joseph's camp followed. In the dim radiance of the stars they saw the dark mass of mounted Indians and pony herds enter the deep shadow of the canyon's mouth. The settlers knew that there was a good pack-horse trail all of the way up through the canyon and out at the head. The steeply sloping sides were bisected by lateral ravines.

Joseph had chosen White Bird Canyon knowing that within its depth he could set a trap for the soldiers and give them such a beating that they would keep at a respectful distance for a while. Joseph needed that interval so that he could call in the few young warriors who still roamed the settled country. Also in his retreat he needed a long start so that he could double back beside his own trail before camping for the night. It was essential that he choose his own course instead of being driven by a hot pursuit. Indian mothers with babies strapped to their backs and children to watch besides could not become successful fugitives. Therefore the departure of the Wallamwatkins must indeed be a retreat, not a flight.

Meanwhile Captain Perry with his command riding all night had crossed Craig's Mountain and Lawyer's Canyon and reached Grangeville. The cowboys who had acted as voluntary observers met Perry at Grangeville and urged him to attack at once the Indian camp in White Bird Canyon. They assured him that he could exterminate the entire band with ease, that there would be only a token show of resistance and that the great danger was that the Indians would be gone before he could catch them. Since Perry's command was not equal to one full company, the cowboys offered to go along and help him. Not that he would really need them, but it would afford them an excuse for shooting Indians off of their ponies, a sport supposedly forbidden by law.

Perry foolishly listened to them. His troopers were tired. They should have been allowed an adequate rest while Perry himself rode to the canyon's rim and followed along a few miles of its length, using his binoculars to acquaint himself with the location of the Indian camp, the lateral ravines and the dispersal of warriors in those ravines, and some idea of the number of Indians. Instead Perry led his troop to the head of White Bird Canyon. Because it was not yet light Perry dismounted his men and told them that they might lie down on the ground and sleep for two hours.

At sunrise Perry, who had not attempted to sleep, saw hilltops peeping above the quilt of white ground mist. As the mist lifted he could see the Indian camp.

At the same time Joseph and his brother Alokut had just emerged from their tepees and were watching the sunlight descending slowly from the peaks until it touched with color the sloping surfaces of the west side of the canyon. Alokut saw their enemy first, two mounted Indian scouts, motionless as if painted on the skyline. Alokut ran to White Bird's tepee and awakened him, then to his own tepee and fetched a pair of binoculars which he used, then handed to Joseph. Alokut had carried those field glasses for keeping track of the Wallamwatkins' cattle and ponies. Now they served a military purpose. Three Eagles later described the incident:

□ "Two of our men (Joseph's men) started riding up the hill. We saw a man (Chapman) shoot at them. Then our men fired. Jonas Hayes (a reservation Nez Perce) was with the soldiers. He had come with the intention of talking to Joseph to see if he could not bring him back in peace. If Chapman had not fired, Jonah Hayes would have come and talked with Joseph and the whole war would have been avoided." □

This was Three Eagles' opinion. Joseph was proud and dignified. To protect his people from war he had swallowed insults and endured abuse, but when by looking through binoculars he could see a fight coming his way, he was not the sort of man who would sit down and talk about peace. The Wallamwatkins were now in a state of war. Because of that condition they were all willing to take orders from Joseph while the war lasted, and while they continued to be of the Wallamwatkin band. It was their privilege as individuals to forsake the band and go to the Lapwai Reservation or for that matter anywhere they pleased. But as long as they were of the band Joseph was their war chief.

Mox Mox* who had been keeping watch up on the plateau came running down a lateral ravine confirming the arrival of

* Another authority states that Itskimze Kin (Feet and Hands Cut Off) carried the message of alarm to the Nez Perce.

Captain Perry's troop of cavalry. Joseph received the news calmly and told Mox Mox to take charge of the striking of the tepees and packing them, together with the household goods, on the ponies; also the driving of the pony herd down the canyon until they were out of sight. That work could be done by the women and older children.

Joseph then sent enough warriors down to the mouth of the canyon to protect his rear. He posted a number of warriors led by White Bird behind a ridge at the left of what had been the camp ground and based his line of battle on that. Joseph took charge of one end of the line, Alokut the other. About fifty warriors had rifles. The others were armed only with bows and arrows. All of the warriors with their ponies immediately took cover behind rocks.

Joseph's disposition of his warriors was well-considered. It was likely that when Perry attacked, his heaviest pressure would be exerted against Joseph's center. As the center retreated, it would pass in front of the ridge concealing Joseph's hidden force. Perry's right flank would receive an onslaught while Joseph's right and left wings closed on Perry's rear like the jaws of a trap. The only thing the matter with that ambush was the bows and arrows, and that Joseph couldn't help.

Perry's troop in single file rode four miles down into the canyon. When the trail widened they formed a column of fours. Lieutenant Theller with a squad of eight rode a hundred yards ahead of Captain Perry, who led the main body of the cavalry and the cowboys. Captain Trimble with a few troopers brought up the rear. The three groups kept a spacing of about fifty yards. This was a smart order of march, but there was one flaw. Perry was attacking too precipitately. He still had not taken the precaution of informing himself about the strength and disposition of the Indian forces. He was soon to acquire that important information—the hard way.

When Indian heads began bobbing up behind the rocks and boulders strewn across the canyon about a hundred yards in front, Lieutenant Theller ordered his small detachment into skirmish line. The cowboys trotted to a butte on their left, dismounted, and formed an extension of Theller's line. Perry ordered Trimble to move up and extend the skirmish line still farther. For a moment it seemed to the cavalry that they would burst the Indian line and chase the Indians into the Salmon River beyond the mouth of the canyon.

Perry held his main body in reserve. His troopers began firing between their horses' ears at the Indians. The Indians didn't like it. Neither did the horses. They reared, bucked and kicked, tossing their riders. During this diversion the Indians moved up the sides of the canyon to higher ground where they could look down on the cavalry.

At the same time White Bird attacked Trimble's right flank. Then two cowboys stopped Indian bullets. Protective instinct caused the rest of the cowboys to flee up the canyon. The Indians wanted very much to catch the intrepid cowboys, but they couldn't even get close enough to them for another shot.

Theller saw a lateral ravine and led eighteen troopers in there, believing that at the head of the ravine he could climb back to the plateau above. The ravine proved to be dead end. The Indians closed in. Theller and all of his men were killed.

Flanked on both sides and fired on from above, the cavalry very sensibly ignored the commands of their officers. The bugler was dead. The officers had lost their trumpets. The officers shouted and bawled to their men to reform their line and make a stand to cover a retreat. The troopers responded by concentrating on getting out of that canyon. Some of them reached the plateau, turned and fired at the pursuit. This checked the Indians long enough to permit other troopers to ride out.

Mount Idaho, and safety, was eighteen miles away. To reach it they had to cross one last ravine. Parnell and a few troopers made a stand to hold back the Indians while Perry led the remainder across. Having reached the opposite side the remainder were supposed to shoot back at the Indians while Parnell's detail crossed. But the remainder didn't remain. They kept right on going. Parnell and his set-ups had to cross with the Indians on their heels. And it wasn't as funny as it sounds.

Three miles beyond at Johnson's abandoned ranch Perry ordered a halt. He told Parnell that they would hold that position for a couple of hours, when it would be dark. Then they would continue their retreat. Parnell patiently explained to Perry that they had started fighting at sunrise and that they had been fighting and running, mostly running, for four hours, that it wasn't seven P.M. but seven A.M., and they were nearly out of ammunition.

Then Perry had another happy idea. He could see Indians rapidly closing in from all sides among the rocks and along the fences. So he asked Parnell to make another stand and cover the retreat while he with what was left of the main body got a good head start toward Mount Idaho.

Parnell looked at Perry very skeptically, but he obeyed until, with the Indians running right at him, he tried to turn his horse to ride after Perry, only to find that he wasn't on one. His horse, having had experience, had slid out from beneath him and followed Perry and his men. The Indians wore moccasins. Parnell wore heavy cavalry boots. Even so the Indians couldn't catch him. They were good runners too.

Some of Parnell's men glancing back saw his predicament and were finally able to point it out to Perry. Perry halted the troops, had Parnell's horse caught and taken back to where he could mount it. Parnell, thoroughly angered, turned and faced the Indian charge. He was supported by a few of his men. At the right moment they fired a volley which brought down several Indians and their ponies. The warriors veered off. Parnell galloped after Perry. When the Indians again came close, he halted and gave them another volley. Meanwhile White Bird again flanked Perry and tried to push him off the plateau into Rocky Canyon. White Bird might have succeeded at that, if valiant Captain Perry hadn't followed Parnell's example and given White Bird a few volleys.

Four miles from Mount Idaho the cavalry were met by a lot of cowboys coming to their rescue. The Indians gave up the pursuit and returned to rob the dead cavalry men of their rifles and ammunition. There were thirty-three dead soldiers. Perry's men had wounded a few warriors and killed none. With the loss of over one-third of his command Captain Perry was luckier than Custer at the Battle of the Little Big Horn in 1875, but not much. They both made the same mistake. They failed to recognize that the Indians are brave, very intelligent and think and act quickly.

Long afterward Joseph in speaking of the battle in White Bird canyon said: □ "Until the first fight had been fought and the victory had been given to the Nez Perce I did not think that we would go farther than the buffalo grounds. After the fight I knew that I would have to lead my people to the country where Sitting Bull had found a refuge when pursued." □

Joseph remained near the mouth of White Bird Canyon until his scouts informed him five days later that General Howard, with two hundred and twenty-seven cavalry, was approaching the Salmon River.

Joseph led his people down the Salmon River to Horseshoe Bend, took them across on rafts made of willow-framed buffalo hides, guided them up into some low rocky hills and pitched camp.

General Howard with Captains Marcus Miller and Nelson Miles and a well-equipped body of cavalry filed into White Bird Canyon and buried the dead soldiers. On June 27th and 28th the cavalry rode to the crossing of the Salmon River a mile and a half above the mouth of White Bird Creek, where the arrival of reenforcements augmented their number to four hundred. A few warriors came down to the opposite bank and taunted the cavalry. A few shots were exchanged. No one was hit. Several troopers swam the river. The current was unspeakably cold and very swift, but they managed it encouraged by the cheers of their comrades. Naked and shivering they climbed the bluffs on the opposite bank, but there was not an Indian in sight. It was a pleasant afternoon outing and kept Howard and the boys interested and amused while twenty miles downstream

Joseph and his people recrossed the Salmon River, got behind Howard and cut his supply line.

Indeed Howard became so intrigued with the sport of crossing the river, first by lariats which burst, then by a cable and boats, that he spent several days at it. While thus happily engaged some friendly Indians appeared and said that some of Looking Glass' young warriors had joined Joseph.

Howard paused long enough to dispatch Captain Whipple with a dozen or so of calvary and a few casual cowboys to investigate while he continued transferring his command across the Salmon.

Howard's orders to Whipple were to surprise Looking Glass in his camp, make him prisoner and ○ "all that belonged to him and turn over all prisoners for safe-keeping to the volunteer organization at Mount Idaho." ○

Looking Glass at the moment was camping in what he considered his own territory on the banks of Clear Creek, a tributary of Clearwater River, four miles from Kooskia and northeast of Mount Idaho. Some of the young warriors in Looking Glass' band had joined Joseph. Others were considering it. Looking Glass by conduct and persuasion had done what he could to prevent hostilities, although he was an able leader and a first class fighter and undoubtedly yearned to join in the fight. Certainly his forbearance deserved better than the unannounced arrival at the edge of his camp at dawn on July first of Whipple's detachment with bugle blowing and a demand that the Indians wake-up, get up and surrender.

Looking Glass came forward and in a dignified manner explained to Whipple that he could see no cause for a demand that he surrender. He had not been involved in any hostilities. His people were already on reservation. Why should they become prisoners of war?

While Looking Glass was talking a cowboy named Holmes tried to create a little bit more urgent atmosphere by fanning his six-shooter into the Indian camp. He killed outright an Indian baby. The warriors attending Looking Glass supposing that they were at a peace conference were unarmed. With bare hands they beat up the troopers and cowboys. Then abandoning all of their tepees, seven hundred ponies and every other possession, they fled with their families to the hills to join Joseph. The baby was the only casualty on either side, but Whipple did get the seven hundred ponies. He left them at Mount Idaho. There he received a message from General Howard that Captain Perry would shortly arrive at Norton's Cottonwood Ranch with an ammunition train. Whipple's orders were to hasten to the Cottonwood Ranch to act as a guard for that train.

It was possible that by smoke signals and by runner Looking Glass would inform Joseph of his location. Naturally Joseph's scouts would see the ammunition train and report it. Howard was concerned about the possibilities. He had reason for concern. While Howard was pondering, Joseph emerged from the hills, recrossed the Salmon River at Craig's Ferry and, turning eastward, took a strong position on Craig's Mountain northwest of Cottonwood Ranch.

Whipple's detachment arrived at Cottonwood Ranch on July 2nd and dismounted, lighted their pipes and sat down to wait for Perry and his twenty men convoying the ammunition train. The next morning it occurred to Whipple that it would be useful to know how many Indians were in the offing and where they were. So he dispatched two cowboys, Blewett and Foster, to find out. Doubtless Whipple reasoned that if the cowboys failed to find the Indians, the Indians might find them. Either way would do.

Toward evening Foster returned with the information that to cover a wider area they had separated. About twelve miles away he had seen a large party of Indians before they saw him. He had immediately pointed his horse toward Cottonwood Ranch. There had been no need to whip his horse. The Indians' rifle bullets whistling close to the horse's ears had sufficed. As for Blewett, he could only surmise that the Indians had seen him first. Too bad!

Whipple stroked his whiskers. Maybe the Indians had also seen Perry. Whipple believed that a time of crisis called not for retrenchment but for action. He might get off on the wrong foot, but at least he would start. First he ordered Lieutenant Sevier Rains with ten picked men to follow Foster to the spot where Foster and the Indians had had a good look at each other. Whipple instructed Rains to ascertain the strength of the enemy and to find Blewett if he could; also to stay on high ground, not go very far and to send back a rider to report his first contact with the Indians. After Rains had gone Whipple followed at a sufficient interval. "Sufficient" meant that there was enough intervening space so that if the Indians suddenly materialized and gobbled up Rains, Whipple with the remnant of his command would have sufficient time for a jack-rabbit start toward the camp.

Two miles north of Cottonwood, Rains followed his instructions to keep on high ground by entering the bottom of a ravine. It was analagous to a dog walking into the wide open mouth of an alligator. At least that was the way it sounded to Whipple whose troopers were in the act of mounting. There was also a lot of shooting. Whipple gave the order to charge. The troop galloped to within a half mile of the ravine, stopped galloping and sat in their saddles watching the extermination of Rains, Foster and the ten picked men. As they fell shrieking beneath tomahawk and bullet, it is possible that some of the troopers with Whipple became convinced of the disadvantages of becoming "picked men."

After the show was over Whipple selected a wide open spot in which to spend the night. He deployed his men in two long lines, placed his mountain artillery in the center and prepared for attack. There was none. Having no interest in charging across a wide open space into flaming artillery and salvos of grape and rifle bullets, Joseph prudently withdrew to his camp back in the hills.

During the skirmish General Howard was riding through the hill country west of the Salmon River under the illusion that because Joseph had been there he must still be there. It was therefore something of a shock to him when a band of cowboys known as McConville's Company found him and informed him of

Joseph's actual location, the massacre of Rain's detail and the almost fortuitous junction of Whipple, and the twenty cavalry men he had managed to save, with Perry and the ammunition train. However, he must have been relieved to know that they were now safe in a fortified position at Cottonwood. Howard immediately dispatched a cowboy to Cottonwood with instructions for Perry to stay put.

While acquiring his information McConville had been riding momentarily along the edge of Rocky Canyon. A few Indians had flushed ahead of him and ridden down into the canyon. Rightly assuming that their purpose was to lead him into an ambush in the canyon, McConville led his men away from the canyon at a gallop, thereby saving them from a large and well-prepared ambush.

The ambush was not Joseph's only tactic. He knew that the covered wagons which Perry was escorting contained a great deal of ammunition. The very existence of his people depended upon his capturing it. Therefore at noon on July Fourth Joseph's warriors surrounded the combined forces of Perry and Whipple at Cottonwood. As senior officer, Perry was in command. With his troopers dismounted and in rifle pits, and artillery served with abundant ammunition Perry was able to beat off the warriors' attacks. At sundown the incessant, shrill war whoops died away. The Indians gave it up and rode back to their camp about three miles off.

During the night Perry maintained a strong guard around his camp, but there were no attacks. The next morning Indians assembled in small groups which increased in size as more and more warriors arrived. By threatening gestures, continuous shrill ululations and prancing about on their ponies they tried to intimidate the cavalry.

Some cavalrymen setting up a cheval-de-frise of sharpened stakes on the east side of the ranch house became aware of "yip-yipees" punctuating the wahoos of warriors. Sure enough. From the direction of the Johnson ranch two cowboys with mustaches pressed to their horses' necks were galloping toward Cottonwood with whooping warriors also galloping only a few yards behind, and they weren't fooling. The cowboys' horses, although larger and stronger than the lean ponies of the Indians, were nevertheless barely holding their lead. There was a reality—and finality about the scene.

When they came within rifle range of Cottonwood, the Indians swerved. The cowboys rode in unscathed. They proved to be the messengers General Howard had sent to Perry ordering him to stay put at Cottonwood pending further orders. That order was all right with Perry, and Whipple too. They were not going anywhere.

About noon Indians charged simultaneously all of the exposed sections of Perry's fortifications. Then they crawled through tall grass to within sixty feet of Perry's line. The warriors were brave and resolute. They all knew the importance of that ammunition, but they hadn't a chance. Like Custer, Perry had chosen an elevated area for his fortifications, but unlike Custer he had adequate artillery solidly mounted and expertly served.

After several assaults which must have cost Joseph more warriors than he could afford to lose, he called them off. Meanwhile a diversion had presented. A relief force of seventeen cowboys from Mount Idaho led by Randall had appeared about two miles from Cottonwood. There the cowboys collided with a band of warriors driving herds of cattle and ponies across the prairie. Joseph had already put in motion the advance elements of his people on their long journey to Canada.

As the line of warriors swept toward the cowboys, Randall ordered a charge right through them, hoping that momentum would carry the cowboys through to Cottonwood. He shouted to each cowboy to hold his fire until the clash and then shoot the Indian in front of him and squeeze through. When the lines crashed Randall and Evans fell. The rest did squeeze through, but the Indian line turned and came after them so quickly that they had to scamper upon a knoll, dismount and, forming a circle, try to repel the Indians.

From their knoll Perry and Whipple could see that the cowboys from Mount Idaho were certainly in trouble. Whipple wanted to lead a detachment to their rescue, but Perry refused. With a much more numerous command in White Bird Canyon he had had it—and how! The memory was still green. He had barely enough men to protect the ammunition. Even a small detachment could not be spared, although the Mount Idaho cowboys had sortied and rescued him once and were trying to do it again.

For an hour the soldiers and cowboys at Cottonwood listened to the war-whoops and anguished yelps from the knoll two miles away. Then twenty-five cowboys, in defiance of orders, mounted and were about to ride to the rescue, when Perry halted them. Captain Whipple and a detachment of cavalry, also in defiance of orders, resolved to join them. Then Perry changed his mind and sent them all on.

Whipple led his detachment in an arc, approaching the attacking Indians from behind. At the same time the Mount Idaho cowboys charged them in front. The Indians gave way. Before the Indians could mount a counterattack Whipple, the cavalry, and the cowboys who had survived, were all safe at Cottonwood.

Convinced that he could not take the ammunition wagons at Cottonwood by any sort of assault, and aware that it wouldn't be much longer before Howard would suspect that Joseph was not west of the Salmon River, as indeed he hadn't been for about a week, Joseph focused his attention upon transporting his people across the prairie and into the hills where he would have more natural advantages. Looking Glass and his people had already taken refuge in those hills. Joseph wished to join them.

Had the Nez Perce and all of the other tribes in the Columbia River basin been ethnically cohesive, the demonstrations of mastery of military tactics which Joseph had already given would have sufficed to rally thousands of fighting men to his camp. The ensuing war might have eventually involved all of the tribes west of the Mississippi. The ultimate consequences of such a war can only be surmised. But Indians are not like white people. They are not greedy and, while they will fight when necessary, they are by nature a peace loving people. They did have inter-tribal wars, but their wars were more like rough games, such as the Irish at Donnybrook. Of course a few were killed, but mostly it was bruises and bumps.

Joseph had no thought of conquest. After Looking Glass had joined him his warriors raided the farms of reservation Indians as well as those of the white settlers. But they did not destroy. They took only what they needed to repair their losses.

So, two friendly Nez Perce scouts attached to Howard's cavalry tactfully suggested to him that although the transferral of his force across the torrent of the Salmon River had been a fine bit of military engineering there was no use in continuing his search for Joseph on the west side. The reports that Joseph had recrossed the Salmon were true. For many days Joseph had been between Howard and his supply base at Fort Lapwai. If Howard wanted that ammunition train, he had better follow Joseph by recrossing the Salmon and riding to Cottonwood Ranch. It is possible that the two scouts had relatives among those whose farms were being raided by Joseph's foragers.

General Howard was a God-fearing man, not as devout as General Thomas Jonathan (Stonewall) Jackson, but he was fearing. It would be interesting to know whether he swore when he realized that Joseph had made a monkey of him. At any rate he retraced his steps through the Salmon Mountains, enduring rain, fog, and snow. Several mules missed their toe-holds while hauling artillery up steep muddy hills and vanished over the edge of a two-thousand-foot precipice in a snow storm on the Fourth of July.

On the afternoon of the Fourth the cavalry troop recrossed the Salmon at the confluence of Billy's Creek. The infantry, led by Captain Miles, followed as fast as they could. Howard led the cavalry up through White Bird Canyon and on toward Craig's Mountain. He rode into Cottonwood on July 9th and immediately replenished his stock of food and ammunition. Captain Miles with his infantry marched in late that night.

The same night McConville discovered the Wallamwatkin

camp. A friendly Indian informed him that Joseph had in that camp 313 warriors. McConville sent a cowboy to warn Howard, then dug in on a hill about a mile from the South Fork of the Clearwater River. Howard had crossed on Jackson's bridge. He was ten miles away and of course on the opposite side of Clearwater River. Joseph's reconnaissance soon discovered McConville. Shortly afterward the warriors attacked and drove away all of the cowboys' horses. For two or three days McConville beat off Indian attacks. Unquestionably Joseph could have gathered in McConville & Co. like poker chips. There were only forty-three of them. But he left them there as bait, hoping that Howard would come to their rescue. However, Howard was too smart to be drawn into such a trap. The cowboys stuck it out for two or three days, then, having no horses, they walked to Three Mile Creek near Mount Idaho and again dug in to protect the town—and themselves.

The South Fork of the Clearwater flowed in a deep current between steeply sloping banks which seemed to brace sheer cliffs rising a thousand feet or more. At irregular intervals the cliffs on either side were indented with deep ravines and narrow canyons. From the tops of the cliffs back to the foothills stretched a plateau on either side of the river. Ravines cut the plateaus. The floors of the ravines arose from their mouths, gradually sloping upward until they came up to the plateau level a mile or so back from the river.

With his people and herds Joseph had gone into one of the ravines on the west side of the South Fork like boys disappearing down an outside cellar staircase. Because all of the Wallamwatkins and their ponies needed a few days of rest Joseph hoped that Howard would not immediately discover his whereabouts. The cowboys, knowing the hiding places from their searches for cattle, notified Howard. At noon on July 11th cavalry appeared on the edge of the cliff on the east side of the south fork of the Clearwater. They were looking down into the mouth of the ravine where about half of the Indians' ponies were grazing.

The Indian families were in tepees farther up the ravine. The other half of the ponies were in a ravine on the opposite side of the river. If the soldiers had ridden a little farther, they would have looked directly down upon them. Joseph had divided his pony herd thus for greater flexibility of maneuver in event of attack.

When shells from howitzers exploded above their heads the Indian herdsmen did not wait for Joseph's order. On both sides of the river they drove the herds upstream on the steeply sloping banks and around a bend where they were out of range and temporarily safe.

Deep in the ravine on Howard's side of the river Joseph had posted a large number of warriors to guard the herdsmen. These warriors swarmed out like angry bees. Taking cover behind boulders, they formed a circle around a spring. Firing continuously they extended their line into a flanking formation. Parched with thirst, the soldiers tried to take the spring by assault. The Indians retreated, then counterattacked and retained the spring. The artillery laid down a barrage to cover an attack, but the barrage was ineffectual because of the many boulders. The Indians retained possession of the spring. Shooting and whooping, the Indians made so much noise that the infantry and artillery became confused and shot at each other. Firing ceased with darkness. The soldiers spent a chilly, thirsty night. At dawn the soldiers charged the spring and took it, but they paid a price.

The second day of the battle saw sharpshooting and sniping by both sides and charges by the Indians. Joseph was everywhere, exposing himself recklessly. All of the soldiers were shooting at him. Several horses were killed under him, but he was not scratched.

In the afternoon a string of pack-mules with ammunition and supplies from Fort Lapwai approached. Mounted warriors swooped down upon it, but Captain Miller with a company of cavalry swooped at the swooping Indians and kept them so busy dodging saber thrusts that their attention was completely diverted from the pack-mules. Without stopping Miller led his troop between the two battle lines, struck the Indian line at an angle and rolled it up.

Howard saw the Indian line waver under the impact of that old Civil War trick and promptly ordered a general charge. Indians had no particular dread of the cavalry saber, but they have uniformly disliked a bayonet charge. When the Wallamwatkins saw that a last minute effort to turn Miller's left flank had failed and that the infantry with flashing bayonets was closing in they fled to the river and swam across.

General Howard ordered Captain Perry to lead the cavalry along the cliff until he found a slope not so steep but that the horses could slide down it, then to ford or swim the river and attack the Indian village in the canyon below. Lieutenant Parnell afterward wrote that if Perry had executed that order promptly the Indians would have surrendered. But Perry had not forgotten his attempt to do just that four weeks previously in White Bird Canyon. To Howard's great annoyance Perry proceeded so slowly that by the time he reached the tepees the Indians had gone. They had abandoned their tepees, flour, kettles, buffalo robes, knives and axes, but they had retreated in good order northeastward toward Kamiah.

The quantity of baggage which the Indians left suggested that they had hoped to stand a siege in that canyon, but had changed their minds and resolved to seek safety in flight.

Howard's burial party interred twenty-three warriors and thirteen soldiers. Two officers and twenty-two soldiers seriously wounded were returned to Lapwai under escort.

General Howard had indeed driven the warlike element of the Nez Perce, the Wallamwatkins, out of Oregon and Idaho, but he had not put them on reservation. Therefore as soon as he could reorganize his forces he doggedly followed their trail.

YELLOW WOLF'S STORY
OF
THE CONFLICT

White Bird Canyon—Whither L. V. McWhorter had conveyed Yellow Wolf for an on-the-battlefield description of the Battle of White Bird Canyon, the first of the war.

IT WAS THERE under that rock-ridge that I saw the first enemies. Five warriors, led by Wettiwetti Houlis (Mean Person, known to the whites as John Boyd), had been sent out from the other (west) side of the valley as a peace party to meet the soldiers. These warriors had instructions from the chiefs not to fire unless fired upon. Of course they carried a white flag. Peace might be made without fighting.

MCWHORTER'S COMMENT:

Yellow Wolf paused, scanning the west buttes which hid the canyon paralleling White Bird Creek. It was up this west-side canyon that the Nez Perce peace embassy was dispatched. Not satisfied with the outlook, Yellow Wolf signified that we should go to the other, the more northern, Cemetery Butte, only a few rods away. The transfer was not accomplished without difficulty. The smooth, rounded knoll, coated with dead midsummer range grass, rendered the climb most laborious for the once strong warrior, now weakened by a life of hardships and penury and by old age. After a few moments of rest on the summit, Yellow Wolf called attention to the largest, loaf-shaped butte in the distance. The fires of other days lit his restless eyes, as with outstretched arm he resumed his story:

Back of that largest butte, near fifty warriors were waiting. From around its southern point I saw a tall warrior, wearing a commander's sash, ride out on a fine cream-colored horse. All knew that easy rider, Chief Alokut. Slowly—not hurriedly—as if reconnoitering, he loped northward to midway the butte. Just then, at that time, that moment, broke the *Qoh! Qoh!* of a raven. Alokut turned back and disappeared where we first saw him. The warning came from an Indian lying close on top of the butte. It reached across to where we were watching. It told, "Soldiers close approaching!"

From the north echoed a rifle report, and right away a white man on a white horse came riding swiftly south. He crossed that bench-flat along the foot of the rockline crowning the ridge. He did not look like a soldier. A big white hat, he was dressed more like a citizen. When he came closer, we knew him. Yes, he had the big-four hat (sombrero). A *big* hat! It was Chapman, called by the whites a squaw man! Having an Indian wife was why we had been friends. He and my uncle, Old Yellow Wolf, had lived in the same house, just as brothers. Now he was first enemy we see. Changed, and trying to kill each other. It was he who fired the first shot we had just heard. Fired on our peace party.

The chief's peace offer was not respected.

About twenty soldiers charging after Chapman were not firing. When Chapman got closer, he fired across at us. Then the soldiers began shooting. That was how the battle started. Chapman made first two shots.

The three men with me now began shooting. A long distance! I, with only bow and arrows, could do nothing. The soldier bugler rode close to the brink of that rounded cliff, north edge of the gorge.

Twelve other warriors joined us. One, an old man, Otstotpoo (Fire Body), made a good shot and killed the bugler. When the bugler fell from his horse, Chapman rode swiftly out from there. His soldiers went with him. We did not try to stop them.

We ran to our horses. Mounting, we rode at swift gallop up that draw you see, leading north. The low, broad ridge on our left hid us from the soldiers. We came out on higher, more level ground which we cannot see from here. It was there the real battle was fought.

McWhorter's Transitional Comment:

Three days later we motored to where Yellow Wolf and his war mates had rushed to join in the defeat of Captain Perry's numerically superior and far better armed forces. Selecting his spot of observation, Yellow Wolf cast a rapid glance south to the rock-crowned ridge already mentioned, at the northern foot of which the Nez Perce peace embassy of six had been fired upon by "Ad" I. Chapman, captain of the volunteers. It has been shown that it was along the eastern base of the rocks topping this ridge that Captain Chapman, leading his company and some regulars, had disappeared, and it was there that Trumpeter John Jones, First Cavalry, was the first man to fall. Seemingly content with his survey in that direction, Yellow Wolf turned to the northwest and stood for some minutes in silent reverie. It was easy to imagine that he visioned the stirring scene there enacted half a century before. His story was now resumed.

✓ ✓ ✓

When our party rushed to where we now stand, everything could be seen. We were on the soldiers' left flank. Their right flank was in that low saddle ground over there, where our peace party had been fired upon by Chapman.

The warriors charging up the west canyon struck that flank hard. Hanging on the side of their horses where not seen, they gave the soldiers a storm of bullets. Warriors dismounted, and from hiding dropped soldiers from their saddles.

No wild horses were in this battle, as you say claimed in white man's history. Every horse carried a rider. In all there were not as many as seventy Indians in that fight.

In the meantime, our smaller party, sixteen in number, attacked the enemy's left flank. It was just like two bulldogs meeting. Those soldiers did not hold their position ten minutes. Some soldiers (citizen volunteers) on that low, rock-topped butte you see ahead there, were quickly on the run. Then the entire enemy force gave way.

We nearly headed them off. We mixed them up. I did some bow shooting. Two of my arrows struck soldiers only five steps away—one in the shoulder, the other in the breast. We did not stop to fight the wounded. We chased hard after the others.

✓ ✓ ✓

(Interpreter's Comment)

Wanting to bring out some latent phases of this first battle of the war, I asked Yellow Wolf, while he was relating the quick defeat of the soldiers, if either side had occupied the rock-crowned ridge where Captain Chapman was first seen, to which he replied:

When Chapman and soldiers ran away, no more soldiers got that far south. No Indians were on that butte.

✓ ✓ ✓

(Interpreter's Comment)

Asked if he thought the soldiers might have won had they gained possession of that butte—since it commanded the entire field—he explained:

✓ ✓ ✓

Had the soldiers gained that far south and divided their army at north end of the butte, one division fighting on west side, the other division taking that small, rocky butte off northeast there, they could have put up a stronger fight. But the soldiers could not do that. They were stopped too quick. Had they gone on that high butte, we could have starved them for water. Fighting makes bad thirst. The wounded die of thirst.

About a mile from the main battleground, five soldiers dismounted and took shelter among rocks. I did not know. I had not seen them go in there. As I drew near and dismounted, I heard a voice—somebody calling, "Heinmot Hihhih! Get to the rock! You will be shot!"

I saw and became mad. I ran to strike one soldier with my bow. I leaped and struck him as he put a cartridge to his gun. I grabbed the gun and shoved hard. The soldier went over backward, but he was not hurt. I wrenched the gun from him, and at same time a warrior back of me killed him. That was the Nez Perce way of war.

I now jumped down a bank where was another soldier. About a seven-foot jump. My feet slipped, and I slid in front of him. He was on one knee, pointing his rifle. The bullet passed over my shoulder. I grabbed the barrel of his gun. While we wrestled, a Nez Perce fired from the bank, and the soldier fell dead. I had the gun, and I took the belt of ammunition.

I was partly winded. I glanced around. A soldier was pointing his rifle at me. In that I saw danger. I jumped and ran, springing from side to side. I did not look back. Before the soldier got sights on me, a warrior threw a rock. It struck the soldier above the ear and killed him.

Farther on, we came upon two white men, dismounted. They hardly slowed us. They did not last any time.

Keeping after the runaway soldiers, we made a stop to fight seven or eight who had dismounted. Their horses were played out. They were in a ravine where grew thornbushes. Those soldiers put up a fight.

I saw Moositsa (Salish for Four Blankets), about my age, riding on opposite side of the soldiers. He had no gun. Was not fighting. He rode too close. Someone called, "Moositsa! Dangerous there!"

Just then a soldier fired. Moositsa fell off his horse, but was only slightly hurt. The bullet cut across his thigh, a light wound. It did not lay him up. He went through the war, to the last battle, and was among those exiled to Eeikish Pah (Hot Place; i.e., Indian Territory), where he died.

Those seven or eight soldiers in the ravine were wiped out. We chased the remaining soldiers. Fought them running for several miles. We drove them back across the mountain, down to near the town they came from (Mount Idaho). Then some of the chiefs commanded, "Let the soldiers go! We have done them enough! No Indian killed!"

The warriors have to mind what the chiefs say, so all stopped. Not one Indian killed! But three wounded. Moositsa's hurt was small. Chellooyeen (Bow and Arrow Case; afterwards known as Phillip Evans) was shot through the right side while wresting a gun from a soldier. Auskehwush was shot in the belly when he reached for a gun held by a wounded soldier. That soldier played as dead. Auskehwush's mother sang medicine songs over him, and he recovered.

About eleven soldiers escaped from where I last saw them retreating.

We returned to the main battlefield. There we counted thirty-three dead soldiers. We did no scalping. We did not strip them naked. This may be in white man's history, but it is not true. We did not hurt the dead. Only let them lie.

I heard that one hundred soldiers and twelve of General Howard's Christian Indians fought in the battle. Those Nez Perce were fighting against their own people. Three of them were captured. They begged not to be killed. They cried, holding up both hands. One man said, "Do not kill them. We will take them before the chiefs. Whatever they say will be done to them."

The chiefs held council just below our village. They took pity on the three Indian prisoners and said, "These three Christian Indians! Poor fellows! They are crying about what they are doing to us. Let them go home."

The three were told, "If you help the soldiers again, if we catch you again, we will whip you! We will take hazel switches and beat you good!"

Then the chiefs said, "Bring all guns you take from the soldiers."

The guns were brought, and one man appointed to count them.

He counted and reported, "Sixty-three guns!"

There were not so many pistols, and not much account taken of them. They were picked up mostly by women. I took one, a six-shot, off a dead soldier.

We stayed two suns at Lahmotta camp near the battlefield. It was at Lahmotta that Pahkatos Owyeen (Five Wounds), Wahchumyus (Rainbow) and a few other buffalo hunters joined us. They were just from Montana. Buffalo hunters were the best warriors, bravest fighters.

Then we moved to south side of Salmon River, crossing at Horseshoe Bend. You have asked me how we crossed the Salmon and other deep, swift streams with our families and goods. I will tell you all, how done. Owning that country, the Nez Perce knew all such streams. Crossed them often without difficulty. They understood to manage.

At this crossing was only one canoe. But we had plenty of buffalo robes. With them we made hide boats.* In making such boat, the hide, hair side up, was spread flat on the ground. Across the hide were laid green willow or other limber poles about the thickness of your thumb. The hide and poles were bent up and lashed to other bent poles forming a long circled rim. This rim was on outside. That was all. Such boats carried big loads, and children and old people rode on top of the packs. Everything—tepee covers, cooking pots, pans, blankets—all were ferried in these boats. No paddles used. Boats were hauled by ponies guided by men. Two, maybe three or four, ponies to a boat. Two men swam at the sides to steady it.

In a strange country Indians might have trouble crossing bad streams. We knew, and we had no trouble with water during the war.

You asked if we were trying to go to Imnaha and Wallowa country. When we crossed the Salmon we had no intention of going to either of those places. The chiefs planned to cross

---

* Alexander the Great ferried his army across the Euphrates River in similar boats.

the Salmon only. If soldiers followed, we would cross back and go to the Clearwater. Just to get soldiers out of way, did we cross the Salmon.

All the people, old people, children, everybody, crossed the Salmon, except thirty warriors. I was one of the thirty. We turned back to Tepahlewam to scout the country, to watch for soldiers.

One evening we were riding along in the dark. Our leader, Teeweawea, stopped suddenly. He pointed towards the White Bird trail. There we saw lights moving, as if carried by men. Must be soldiers!

Kosooyeen (Going Alone) and I were sent to spy. Whatever we learned we must carry to the chiefs across the Salmon. We rode away in the darkness, in the direction where the lights had been seen. We could see nothing. But soon we heard a gun report up the mountain trail. We went that way to see who made the shot.

Sure enough! Soldiers traveling the trail to Lahmotta.

We crossed the mountain by another way, and hurried toward the Salmon. It was morning when we reached the river about two miles below mouth of White Bird Creek. On the opposite side of the river was a boat belonging to a Chinaman. Kosooyeen had a good swimming horse, so he crossed and brought the boat. I got in with Kosooyeen and towed my horse with a rope. Landing, we went up the river a few miles to a butte overlooking the Nez Perce camp, pitched near Deer Creek.

From the butte we waved a blanket, "Soldiers coming!"

Of course, guards were out on the hills, and the camp was not much excited. The next sun, scouts brought word, "Soldiers on both sides of the White Bird and Skookum Chuck."

This was true. But it was another sun before they came in sight of our camp. They came over the mountain, opposite side of the river—a great string of soldiers. Some thought there must be a thousand—cavalry, walking soldiers, and big guns on wheels. With them were a few Indians, General Howard's Christians. Chief Lawyer, Chief Timothy, Chief Jason, Chief Levi, and other headmen of the Upper Nez Perce had sold our homes. Sold our country which they did not own. This stayed in our minds, and now their followers were helping soldiers take all from us.

Annihilation of Rain's Scouting Party in White Bird Canyon

UP THERE the soldiers appeared on top of the mountain. The families, the entire camp, had crossed the Salmon at Horseshoe Bend. They were camped on Deer Creek. This stream joins the Salmon about two miles above here. Our scouts had kept close watch on movements of the soldiers. From our hiding place across the river we were watching. The cavalry came first, strung from top of mountain to more than halfway to the river. As they came closer, we rode out from buttes and ridges, out from canyons and gulches. Forming, we galloped down the slopes toward the Salmon, yelling as we charged. Some enemies were so near we heard orders given.

James Reuben, one of General Howard's Christian Nez Perce scouts, called to us, "You cowardly people! come over here. We will have it—a war!"

Lakochets Kunnin (Rattle on Blanket) shook his rifle at him and yelled, "You call us cowards when we fight for our homes, our women, our children! You are the coward! You sit on side of Government, strong with soldiers! Come over. We will scalp you!"

Reuben made no answer. Another man called to him, "Cross the Salmon yourself! You are the fellows starting this war! Come on if you want to! You are ready mounted for riding the water! Do not be scared like a woman! You are growing fat, eating Government food!"

Chapman was there to interpret to soldiers what was said. When the warriors made that answer, the cavalry showed mad. They fired at us across the river. Then we saw one ridge behind the cavalry covered with walking soldiers. We saw big guns on wagons, hurrying down. We dashed about on horses, playing war, doing a little shooting. We wasted only a few cartridges, and let the soldiers do most of the shooting. Their bullets did not hurt us. The chiefs now ordered, "We will give them the road. Do not bother them. Let them come across the Salmon. We do not have to cross to them. We are not after them. They are after us. If they come to our side, we can fight them if we want."

The women could not sleep when soldiers were so near, so we moved camp high into the mountains. Up to the country of the *pottoosway*, the medicine tree. Its branches are good for perfuming tepee homes. It keeps bugs (moths) from furs and robes.

But the warriors remained behind, hiding among ridges, waiting for soldiers to cross. Waited until the sun went down, and the darkness came. Then we all went home, to the camp.

Came the morning, and when some of us scouted back we saw the soldiers still on north side of the Salmon. They were making a cross. A white man had a boat there—not a regular ferry. We had not bothered that boat. General Howard could use it if he wanted to. We waited half a sun for the soldiers, but none crossed. Then the chiefs said, "We will move out of their way."

Scouts remained to watch, and the families packed up and moved about twenty miles down the Salmon and camped. In the afternoon we had seen two boats drifting down the Salmon. They may have broken loose, or maybe set adrift by General Howard after using them for crossing.

Next morning scouts brought word the soldiers were on our side of the Salmon. This was good. We immediately crossed back to the north side. We used the skin boats to carry our packs, the old people, and the children, as when we crossed before.

McWhorter's Comment:

To the inquiry as to why this hasty return, came the reply:

It was from first so fixed. We intended turning back if soldiers followed us south. That was how the war was planned to be carried out. The chiefs wanted the soldiers out of the way. The two great warriors, Pahkatos Owyeen and Wahchumyus, counseled that trick. Counseled it while in Lahmotta camp.

Leaving the Salmon, we moved to Aipadass, a flat where the women dig *kous* (an edible root). All desert land. The ridge there is called Tepahlewam. It is not far from Split Rocks, and that is why the same name. We camped there that night.

When morning came, I heard a gun report and the echo of a song. I saw a warrior on a horse and Indians all about him. I took my gun and hurried there to see what enemy had been killed. Seeyakoon Ilppilp (Red Spy or Red Scout), the mounted warrior, said, "Some white men almost kill me. I suppose scouts—two white men coming this way. They didn't look like soldiers."

The white men had seen him, Seeyakoon told us, as he was watching on guard away off from camp. They made for him. Seeyakoon jumped from his horse and dodged behind rocks. They fired at him. When they did that, he ran toward them, keeping hid by rock protection. He was not afraid! He killed one of them, shot him through the head. The other man got away.

That was what I heard Seeyakoon telling, and he added, "I tell you, furthermore, soldiers are now close upon us."

"Yes," answered the chiefs. "What are the soldiers doing? Moving or camping?"

"Camping," said Seeyakoon. "Solidiers are ready for the battle. They have embankments and dugout hollows fixed up. All ready for war."

Some said, "Let us go see," and they went.

After they had gone, I followed alone. In a draw I saw my friends gathered together. When I got where I could see them better, they made a left swerve. I looked in this new direction, and saw a blanket waving, a signal of war. I ran my horse that way and, reaching a small lump, I saw about twelve soldiers. When they saw the warriors they became scared and tried to escape.

My friends went after those soldiers, and I overtook them. There was shooting, and one soldier fell from his horse. Then another went down a little way from us. Soon a third fell; and another and another, not far apart, went to the ground. Some distance on, a man—maybe wounded—got down from his horse and was killed. I will not hide anything. That part of the fight was not long. Those six soldiers did not get up.

The remaining six soldiers ran their horses up a hill, maybe one half mile. Then they jumped off and lay among some rocks, and began shooting.

McWhorter's Transitional Comment:

We proceeded to an impressive group of large isolated boulders [on land now owned by Vincent Duman] which has become recognized locally as the scene of the wiping out of Rain's detachment. John L. Rooke, postmaster of Cottonwood, informed the writer that as a boy he played about this boulder formation, and that he saw bullet marks in many places. It would seem that such scars should still be discernible, yet the most searching examination by our party failed to reveal the slightest trace whatever. Yellow Wolf animatedly resumed his narrative:

Not true that this place is where the soldiers stopped. They did not pass by here, but struck more to the right. We were not crowding them very close, and had they kept on they might have gained the timber, although Indian scouts were ahead, watching to catch mail carriers (Army couriers) going either way. The soldiers may have seen those scouts. It was Tipyahlanah Kapskaps (Strong Eagle) they began shooting at. He was what you call a decoy, guarding the road. He let the soldiers see him behind a small dead pine.

Those soldiers were trapped. They had no show. When they began shooting, it was just like their calling, "Come on! Come on! Come on!" A calling to death.

Our leader, Pahkatos, threw up his hand, and we stopped.

The soldiers were shooting at Tipyahlanah in the canyon on their left. We dropped back out of sight, then circled the hill to the right. A little beyond the soldiers we dismounted. Some men stayed with the horses, and the others crawled toward the soldiers. I was one of the crawlers. The soldiers were still firing, but not at us. They did not see us, and we got close to them. I will not hide it. Those soldiers were killed!

I was soon there with the others. One soldier was sitting up, leaning against a rock. He was shot in the forehead, almost level with the eyes. He had two other shots, through the breast, and he still lived. He washed his face with his own blood, and looked around. He made a clucking noise, a sound like that of a chicken. The Indians, hearing, wondered! They asked one another, "What about him? He must be more like us!"

From that day the warriors who are left remember what they saw and heard. All stood around that soldier, many of them saying, "He can not live. His body is too bad hurt."

But one man thought differently and he said, "He can live if he wants to!"

"He is too many times shot," answered one. "Head too bad shot!"

Then one oldlike man named Dookiyoon (Smoker), who had a gun with flint to set the powder afire, spoke, "We shall not leave him like that. He will be too long dying."

With those words, Smoker raised his gun and shot the soldier in the breast. The bullet knocked him over, but he raised up again. He sat there, still calling to his Power. Calling with that same clucking. He washed his face again with his running blood, and still looked around.

The warriors, all silent, said nothing. Then some of them taunted Smoker about his gun, that it was not strong. Smoker reloaded and shot once more, but it did no good! The soldier still sat against the rock, still making the clucking of the hen.

While the warriors stood silent and wondering, one man stepped forward and knocked the soldier over with his *kopluts* (war club). Others spoke to save him, but our leader said to us, "We have no doctor. Poor fellow! He is suffering. We better put him out of trouble."

When our leader made this talk, we all became one-minded. I then helped with my *kopluts.*

We started for where the other soldiers were camped, the camp that Seeyakoon had told us about. But the chiefs commanded the warriors to stop. "Let's not go farther," they said. "This sun we have killed thirteen enemies, and none of us hurt. It is good to quit now."

The warriors stopped, for they had to listen to the chief's orders. We all went back to camp. We wanted to see where Seeyakoon killed the white man that morning, so we went that way. I saw him lying where he fell some hours before, shot in the head. He was killed in a draw west of where we killed the last six soldiers in the rocks. I do not know the distance, but it was not far. There was timber scattered in and about the draw.

I heard, too, that Pahkatos Owyeen (Five Wounds) killed a white man, thought to be a scout, that same morning. All white people were spies for the soldiers. Five Wounds was with us in that running fight with the soldiers. He was our leader.

Fight with Captain Randall's Volunteers and Its Sequel—McWhorter, Yellow Wolf and the interpreter ride on to the location of another skirmish. Yellow Wolf continues his narrative.

We held our camp, going nowhere. But next sun the families moved to a spring. Piswah Ilppilp Pah (Place of Red Rock). While this was doing, a small bunch of young warriors went separately. No old men among us. Coming to the wagon road, we looked in direction of the ferry (Craig's Ferry). We saw them—about twenty armed horsemen. Not uniformed soldiers, but more like citizens. Not riding a close company, but strung out along the road. When they saw us, they bunched and came a little faster. Came straight towards us! Seemed to me they cared not for us. Drawing closer, they appeared mail carriers (couriers). We now knew there was to be a fight.

Then those men made for us. We were lined across their path. As they charged we gave way—let them go through. We then struck after them, racing to flank both sides. The shooting became faster, and soon those whites stopped and dismounted. The fighting was from about half-past ten o'clock to middle of afternoon. We did not know why the soldiers in their dugout rifle pits did not come to the fighting. We could see them where they were on higher ground. They seemed a little afraid.

One young white man among those fighting us was brave. I did not recognize him, but some said he had been raised right among the Indians—that his father was Cooks, or Crooks; I do not know. But his father was a friend to us. Had always been our friend.

When we were mixing close, this boy killed the horse of Weesculatat. Then this same young man shot Weesculatat in the leg below the knee. He then shot him through the breast and again a little lower down. But the bullets did not go through his body.

Scattered, the warriors were on every side of the enemies. Plenty of shooting. We gradually crowded in on them. Some of those whites must have been killed. The sun was halfway down the afternoon sky when, looking back, we saw soldiers coming, their big gun in the lead.

The chiefs now called out, "Let us quit for a while!"

Hearing that order, we left the fighting, taking Weesculatat with us. Three times wounded at beginning of fight, he lived until about dark. With two bad wounds, he could not hold his life. Not old, about middle-aged, he was first warrior killed. We lost a good fighter.

Next morning, a funeral was held for Weesculatat. It was not what you call a Christian funeral. He was wrapped in blankets with some weapons and a few objects sacred to him. He was buried at Piswah Ilppilp, and his grave was hidden from finding.

After we buried Weesculatat, we packed up and moved to the Clearwater River bottom, a place called Peeta Auuwa. An Indian, an old man named Peeta, lived there. That was how the place was named. It is not far from present Kooskia, on the same river. We camped above where town of Stites has been built.

That same sun when we got in camp nearly one hundred of us went down to Kamiah. We made James Lawyer, son of old Chief Lawyer, who was leader in helping steal our lands and homes, ferry us across the Clearwater. Had he refused, we would have cut his boat loose. We were going to a Dreamer religious meeting at the camp of some Lapwai Indians just returned from Montana. Those people who wanted to join us went up to our camp afterwards.

Chief Looking Glass joined us here. All his band came at same time. My mother was with them. She was with Looking Glass's family when soldiers attacked his village. His tepee was burned, but my mother escaped with the others. She remembered to save my rifle. Took it apart and hid it in her pack from being seen by whites. I was glad to see my rifle. My parents had bought it for me with one good horse. I now had my own sixteen-shot rifle for rest of the war.

My mother could use the gun against soldiers if they bothered her. She could ride any wild horse and shoot straight. She could shoot the buffalo and was not afraid of the grizzly bear.

My stepfather, Tommimo, three-quarters French, was not at Chief Looking Glass's camp at time of attack. Herding horses near Lewiston, he was arrested and jailed to keep him from joining in the war. He belonged to Chief Joseph's band.

McWhorter's Comment:

Wanting to obtain the Nez Perce version of the status of Chief Looking Glass at the outbreak of hostilities, I interposed, "General Howard states that some of Looking Glass's men had joined Chief Joseph's band before this time, either before you crossed the Salmon or while you were south of that river." To this came the quick response:

Not true! None of Chief Looking Glass's people joined us until coming to our camp on Clearwater. Looking Glass refused joining with the other five chiefs. He moved to his own camp to get away from war. The soldiers drove him to us when they attacked his village. Those Indians then had gardens planted on the Clearwater.

At this time we heard of soldiers on the hill called Possossona (Water Passing) near Kamiah. We went back over the hill to where they were. It was to be a battle about the middle of afternoon. We surrounded those soldiers. There was fighting until sundown. Near dusk we quit and returned home to camp.

It must have been about nine o'clock that same night when somebody said, "Let us go where the soldiers herd their horses!" A small bunch of us went. When the soldier-herders heard us coming, they ran away. Left their horses. We took them all, except a few we did not want. They were no good for us.

We had those soldiers surrounded, and they kept firing. We skirmished awhile. It was just like fireworks cutting the darkness. It was about middle of night when our leader called out, "Let's quit! We have got horses."

We then went home, taking the horses with us. They were horses stolen by soldiers. Good horses taken from Looking Glass when soldiers came and attacked his village. We returned them to warriors who claimed them.

Next morning some of us—I do not know how many—went back to where the soldiers were. We would make another war. We found no officers, nobody there. We thought we must have killed or wounded some of them. They had lain close in dugout trenches, but we had crept within a few steps of them. No time did we see any of them. We had fired at close range, and they knew where to find us. But they would not raise up to shoot. Nobody there now to fight. We returned to camp. We stayed here three days.

Battle of the Clearwater—L. V. McWhorter and Yellow Wolf rode to the scene of the battle on the banks of Clearwater River. As he told the story of the battle Yellow Wolf pointed to spots where various incidents had taken place.

IT WAS ABOUT TEN O'CLOCK in the morning, a sun or so after we took horses from soldiers, on Possossona. Some boys and men were racing horses on the narrow strip of level land along the Clearwater below our camp. I was sitting on my horse watching them, when Wemastahtus called to me, "Yesterday a soldier was killed below here. I saw him."

I rode down to see the dead soldier. I found him lying by the trail. He had a mustache, but nothing else appeared about him to note. It was afterwards thought he had run away from the army. Alone, he could not defend himself.

Just then I heard a noise at the races. I moved away a short distance, dismounted and sat down on a boulder. I could still hear an excitement at the races. I sat there some time, thinking. Then I heard the boom of a gun report. Sounded like the shot of a big gun—a distance away. I listened hard! It was a strange sound passing through the air that I now heard.

Then came a loud explosion near the racers. That shell-shot was from the high mountain bluff beyond the river—north side of the canyon. Immediately a scout came riding hard down the slope from that direction. Waving his blanket, he called across the river, "Soldiers surrounding us! Soldiers surrounding us!"

It was sure enough! I saw soldiers strung out a long way off; far up along the mountain's brow.

I jumped on my horse and galloped to camp. I stripped for the battle. I got my rifle and cartridge belts, two of them. One I wore around my waist; the other, across my left shoulder and under the right arm. I always carried them that way.

The chiefs called an order, "Split up! Make three bodies!"

About twenty of us young warriors joined together. Chief Tulhulhutsut was our leader. The other two companies must stay at camp. We hastened upriver a short ways. We crossed and rode into the timber. We hurried up the wooded slope of a canyon, leading to south side of this battlefield.

I was ahead as scout, and reached the ridge-brow first. Looking north, I saw many soldiers. They were getting ready for the war. I saw a big bunch of them heading down toward our camp across the river. Pointing, I called to the others, "Can you not see the soldiers? What they are doing? Let us go closer and do shooting!"

We ran our horses across the flat, down into this canyon and up the other side a ways. We tied them in some small, scattered timber, and hurried afoot up to the flats.

We had to stop those soldiers going to our camp!

A few other warriors joined us, making about twenty-four to fight General Howard's army.

You see a white house far away to the left yonder? It is in the foreground of trees. That black spot to its right is a thorn-bush clump. We were left of that thicket only a few steps.

I heard our chief call, "Come, boys! We will make a rifle pit."

At that place we worked fast. Piling up stones, we soon had a good shelter.

Chief Tulhulhutsut then said, "Stay here. I am going up a short way."

Holding close to earth, the chief crawled up the hill. He did not pass from our sight. Soon we heard a rifleshot. Our chief had killed a soldier.

His rifle a muzzle-loader, it was a little time before we heard a second shot. Another soldier had been killed.

Some of that last shot drew a storm of bullets. But they did no harm. Chief Tulhulhutsut's *Wyakin** was strong.

We were firing whenever soldiers could be seen. Bullets were striking our stone fort. Chief Tulhulhutsut crawled back to us. The firing was making our horses uneasy. They might break loose. Tulhulhutsut gave command that four go hold them, the rest to

* The word means "luck"—like the luck of the Irish.

stay and beat back the soldiers. None of us were hit, but we saw some of our bullets found marks.

Soldiers were strung out a long ways and advancing. Some were close to us. Indians and soldiers fighting—almost together. We could not count the soldiers. There must have been hundreds. Bullets came thicker and thicker.

Our chief looked around. It was early afternoon. A long while before dark would come. He saw we were hemmed in on three sides and gave orders that we go. He was last to leave. We crawled a ways, then ran. We hurried, for bullets were singing like bees. My heart beat fast. Thinking only for escape, I ran away from my waiting horse. Nobody stopped for horses. All were running to cross the ridge about where we are now standing. I, too, kept on for a little ways.

Then I came to myself. I missed my horse, and I grew hot with mad! I made myself brave! I turned and ran for my horse—many soldiers shooting at me. Why, I did not care what I ran into! I got my horse and led him away. The boys caring for the horses had escaped on their own. The enemies got all the others.

With soldiers still shooting, I jumped on my horse and galloped down the hill. Crossing the canyon, I came to left of here. As I drew up to higher ground, bullets fell about me. I could see dust spurt up where they struck the earth. I whipped my horse for all in him. A swift horse, light black (brown) in color. He began slowing down, breathing hard. I whipped the more, and finally we passed over the saddle ridge just west of here. Out of sight of the soldiers, my horse could take a good rest.

While making that ride, I thought it my last day. My feelings were that I was not much excited. Before that time, my uncle, Old Yellow Wolf, had said to me, "If you go to war and get shot, do not cry!"

I remembered that instruction. It helped me to be brave. If we die in battle, it is good. It is good, dying for your rights, for your country.

When I reached timber south of this saddle ridge, I dismounted and tied my horse. I came where some older men had built the big "Smoking Pit." Sheltered from all danger, I saw lots of people there smoking. Most of them old, they were not fighting. I passed them. I did not like tobacco or any kind of smoking. I was afraid to smell it. I ran eastward to where I heard shooting.

I came where four men were fighting. They were my uncle, Old Yellow Wolf, Otstotpoo, Howallits (Mean Man) and Tomyunmene. The three older men's faces were bleeding. Rock chips from flying bullets were doing the work.

These warriors had rifle pits among some boulders. Not too big, the rocks, but about right size for concealment. I dropped down behind one of them. We were now five, all fighting in thick smoke. Like smoke rolling up from burning woods. My uncle was shot in the head and lay dead for a while. But returning to life, he helped on with the fight.

This fighting was with the cavalry only. Later, foot soldiers came. I did not know which officer was in charge, unless General Howard. I watched for him, but did not see him.

Most shooting was now from the whites. I heard the cannon guns and was scared. I lay close to the ground. I did not know to shoot or not. I heard my uncle say, "I am thirsty! I will crawl to the *koos* (water) and drink."

He did so, and came only part way back. I saw him crawling slowly, rolling a boulder ahead. Hidden behind that not large boulder, he advanced for closer shooting at the soldiers. He passed from my sight. I heard him shoot a few times.

McWhorter's Explanatory Comment:

Wishing to check statements from other warriors, I interrupted here and asked if it were true that the soldiers were unable to determine from what point the Indian bullets came, even in open ground. Yellow Wolf replied, "The little boulder is good for hiding behind. Our rifle pit was already made." I could see he meant that the outcropping rocks served the same purpose as a dugout rifle pit.

I lay flat, seeing nothing, hearing only the battle. I did not know all had left when the soldiers' firing was the hottest. Other warriors all gone, and still I lay there.

One of the brave men, looking back, saw me and thought, "Why is he lying there? Must be wounded!"

Sounds came to my left ear. A voice speaking, "Who are you, lying flat? Soldiers are close coming!"

I looked to my left. I saw nobody. I did not get up. I heard the same voice again, and a whip struck me. What I heard was, "Heinmot Hihhih! Are you wounded? Why you not shooting? Kill some soldiers. They will kill you if you do not defend yourself!"

When I heard that voice, I was convinced what to do. I raised up. It was Wottolen (Hair Combed Over Eyes) who had called me, who had struck me. He was one of the commanders. Soldiers, armed, were about thirty steps from me. I grew mad to see them so close. Struck with the whip, I showed myself brave. I now was not afraid of death. From between the boulder rocks, I pushed my rifle. I fought like a man, firing five or six shots. Just then I heard heavy breathing. Otstotpoo had come back to me. Hearing the firing, he knew I had been left alone.

He said to me, "Dear son, we are going to die right here! Do not shoot the common soldier. Shoot the commander!"

I understood. I looked for an officer. He was just back of his men. All were crouching. I fired, and that officer went down. Another one seemed taking his place, I dropped him. Those officers did not get up. No one now to drive the common soldiers, they fell back in retreat. Those two officers killed, common soldiers retreating, the warriors returned to their rifle pits.

The soldiers were being whipped in another part of the field. A supply train coming from the south was nearly captured by warriors of the other two bodies who came up from the camp. They almost took that train. Of course I was not in the fighting there. Not all three companies of warriors could leave camp until they saw the soldiers being held on the mountain.

Came complete sundown. The firing almost quit. With darkness was heard only occasional shots. The five chiefs gave order, "Warriors, do no more fighting tonight!"

Half the warriors went down to camp. Women, children, and old people to be guarded. Horses must not be lost. The others of us, we did not run from the soldiers. Only did what the chiefs commanded.

I had only moccasins and breechcloth. But with the darkness, I did not leave. About midnight came stronger cold. It was then I left my pit. The big Smoking Lodge where no-fighters stayed, smoking and counseling, safe from bullets, was many rods southwest. I found several men lying there. I did not stop. I saw one man lying where horses were tied. I asked to sleep with him on account of the cold. He answered "Yes." Then I knew my own brother (cousin), my aunt's son, Teminisiki (No Heart). As I lay down with him, I heard a woman speaking, "May I stay with you? I have no blanket. I get cold!"

My brother replied, "Come on! Get between us! You will keep warm."

The woman did as invited. I remembered instructions from old people. In wartime man cannot sleep with woman. Might get killed if he does. Because of this, I got up and went back to my rifle pit. No shirt. No leggings. Only breechcloth and moccasins. Just as stripped for war. I stayed there until daylight. Stayed until the fighting began again.

My brother Teminisiki was killed in our next hard battle, the Big Hole!

Indian Withdrawal from the Clearwater.

Next morning began the fighting again. In first skirmishing it seemed soldiers had drawn a little nearer. Had made barricades during the night. Four of us were fighting from behind our boulder shelter. The same warriors, same barricade as the night before. Shots from the soldiers were not scattering. Their volleys became one continued roar. I paid attention to myself only, what I was doing. I thought nothing about the warriors with me.

I got a bullet here in my left arm, near the wrist. When it struck me, I rolled on the ground, it hurt so. But I said nothing! Then I was hit just under my left eye. It was a piece of bullet or a chip from the boulder. Blood ran down my face. That eye was dimmed for the rest of my life.

The battle continued some hours. It must have been about ten o'clock, and soldier bullets still rained. Of course there was some cannon shooting. The soldiers began leaving their shelters, coming towards us.

Suddenly I heard my partner, Wottolen, call to me: "Nobody here! We will quit!"

I raised partly up. No Indians could be seen fighting. All had left the battle! Wottolen and myself were holding back the troops.

I now understood why soldiers crowded so. *No warriors opposing them!*

All yesterday fighting; all this morning they did not crowd us. But now, meeting no Indian bullets, they came charging bravely.

Then I ran, again forgetting my horse. I ran back where he was tied in the timber edge. Mounting, I started down the mountainside. It was through woods, open places, over rocks and steep bluffs. But my horse never missed footing. Crossing the river and reaching where the now empty camp stood, I heard a woman's voice. That voice was one of crying. I saw her on a horse she could not well manage. The animal was leaping, pawing, wanting to go. Everybody else had gone.

I hurried toward her, and she called, "Heinmot! I am troubled about my baby!"

I saw the baby wrapped in its *tekash* (cradleboard) lying on the ground. That mother laughed as she took her baby. It was the cannon shots bursting near that scared her horse. She could not mount with the little one. She could not leave it there. Riding fast, we soon overtook some rear Indians entering the canyon. We were then out of reach of cannon shots fired from the high mountain bluff.

This woman with the little baby was Toma Alwawinmi (possibly meaning Spring of Year, or Springtime), wife of Chief Joseph. Her baby girl was born at Tepahlewam camp a few days before the White Bird Canyon battle, but it died in the hot country (Indian Territory) after the war.

I did not ask why she was as I found her. Chief Joseph left the battlefield ahead of the retreat. Seeing it coming, he hurried to warn the families. He could not leave his wife had he known. The women were all supposed to be ahead. A bad time—everybody busy getting away.

McWhorter's Comment—*through the interpreter he needles Yellow Wolf to get his reaction:*

Here, taking advantage of a pause in the narrative, I informed Yellow Wolf of General Howard's claim that in their abandoned camp many dead and wounded horses were found as a result of the cannon fire, to which he replied:

I am telling you all I know about the cannon fighting. During the battle one shell exploded west of the barricaded Smoking Lodge. When I came down from the mountain, only two Indian men were in sight. They were a good distance away, riding hard to escape. Joseph's wife and baby only were left in camp. No dead horses killed by cannon shots were there. Usually at all camps a few lame or sick horses were left.

McWhorter's Comment—*Apparently there was some doubt in McWhorter's mind about the accuracy of the record's statement of the number of Indians killed at the Clearwater. So through the interpreter he again needled Yellow Wolf:*

This fact being amply verified by different warriors questioned, I continued, "General Howard states that fifteen Indians were killed in this battle, and eight others were found dead on your trail as a result of wounds received in fighting, making twenty-three in all, and that about forty were wounded and forty taken prisoners." There came the quick retort:

Not true! Only four warriors killed. First was Wakakat (Going Across), killed instantly. Second man, his partner in the fight, was Yoomtis Kunnin (Grizzly Bear Blanket) who lived a few hours after shot. Howallits, also fighting there, was slightly wounded. He died years later on lower Snake River. The three were fighting near where we are now sitting. A few trees, three, maybe five, stood there.

Third man killed was Heinmot Ilppilp (Red Thunder). Killed in timber edge at break of canyon, south side of battlefield. Many small bushes there were nearly cut down by soldier bullets. These three men killed and one wounded in earliest fighting.

Lelooskin (Whittling) was fourth man killed. Killed in his rifle pit after dark. His partners, Kosooyeen and one other (name unknown), escaped to safer rifle pits. Wayakat and Lelooskin were so close to the enemy lines when they were killed that both bodies were left.

No Indians died on the trail from wounds. Just one man was bad wounded, Kipkip Owyeen (Shot in Breast). Bullet went in back of shoulder and came out through his breast. That is how he got his name. Had no good name before that time. Pahkatos was wounded in right hand. Three others were lightly wounded, two of them warriors. One was my uncle, Old Yellow Wolf, in the rifle pit as I have told; the other one was Elaskolatat, known to whites as Joe Albert.

The oldlike man, Howallits (Mean Man), was hurt by cannon firing on camp. No other person was wounded at camp that I ever heard.

Not one prisoner taken by soldiers in Clearwater battle.

McWhorter's Comment—*showing that in his mind there was further doubt about the accuracy of the record—So more needling.*

One other phase of General Howard's summary of the Clearwater fight was in my mind, and I said, "General Howard claims that you were badly whipped at the Clearwater, and that to get away from him, you hurried across the Lolo Trail into Montana."

The old warrior's rebuttal was fraught with fire:

We were not whipped! We do not acknowledge being whipped! When counted, we had many young fellows who should have been in that fight. They held lots of councils, while some—not many—were in the rifle pits. There were big smokes in the Smoking Lodge. That is good, if old people alone!

Our commanders were not scared of bullets, not afraid of death. The Three Red Coats* wanted all the young men to go on horses to fight the left wing (cavalry) of General Howard's soldiers. Make it the last fight. Whichever side whipped, to be the last fight. But it was not to be. Many fewer than one hundred warriors met the hard fighting here, as throughout the war. The families were camped across the river from the soldiers. Many of the Indians talked, "Why all this war up here? Our camp is not attacked! All can escape without fighting. Why die without cause?"

We were not whipped! We held all soldiers off the first day and, having better rifle pits, we could still have held them back. Not until the last of us leaped away did soldiers make their charge. Some tepees, robes, clothing, and food were left. The women, not knowing the warriors were disagreeing, quitting the fight, had no time to pack the camp. Chief Joseph did not reach them soon enough.

But we were not whipped! Had we been whipped, we could not have escaped from there with our lives.

We could not have stopped General Howard at Kamiah crossing. We were not scared at that crossing. We did not cross the Clearwater until next morning. We then waited into the third sun for General Howard to cross and give us war.

He would not cross. It was then we started over the Lolo Trail.

---

* The select warriors, distinguished for their military skill.

Had we been whipped we could not have passed the Lolo barricade.

We could not have beaten General (Colonel) Gibbon at Big Hole.

We could not have captured 250 good horses at Horse Prairie.

We could not have captured General Howard's pack mules at Camas Meadows.

We could not have held off the new army (Colonel Sturgis) at Canyon Creek.

We could not have captured the big supplies at Missouri River Crossing.

We could not have stood against General (Colonel) Miles during four days.

No, it would not have been best to fight to the death at Clearwater. Standing before General Howard's soldiers was not too dangerous. Nothing hard! Wottolen and myself alone held them back after all Indians had quit the fight, left the ridge!

3 THE FLIGHT

On July 13th the Wallamwatkins crossed the Clearwater a mile above the Kamiah Ferry. As in former crossings they used rafts made of buffalo hides. Joseph led them downstream to the ferry and ordered stone barricades to be built there so that his riflemen could shoot Howard's soldiers when they were on the ferry or swimming over on their horses. But before the Indians could build the defenses Captain Jackson with cavalry and gatling guns appeared on the opposite bluff. Since barricades could not be built under the direct fire of gatling guns, Joseph abandoned what might have been a very favorable defense and led his people eastward toward the Lolo Trail in the Bitterroot Mountains.

By this time Howard had sensed that the Wallamwatkins were in acute need of a rest, time for the hunters to kill some game, time for the mothers to cook food, repair clothing and moccasins and to wash their babies. As a feint Howard led his forces northward as if he had abandoned pursuit and was withdrawing to Fort Lapwai. Joseph, keeping track of Howard through scouts, was aware that as Howard rode northward he was following the Clearwater downstream, that he would reach Dunwell's Ferry where he could easily cross the river. From Dunwell's it was only a day's ride to the junction of the north fork of the Lolo Trail and that was a mere fifteen miles from the camp of the Wallamwatkins. By moving swiftly Howard could cut off their escape.

Joseph gained time by sending a messenger to Howard under a flag of truce to ask him upon what terms he would accept a surrender. Actually Joseph, although he did not wish to surrender, would have done so because he wished to spare his people from further misery. Because of the Wallamwatkins' military success it is likely that Howard could have arranged favorable terms for them with Washington, but Looking Glass, White Bird and Tulhulhutsut would not listen to Joseph. Since the only terms Howard was authorized to give were "unconditional surrender" nothing further was said.

Howard was detained by the talk of surrender. He was further detained when his cavalry reached Dunwell's and discovered that the ferryboat had been cut adrift and had lodged on a snag far down the river and that Joseph's scouts had not neglected the buildings. They had all been burned.

When Howard suspected that Joseph was trifling with him in the matter of surrender he ordered his troops to cross with their baggage at Kamiah. Because this would take several days McConville and a large band of cowboys swam their horses across the Clearwater and picked up the tracks of Joseph's people. Their purpose was to overtake and harry Joseph's rear.

Anticipating that human wolves would be following his people, Joseph had an ambush prepared near Orofino Creek. Large trees beside the trail at two points about a mile apart were sawed at their bases until a hard push would tip them over. The Indian rear guard covered all signs of their work with dirt, bark and leaves, then hid, watching for white men to enter the trap. Because of the extreme density of the forest on both sides of the narrow road it was indeed a trap. The forest trees stood so close together that a pair of wheels could not possibly pass between them. A soldier mounted on a saddled horse could squeeze through slowly, but only with difficulty. If Howard's column had been caught in the mile long space between those two dead falls, he would have been completely at Joseph's mercy.

The sun had passed from the east toward the west when the cowboys came clattering over the stones. A few of them had entered the trap when shots rang out farther up the canyon. The cowboys halted. Their horses nervously pawed the ground pulling back the dead leaves. This uncovered a quantity of fresh saw dust. That took the cowboys off of their horses. They quickly found the partially sawed trees. Just as quickly they mounted, turned their horses around and galloped back to Kamiah without the loss of a cowboy, although one of their Indian scouts, riding ahead, was killed when the shots rang out. But it was all right. Cowboys considered Indian scouts expendable.

The experience of the cowboys satisfied Howard that the Indians were far enough ahead so that he could safely follow them with his forces. However Joseph, not wishing Howard to become entirely complacent, detached a small band to detour Howard and attack the houses in the vicinity of Kamiah. To create the impression that the Wallamwatkins had reversed their decision to escape eastward and were returning westward to Idaho, the raiders burned houses of white people at Kamiah, the north fork of the Clearwater and the homes of both white people and Indians at Kooskia. After a continuous but glorious raid they returned to Joseph smelling of smoke and accompanied by over five hundred captured horses.

At the time, Howard and his cavalry were approaching Cold Spring. Unexpectedly messengers arrived with word that Joseph and his band had circled back behind the soldiers bringing fire and destruction. The settlements were screaming.

Howard expected to be joined at Cold Spring by artillery and infantry. They hadn't arrived. Howard's instinct urged him to push on and overtake Joseph before he could reach the Lolo Trail and let the settlements shriek. If he should delay, the opportunity would be lost. It was reasonable to suppose that whatever harm could be done in his rear had been done, but Howard finally decided that he couldn't take that chance. He led his cavalry to Camas Prairie, camped, and while awaiting reenforcements formed new plans for following Joseph. Of course this gave Joseph the head start for which he had been scheming. It amounted to eight days. Even then, when Howard resumed the pursuit, he had no remounts whereas Joseph had hundreds of spare horses.

It became immediately obvious that if Howard should camp where Joseph had stopped over night, there would be nothing for the cavalry horses to eat. The Indians' ponies had already grazed the country bare.

As the Indians climbed to the Lolo Pass on the Montana border the trail became rough and steep, the soil muddy and the air cold. There were rock slides, washouts and fallen timber. At that elevation it rained daily. There was frost every night. Still higher the trail became narrow where it edged cliffs. Always it was slippery. Man or beast losing balance or missing his hold would fall two thousand feet without bouncing. The trail itself was enough to discourage pursuit.

Before leaving Kamiah, Howard sent a telegram to Captain Rawn at Fort Missoula on the Montana side of the Lolo Pass ordering him to blockade the approaching Indians in Lolo Canyon. Having only a small garrison Rawn sent Lieutenant Woodbridge with four mounted soldiers to Summit Prairie at the top of the pass to stop the Wallamwatkins. When Woodbridge arrived at the western end of the pass where he could look down into Idaho, he could see no Indians. They were coming up the side of the mountain, concealed by the heavy timber. Woodbridge remembering what had happened to Leonidas the Spartan at Thermopylae concluded that since Joseph hadn't arrived he wasn't coming and lit out for Fort Missoula. On the way he encountered Lieutenant Coolidge and another small detail sent out to find him. At that moment a half-breed named Tom Hill appeared. He chilled them by stating that three hours after Woodbridge had left Summit Prairie, Joseph's people had arrived, stared in amazement at fresh boot-prints in the mud and were now coming down the eastern slope.

Woodridge and detail had just dragged their horses along a ledge inches wide jutting out from sheer cliff rising from a gorge thousands of feet deep. Ahead there was another crest to be ascended and beyond that a wider and less rugged descent. Woodbridge, Coolidge and followers passed the next crest in record time. Unlike Leonidas they didn't want to blockade several hundred Indians in a place like that. They wanted to get back to Fort Missoula while they could still truthfully report that they hadn't seen any Indians. Neither they nor any other people gave a thought to Joseph's extreme anxiety and tension when, a few hours later, Indian mothers with babies on their backs, small children who were just learning how to walk, and Indian boys, who were forever daring each other in the most dangerous places, had to creep along those narrow ledges above the yawning chasms. Unquestionably, Joseph suffered agonies until they had all passed safely.

At the foot of the mountain Joseph halted his people so that they could wash in the healing waters of Lolo Hot Springs, Montana. They were then only two hundred and forty miles from Canada and safety. But to ride northward they would have exposed their left flank to a regiment of infantry coming from the northwest to head them off. An eastward course would take them close to the town of Missoula. Joseph decided to go southward up the Bitterroot Valley through the lands of the Flathead Indians. The Flatheads were not friendly to the Nez Perce, but Joseph thought that they would not attack unless they had provocation. Beyond the Flatheads were the Crows. They were friendly and had promised the Nez Perce safe passage to the buffalo country. Of course the Wallamwatkins would have to pass Missoula.

Joseph reasoned that if he did no harm to the citizens of Missoula or their property, they would not molest him. Joseph didn't know his citizens. As the Wallamwatkins rode at a leisurely pace down the Lolo Canyon, the cow-punchers inhabiting the unpainted shacks known as ranch-houses, within the Missoula district, abandoned them and indeed pretty much everything except their hats and pistols and fastest horses and headed for Missoula. Stories had circulated of what had happened to people who were late in getting started when Joseph's people were approaching. They knew all about it.

Captain Rawn of the Seventh Cavalry and commander of the partly finished fort assumed charge. First of all he crammed all of the women and children into Higgins & Worden's general merchandise store making it possible and convenient for the

Indians to burn them all at one time instead of chasing them from house to house. Then Rawn, leading thirty soldiers and two hundred assorted citizens and cowboys, rode twelve miles up the Bitterroot Valley to the mouth of Lolo Canyon and eight miles up the Canyon to a defile flanked by steep rather bare hills on either side. There he ordered his men to build a low breastwork of logs and to dig some trenches. They named this strongpoint Fort Fizzle.

The moment Chief Joseph riding down the canyon perceived Fort Fizzle he ordered his people to halt and set up their tepees. He knew that he could take Fort Fizzle by frontal assault, but he would pay for it with the lives of many warriors. Always Joseph, with no thought for his own safety, endeavored to preserve the lives of all of his people. He sent scouts to determine whether there might be a possible detour around Fort Fizzle. To divert the attention of the Missoula citizens from their worries he went himself with Looking Glass and White Bird to ask them why they were making such preparations for defense. Upon meeting the citizens Joseph expressed astonishment and disappointment at their hostile attitude. He said that his people were merely passing by on their way up the Bitterroot Valley to the buffalo country where they expected to do some hunting. They had no thought of committing depredations. They asked only to be let alone.

Speaking for the soldiers and citizens, Captain Rawn replied that the Indians would be unmolested only if they at once surrendered their arms, ammunition and horses. This was another way of saying "unconditional surrender." Well pleased with his own cleverness Rawn suggested that they meet the next day for further discussions. This was to gain time for Howard to arrive with reenforcements. Surmising what Rawn had in mind, Joseph nevertheless agreed affably. His genial manner was so convincing that about half of the cowboys returned to their ranches convinced that the Indians would ride through the valley without doing them any harm. Their desertion drove Rawn to a pitch of exasperation.

The next morning at ten o'clock Rawn's frenzy was arrested by sounds far above his head like angels singing. Looking up from Fort Fizzle to the top of the steep canyon wall he saw the Wallamwatkins with their ponies and baggage walking along a ledge at a dizzy height. Rawn had been unaware of the existence of that ledge, but he now became painfully aware that if an Indian or a pony should miss his hold, he would be the cushion. It further impressed him that if that was their preferred route for coming down the canyon, they might at least do it without singing. As they descended to ground level at the mouth of the canyon they even twitted him about his inadequate fort. With that the rest of the cowboys and citizens went home after the nudging remark, "Well, we didn't lose any Indians." Rawn with his handful of soldiers returned to continue the building of Fort Missoula, a frustrated man.

The farther Joseph rode from Wallowa the more homesick he became. At a brief council of the chiefs he said: □ "While we were fighting for our land there was reason to fight. But while we are here I have no words to say in favor of fighting for this is not my country. Since we have left our country it matters little where we go." □

The Wallamwatkins on their way up the Bitterroot took nothing except what they bought and paid for at high prices. In one instance, the Lockwood Ranch in Ross Hole, some young warriors looted the ranch house because upon their approach the owner fled. It was on the principle that when a cat runs, a dog will chase it although he devoutly hopes that he won't catch the cat.

Deer Lodge was eighty miles east of Missoula. The Wallamwatkins rode into the town quietly and peaceably. Joseph had the young warriors under strong control. Since leaving the Lolo Trail his people had harmed no one and, excepting the Lockwood ranch, no property. Nevertheless their reputation, like a shadow, had gone before them. The people of Deer Lodge saw them coming. They dispatched William Clark on a fast horse to seek help from the neighboring town of Butte. Then they piled into the town jail and locked the Indians out and themselves in. It was the smartest thing they could have done because when the Indians saw the streets deserted and people sticking out of the jail windows, they rode on up the road without stopping. One of the most outstanding characteristics of Indians is their sense of humor. They are rugged practical jokers. It is safe to say that as they rode past that jail the corners of their mouths twitched.

But no sooner does the sun shine than clouds come up over the horizon. General Howard had telegraphed the Civil War hero of South Mountain, Colonel John Gibbon, at Fort Shaw to take up the pursuit. Gibbon collected one hundred and forty-six men of the Seventh Infantry, and thirty-four citizens of Helena, and with a wagon train marched toward Missoula. One hundred and fifty miles and seven days later Gibbon reached Missoula. There his command was augmented by Rawn's small detachment, and assorted cowboys from Missoula and the Bitterroot, bringing his total to one hundred and ninety-one. Howard, trying to get his men and artillery over the Lolo Trail without losing too many mules off the ledges and the high precipices had not yet reached Missoula. Howard's orders to Gibbon were to follow Joseph without waiting.

YELLOW WOLF'S STORY

OF

THE FLIGHT

Across the Lolo Trail and into Montana

HURRYING from the Clearwater battle, we left many things in camp. We traveled to Kamiah, named for some useful plant growing there. We did not cross the river, but camped on its bank.

With coming light next morning, skin boats were made for the crossing. While this was doing, scouts back on the trail from a distant butte waved the blanket signal: *"Danger!"*

Soon a scout came running his horse and called from the bluff:

"Soldiers following us! Soldiers coming fast!"

Crossing the families to north side of the river was easy. While this was doing, we saw soldiers riding down the distant hill toward us. We found hiding and waited for soldiers. When they reached the riverbank, we fired across at them. Many soldiers jumped from their horses and ran to any shelter they saw. Others galloped fast back toward the hills. We laughed at those soldiers. We thought we killed one.

No more fighting, a few stayed to watch. The others went home to camp. We remained there all day and all night. But the soldiers were afraid to cross and have a battle. Next morning we saw General Howard dividing his soldiers. Some left, riding down the river.

There was another trail.

The chiefs called the command, "We will move camp! No use staying here. They do not want to cross and fight us!"

Then we packed up and went. We left the soldiers on their

side of the river and fixed camp at place called Weippe. Here we found Indians who had not been in the war. They were Chief Temme Ilppilp's (Red Heart) band. Friendly to both sides. Next morning, coming daylight, one of General Howard's Nez Perce scouts came riding in. Before he came, some of our friends advised him, "You better not go over where those warriors are."

But he came and said to these Indians. "It will be best to come on your own reservation. There you will be safe."

"We will go," answered most of those Indians. There were about twenty of them, men, women, and a few children. They had not joined us. Never had been in any of the war. Coming from Montana, they had only met us there. Those Indians not joining with us in the war now bade us all good-by—a farewell, that we would never return to our homes again!

An old medicine man, Hatya Takonnin had come to see his son, Heinmot Tootsikon (Speaking Thunder), who had joined our band to go fight the soldiers. He was a strong young man, and his father said to him, "I want you home with me. Death awaits you on the trail you are taking. I see the future. It is dark with blood! I do not want to know you are killed. All going will die or see bondage."

Heinmot Tootsikon answered, "No! I do not care to return home! I want to go with my brothers and sisters. If I am killed, it will be all right."

Tears visited the old man's eyes. Then, clearing his eyes, he spoke again to his son, "I am willing that you go. It is all right for you to go help fight. But soldiers are too many."

Heinmot Tootsikon went with us, and his father returned home. A good warrior, Heinmot went through all fights holding to his life. Captured at the last battle, he was sent to the Indian Territory with others. He died in that Eeikish Pah (Hot Place).

We did not hurt the scout from the soldiers. He came friendly, as a friend to the Indians. It was all right for Chief Red Heart not to join with us. It was all wrong for General Howard to send them as prisoners to Vancouver. They were peaceable Indians. They wanted no war.

After Chief Red Heart's people were gone, we packed up and moved. We traveled to Siwishnimi (Mussel Creek), high in the mountains. We found some mussels there. When we were unpacked, one scout, Wetyettamaweyun (I Give No Orders) came and gave announcement, "Soldiers coming! I am wounded!"

He was shot through the upper arm. They had nearly killed him! Only short miss from fatal shooting.

One of the chiefs then rode about calling orders, "Soldiers coming! We must move from this place! We will give them this road!"

We moved camp about half mile from the road. When unpacked, the warriors went back to our first stop. Watched for soldiers all night. One of them said, "Half of you go back to camp." This was done. The rest of us stayed there.

The seventeen scouts went back on the trail. I was one of them. It was a small creek we came to where we stopped. We heard a voice, and we heard a second voice. It was our language, talking about horse tracks. We heard, "There are fresh tracks! Tracks made this morning!"

We watched through the brush. Just a few of them, and we got ready to shoot. We fired and killed one. They were General Howard's scouts, some of his "good men." They ran from us. One of the warriors lifted up the one we shot and saw he was not quite dead. Nobody spoke to him, and the warrior shot him through the heart. We recognized those Christian scouts, their white man's names. The one killed was John Levi. Abraham Brooks and Jim Reuben were wounded, but they escaped with others.

For about six days, coming through the mountains we saw no more fighting. Scouting on our back trail, I, with others, saw no enemies. Seventh day one man from scouts ahead came riding hard to our evening camp and reported, "Soldiers in front of us! Building fort! They are heading us off. In a little while we will see the soldiers. They know our camp!"

There are high mountains and a narrow pass where the soldiers were camped. They had built a long log barricade across the trail. That was the trail we had thought to travel. I saw Salish Indians at the soldiers' fort. They seemed quite a bunch. All had white cloths tied on arm and head. This, so as not to shoot each other. So the soldiers would know they were not Nez Perce. They were helping the soldiers. Always friends before, we now got no help from them, the Flatheads. No help any time.

We camped a ways above the soldiers, at Nasook Nema (Salmon Creek). There was no fight. The chiefs met the soldiers. It was a council, a peace talk. Whatever was said, whatever was done, each party returned to its own camp. The chiefs returned, declaring, "We must move our camp!"

Early next morning the families packed to move. We found a different way to go by those soldiers. While a few warriors climbed among rocks and fired down on the soldier fort, the rest of the Indians with our horse herds struck to the left of main trail. I could see the soldiers from the mountainside where we traveled. It was no trouble, not dangerous, to pass those soldiers.

Later two or more Indians, while moving, took the wrong trail, the main trail. Reaching the soldiers' camp, they were captured.

Of course, during that day we rode around the soldiers, some of us young fellows stayed back as scouts. One white man, maybe a scout, bothered us. Two of us chased him. He got away, and we did not see him any more.

We traveled through the Bitterroot Valley slowly. The white people were friendly. We did much buying and trading with them.

No more fighting! We had left General Howard and his war in Idaho.

But there was something—a feeling some of us could not understand. One morning a young man who had medicine power rode about camp, calling loudly to the people, "My brothers, my sisters, I am telling you! In a dream last night I saw myself killed. I will be killed soon! I do not care. I am willing to die.

But first, I will kill some soldiers. I shall not turn back from the death. We are all going to die!"

This young man was Wahlitits, one of the Red Coat warriors. He was killed only a few days later in our next battle, the Big Hole. He killed one soldier, maybe more, before he died.

Lone Bird, a brave fighter, also rode about one camp wanting more hurry. His voice reached all the people as he warned, "My shaking heart tells me trouble and death will overtake us if we make no hurry through this land! I can not smother, I can not hide that which I see. I must speak what is revealed to me. Let us begone to the buffalo country!

We reached the Big Hole, our old camp when going to and from buffalo hunting. Good feed for horses. We would stay several days. The women would cut tepee poles to take with us. Those poles must be peeled and dried for the dragging.

It was next morning, after our first night at Big Hole, that it happened. Two young warriors said to an old man, "Loan us your horses."

"No," said old man Burning Coals. "I will not loan you my horses."

Not getting the horses, nothing could be done. It proved bad.

McWhorter's Comment:

Puzzled by this attempt at horse-borrowing, I asked, "What was bad in the old man's refusing to loan his horses?" Yellow Wolf answered:

One man, Wottolen, had strong powers. That first night he dreamed of soldiers. Ten, maybe twelve, of us wanted to scout back over the trail. If no enemies were found crossing the mountain, we would go on to the Bitterroot Valley. Had the scout been made, many Indian lives would have been saved. The soldiers, trapped before reaching our camp, none of them could have escaped. All would have been killed. Sarpsis Ilppilp and Seeyakoon Ilppilp had no good horses. Best race horses must be for the scouting. Old man Burning Coals had such horses. But he liked his horses and refused to let them go.

Chiefs Looking Glass and White Bull also opposed our going. Looking Glass was against everything not first thought of by himself. White Bull always sided with him. They said, "No more fighting! War is quit."

They would not mind Wottolen. The scout was not made!

That night the warriors paraded about camp, singing, all making a good time. It was first since war started. Everybody with good feeling. Going to the buffalo country! No more fighting after Lolo Pass. War was quit. All Montana citizens our friends. This land had belonged to the Flatheads, our old-time friends. They called it Iskumtselalik Pah; meaning "Place of Ground Squirrels,"–the kind you call "picket pins." Lots of them hatched here.

It was past midnight when we went to bed.

4 THE BATTLE OF THE BIG HOLE

Riding southward toward the prairies and the buffalo herds Joseph crossed the Continental Divide and arrived at a grassy meadow on the banks of Ruby Creek in the Big Hole Valley. In the brook there was an abundance of trout. There was forage for the two thousand ponies. Meanwhile he had been joined by a small band of renegade Nez Perce who were returning from the buffalo country. They were led by a chief whom the white people had nicknamed Poker Joe, probably because he could outsmart them. In small parties the young warriors hunted antelope. Soon the kettles were bubbling with the savory steam of boiling meat and roots. Indian love of fun and gaiety burst forth in games, races and dancing.

They danced one night until after midnight. Then unaware that Gibbon's scouts had been watching them that day from distant treetops they lay down in their tepees and slept soundly.

When Gibbon received word from his scouts he served each soldier with ninety cartridges, and one day's rations. He left twenty men to guard the baggage wagons and pushed on toward the Wallamwatkins' camp. By sundown Gibbon was in a ravine fairly close to the Indians. The soldiers couldn't light fires without revealing their position, so they lay down in a ravine, ate raw pork and hardtack and slept without blankets. They were excessively tired from climbing over trees blown down across the trail.

While it was still dark and very chilly the soldiers were awakened and formed in line of march. Climbing through fallen timber in daylight had not been easy. By starlight it occasioned much swearing. Every time someone cursed, a non-com said "Shush!"

Floundering through underbrush, stumbling over rocky ledges and falling into washouts and ravines, the soldiers warmed up. Wading knee deep through swamps and waist deep in the icy water of the Big Hole River they cooled off. After five miles of the sport, with each man trying to keep near enough to the man in front to at least know where he was, they saw not breakfast but the embers of the Indians' campfires across that deep cold brook. Now and then when a flame flickered they could see the teepees and their bunched poles sticking up into the darkness.

Gibbon led his soldiers upstream for a safe distance and forded. On the other side they walked into a herd of Indians' ponies which snorted suspiciously but did not stampede. In file the soldiers pussy-footed through the bushes and around the ever present rocks, coming to a halt about a hundred yards from the nearest teepees. As it was only two A.M., and they could do nothing further until daylight, they sat down and shivered and shook while the raw pork soured and bucked within them, and those who wore false teeth removed them so that their clicking wouldn't stampede those sensitive ponies.

As the curtain of darkness lifted the soldiers could see a willow slough extending from the slope to the stream. They would have to cross that bog to get at the Indians. Quantities of ponies were wallowing around in cold mud which came up to their bellies. They were nibbling the tips and leaves of the willows. In the rosy light a mounted Indian rode up the slope to learn what the pony herd, perched half way up the hill, was doing. Like the first duck over a blind at the opening moment of the duck season the Indian and his horse were riddled with lead.

The soldiers pulled their legs out of the sucking, smacking mud and ran among the tepees yelling. Responding to the yells warriors crawled out of the teepees yawning and scratching, looked around, crawled back for their weapons and came out shooting. Women screamed, children cried, babies squalled, dogs barked, ponies whinnied and guns banged. The excited soldiers shot the women and children as well as the warriors. But the warriors began shooting back. They ran to the river bank, crouched behind it and picked off soldiers with their usual accuracy. In their aim they included officers.

Captain William Logan led his company across a stream and penetrated the rear of the Indian camp, uncovering a guard of warriors in some willows. Using captured pistols the warriors arose and gave the soldiers the business. Captain Logan shot and killed Chief Rainbow. The Chief's sister picked up a revolver and shot Captain Logan through the head. The Captain was said to have died afterward from the wound. The mortal wounding of their beloved captain so infuriated the soldiers that instead of trying to shoot the Indians they used their guns as clubs. This was unfortunate for the Indians because quite a few were knocked into the river and washed down stream.

Although their losses were heavy the soldiers drove the Indians out of their camp in about twenty minutes. However it was an empty victory. The Indians retreated to the protection of the river bank and the concealment of the willows. The sun was well above the horizon. The light was good and so was the warriors' aim. The soldiers were out in the open space between the converging lines of teepees and feeling very exposed. Besides the officers killed, several officers had been seriously wounded. Colonel Gibbon received a bullet in his leg. The bullet passed on through his mount. The horse sneezed, coughed and foundered.

On foot Gibbon suddenly hatched an idea. While bullets from every direction sang he formed his men in two lines back to back. Then he ordered them to charge with fixed bayonets. As they charged some ran faster than others thus forming an expanding circle. This tactic was employed successfully by Major Forbes against the Delaware Indians during the French and Indian War when he marched against Fort Duquesne. It was less than successful now. The Indians simply retreated deeper into the willows, then shot the soldiers when their circle contracted as they retreated.

Colonel Gibbon was finding, as Captain Perry had found, that he was fighting against a master mind. For every attack that he might develop Joseph had a riposte or a counter offensive. Gibbon looked around. The Indians were certainly keeping the flies off of his men. His casualties were already about fifty per cent. According to the book, when they had reached twenty-five per cent a retreat to a defensible position was indicated. Having retreated, the commanding officer was supposed to dispatch a messenger for help.

It then occurred to Gibbon that if he failed to find that defensible position—and soon, he would be a colonel without a regiment. On the valley slope across the river he saw a streak of small pines in an old washout. He shouted an order to follow and led the retreat across the river and up to the pines. His soldiers followed dragging about thirty wounded comrades by their arms or ankles, whichever happened to be within reach.

Using foresight Joseph had staffed the pine grove with Indian marksmen so that with Indians shooting from the willows and more Indians shooting from the pines, Gibbon's men were receiving simultaneously bullets on both sides of their uniforms.

The Indians among the pines suddenly overwhelmed by numbers, ran to another washout and continued their sharpshooting. One warrior alone, shooting through a narrow gap between two stones, accounted for five soldiers before someone got him with a carom shot.

In the pine grove the soldiers dug fox holes with their bayonets. From this temporary safety they watched, perhaps with amusement, the efforts of a gang of cowboys to separate the pony herd from the Indians. Had the cowboys been successful they could have disposed of the ponies days afterward at an attractive price. The skirmish was sharp but in the end the Indians drove the ponies down river beyond the reach of the white men. Those of the cowboys who were able to withdraw did so. The others may have been posthumously celebrated in cowboy songs.

At about that time there were two loud bangs from the trail a half mile back. After that there was silence. Gibbon correctly inferred that the small detachment left to guard the baggage wagons, hearing the distant racket at Big Hole, had hitched mules to the howitzer and packed most of the ammunition on more mules and come to the rescue. Joseph had thought of that one too. The silence meant that warriors had taken over the rescue party and all of their equipment. Actually two of the soldiers managed to wiggle out of the warriors' clutches and escape. They ran for a hundred miles. Back in the settlements anyone who wanted to know the fate of Colonel Gibbon had to run beside them while they related the story. And the story lost nothing in the telling.

As soon as the fight for the ponies had ended, the warriors returned to the teepees. Then they saw the dead women and children and a few dead warriors. Their howls of rage convinced the soldiers across the valley that each man was now fighting for his life. There would be no quarter. Among the soldiers ammunition was becoming scarce. Knowing that they had to make every shot count, they aimed more carefully. Their situation was similar to that of General Custer when he made his last stand.

Regardless of what the warriors might have in mind for the soldiers, the Indian mothers had had enough. Bravely they had fought the battle side by side with their men. Now the time had come to think about their children. Their strong, skilled hands quickly pulled down teepees, packed them on ponies, saddled other ponies and put the children on them and gathered the most essential articles of equipment. During their preparations for retreat they made no attempts to shield or protect themselves from the sniping fire from across the valley. The toll was heavy. A number of Indian women were killed, including a daughter of Chief Looking Glass and two of Joseph's wives. Several ponies went down kicking, some with their packs. That settled it. The Indian women rode out of there and on down the valley. They left behind quantities of buffalo robes, dried meat and clothing, all of which they would sadly miss later. However there was no help for it.

During the rest of the day the Indian marksmen kept shooting from cover. They killed Lieutenant English and put a second bullet in Captain Williams. Late in the afternoon the Indians started a grass fire which flashed smartly up the hillside. The flames were crackling only a few yards from the soldiers' fox holes when a sudden shift in the wind reversed the fire and put it out. That saved Gibbon's command momentarily from extinction. The soldiers were exhausted, famished, suffering acutely from thirst, their ammunition nearly expended. They could not have withstood a frontal assault during the day, much less a general attack on all sides after dark as Joseph had already planned. No one at the time knew why such an attack was never carried out. Nor would Joseph tell afterward the reason for his change of plan, although his warriors had made several practice charges.

The true reason why the Indians never mounted the big attack would be found in their veneration for Mother Earth. They could see that the soldiers had dug in the ground. The soldiers had amply demonstrated their weakness in battle. They had attacked at dawn with every advantage. Now before sunset they were huddled on a hillside about as defenseless as sheep. And yet they had stopped a roaring flash fire only a spear length from their line. It was a fire that would have consumed them, but they had checked it and flung it back upon itself. How? Obviously they had dug from the earth some very strong medicine. Joseph and his warriors knew that while the soldiers held that position nothing could prevail against them.

Gibbon had advanced upon the Indian camp the night of August 8th. The battle lasted all of August 9th. That night while Gibbon was dispatching messengers to Howard for help, the Indians were packing on their ponies some of the supplies in their camp which their women had abandoned. On the morning of August 10th a messenger from the wagon train brought word to Gibbon that although the Indians had captured the howitzer, the baggage wagon guard had successfully defended the wagons, and they were now approaching. At sundown the wagons arrived bringing ammunition, food, water and blankets. The soldiers who had been living on raw pork, and later raw horse, were given their first cooked food in forty-eight hours.

Meanwhile Howard was approaching rapidly.

While riding through Missoula Howard noticed an Indian wrapped in a red blanket squatting on a shed roof watching the parade. Howard probably considered him as an advertisement or part of the Main Street decorations. After Howard's troop had ridden out of Missoula the Indian dropped from the rear of the shed to the back of a waiting pony and galloped by another route toward Big Hole. He whipped his horse until it fell dead. After that he ran. He reached Joseph's camp a day before Howard. His information caused Joseph to decide to lead the Wallamwatkins on down the Big Hole Valley. Had that Indian failed to arrive it is likely that within another twenty-four hours the remnant of Gibbon's command would have surrendered—unconditionally.

By eleven the night of August tenth Joseph's rear guard was riding down the valley. The morning of August eleventh, soldier fatigue squads were afield counting and burying the dead. They reported eighty-nine dead Indians. That day two wounded soldiers died making the total fatalities for the army thirty-one. Forty soldiers were wounded.

Joseph afterward explained that he had supposed that when he had led his people out of Idaho he wouldn't be followed and attacked. He believed that he had done what Howard wanted him to do, and he had no thought of returning without having first negotiated some sort of agreement and arrangement. Then why, Joseph asked himself, had the army followed and attacked his people so savagely and relentlessly? The Nez Perce had always been friendly. They wanted to be friends. They wanted to live in their own country and mind their own business and not molest anybody. They would have been glad to help the white people and to share what they had with them. Then why—?

One hundred and nineteen Wallamwatkins afterward died from wounds received in the battle of the Big Hole and were buried along the trail. Many of them were women and children.

At ten A.M. August twelfth General Howard with his cavalry arrived at the Big Hole battlefield. Colonel Gibbon seated on a pile of pine boughs to rest his wounded leg greeted Howard with a rueful grin. He said: "Who could have believed that those Indians would have rallied after such a surprise and made such a fight?"

Howard's later comment on Joseph was: □ "He gathered his warriors, recovered lost ground and recaptured his numerous herd of ponies which had already been cut off by Gibbon's men, buried most of his dead and made good his retreat before the force with me was near enough to harm him. Few military commanders with good troops could better have recovered after so fearful a surprise." □

But what about the massacre of Indian mothers and their children?

YELLOW WOLF'S STORY
OF
THE BATTLE OF THE BIG HOLE

At the Big Hole: Surprise Attack

BEFORE LEAVING IDAHO one of the chiefs—I do not remember which one—had ridden all about our camp announcing, "We may first go to the buffalo country, and then afterwards join Sitting Bull in Canada. Crossing this mountain, leaving Idaho, we will travel peaceably. No white man must be bothered! Only enemies here we fight. Trouble no white people after passing the Lolo into Montana. Montana people are not our enemies. Enemies only here in Idaho.

"When we reach Sitting Bull, we will hold council. Whatever is there decided will be done. Delegates will be sent to talk with officers of the Government. If agreed we return to our homes, all right. We will return. If agreed to take land in Montana near the Sioux, that will be done for us by the Government.

"Across the mountains kill no cattle-beeves, while the food we take with us lasts. At Clearwater fight, we lost plenty food for reaching the buffalo country. Only if our women and children grow hungry will we take cattle or whatever food we find—as taken from us. The war we leave here in Idaho."

These were instructions from the chiefs. Strong laws, nor were they broken. The chiefs thought the war ended. To be no fighting in Montana. But not so, the Montana people.

They did not regard the peace made with us there at Lolo Pass.

Because of that lie-treaty we were trapped.

Trapped sleeping, unarmed.

Through the Bitterroot Valley they spied on us while selling us vegetables, groceries, anything we wanted.

Sold whisky to some, almost making trouble.

They spied on us crossing the mountains when we thought not of foes.

McWhorter's Comment—*At this point Yellow Wolf's story was interrupted while McWhorter and Yellow Wolf travelled with interpreter Many Wounds to the battlefield on Big Hole River where Yellow Wolf would continue his story. McWhorter described their arrival at Big Hole battlefield as follows:*

The next morning on our way to the lower river bottom where the Nez Perce village had stood, interpreter Many Wounds stopped at a bank of drifted sand and, under Yellow Wolf's direction, drew a diagram of the ill-fated camp. [Yellow Wolf had no ability as a draftsman, although he was fairly good at wordpicturing.] The tepees were shown in rather irregular, compact form with a partly open court in the center, corresponding in general with a pen drawing by Chief Peopeo Tholekt, made at a later day. Both delineations negated the methodic, straightline V-shaped village so generally described.

The sand-picturing completed, we crossed the stream on the old pole-floored bridge to which Yellow Wolf refers in his narrative, and found ourselves upon the Nez Perce camp site and the battlefield proper. Under Yellow Wolf's guidance we walked north to within a few paces of the apex or tip of the old camp or village.

He designated a spot near the riverbank where the tepee in which he was sleeping had stood when the first gunfire of the attack broke upon them. For a full five minutes he stood, his keen eyes sweeping all points of the field. Then facing west, whence the enemy descent had come, he began in his usual evenly modulated tone:

Before the soldiers charged from the hillside, I heard a horse cross the river slowly. Heard it pass down the camp, out of hearing. Minthon was with me, and we afterwards agreed that it must have been a spy.

But we did not think of enemies at the time. This teepee here was not my home, and I was without my rifle. Chief Joseph's teepee, my home, was near upper end of camp. My gun was there. Only very few warriors had guns ready when the attack came.

It must have been about three o'clock in morning, just before daylight, when I heard it—a gun—two guns! I knew not what was the trouble! The sound was like a small gun, not close. I was half sleeping, I lay with eyes closed. Maybe I was dreaming? I did not think what to do! Then I was awake. I heard rapidly about four gunshots across there to the west. We did not know then, but it was those first shots that killed Natalekin, who was going early to look for horses. This gunfire made me wide awake. Then came three volleys from many rifles, followed by shouting of soldiers.

I grabbed my moccasins and with others ran out of the teepee. I had only my war club. We stopped where we are now standing. Men and women were lying flat on the ground, listening. I saw one woman so—over there only a few feet away. I heard her call out, "Why not all men get ready and fight? Not run away!"

I did not know her. When I heard this, it convinced me she was right. Minthon, a younger boy than I, was also convinced. He gave me his gun. It had but one shell. I walked to here (four paces). I saw a man running this way. It was now nearly daylight. He came close and said, "Wahchumyus (Rainbow) is killed!"

I thought that must be a mistake. But he was killed early, before the sunrise.

A man was standing here near the water. He was wearing a black blanket. It was Pahkatos Owyeen (Five Wounds). He seemed thinking to himself. Stepping one way, then another. Restless and not easy in mind. I knew his feelings. Thinking, but not talking. After a moment, he said, "Any you brothers have two guns? Let me have one."

Pahkatos had been wounded at the Clearwater. Fingers of right hand, but no bones broken. Had his fingers wrapped together. I was standing back there. One man, a little ways off, came stepping. Holding out a rifle he spoke in quick words, "Take this gun. It has five shells in magazine and one in barrel."

Pahkatos took the rifle with the remark, "They are enough." He dropped his blanket. I do not know if he crossed the creek here or up there near the willows (forty feet). He entered the willows on the opposite side of the stream. The last I ever saw of him. He was killed later in the fight. A powerful warrior, he had fought in the buffalo country to the east. Was known to all the tribes.

Watyo Chekoon (Passing Overhead), also strong in war, crossed the creek from the main body of Indians. Later, going where bullets flew like hail, he escaped a great danger. Came through it all.

The soldiers had not reached our part of camp. Never did cross the river at this point. The hard fighting was at upper half of the village.

I ran up that way towards the fighting. I saw a warrior hurrying along the line of tepees, and I went with him. Going only a short ways, another man joined us. We ran, maybe half a quarter mile, when we saw soldiers along the creek, upper part of the village, we were about midway the camp when I saw a man coming toward us. I stopped, the other two men going on. He was walking stooped, blood running from his head. His name was Jeekunkun (Dog), mostly called John Dog. I said to him, "Trade me your gun! You have plenty of cartridges and I have none. Trade, and then get away from danger!"

The wounded man answered me, "No! I must have the gun. I do not want to die without resisting!"

I met another young man wounded in the right arm. He was carrying his gun in his left hand. He, too, refused to trade guns. His name was Temme Ilppilp (Red Heart), and he was wounded worse than I saw (stomach wound). He died at the second camp from the battle.

I hurried on to about here (past midcamp) and saw a soldier

crawling like a drunken man. He had a gun and belt full of cartridges. I struck him with my war club and took his Government rifle and ammunition belt.

I saw teeth loose in his mouth, and easily took them out. I had never seen such teeth. They must be around here somewhere yet.

I now had a gun and plenty of shells. As I have shown you, I was in lower part of camp when the attack came. I hurried to join in the battle, which had grown hot. At first the warriors had no guns, but now a few—a very few—had found rifles. I came near a small willow thicket. I heard yelling, screaming. I recognized Iskatpoo Tismooktismook (Black Trail). He came stooping and said to me, "My nephew, I got shot. I am wounded! Shot through the shoulder."

Iskatpoo was a good warrior, a brave warrior. But he was overcome by the too-numerous enemies.

From here where we stand I saw soldiers come stepping forward. Nothing could stop them! As I said, but few warriors had rifles in their hands. Sleeping when soldiers fired on our camp—there must have been two hundred of them—we knew not at once what to do. Of course, not well awake, it was hard to get arms quickly.

These soldiers came on rapidly. They mixed up part of our village. I now saw tepees on fire. I grew hot with anger. Women, children, and old men who could not fight were in those tepees. Up there above that old pole bridge crossing the creek—about one hundred steps from the blazing tepees—I heard an Indian voice loudly announcing:

"My brothers! Our tepees are on fire! Get ready your arms! Make resistance! You are here for that purpose!"

It was Kowtoliks talking, a brave warrior. He was answered with war whoops by those who had guns. There must have been one hundred soldiers in that part of the camp.

An Indian with a white King George blanket about him was standing farthest up the river, alone. Of the Paloos Waiwaiwai band, his name was Pahka Pahtahank (Five Fogs). Aged about thirty snows, he was of an old-time mind. He did not understand the gun. He was good with the bow, but had only a hunting bow. I thought, "If he had good rifle, he could bring death to the soldiers."

He was just in front of his own tepee. Soldiers were this side, not far from him. He stood there shooting arrows at the enemies. The soldiers saw, and fired at him. That Indian stepped about a little, but continued sending his arrows. Three times those soldiers fired and missed him. The fourth round killed him.

Looks wonderful to me, three volleys—not exactly volleys together—should miss him not more than ten steps away. I do not know if he hit any soldiers.

At Kowtoliks' voice, about ten warriors—not more—started for those soldiers. I hurried to get a closer position, closer and hidden.

McWhorter's Comment:

Proceeding another sixty paces, Yellow Wolf halted where had been the southern extremity or base of the village, and about twenty steps from the riverbank. He stood silent, though keenly alert, for several minutes before resuming his narrative:

What I show you from here was just a few men who drove the soldiers back at this point. Only about ten brave warriors made here a desperate stand after Kowtoliks called that the tepees were afire. Some had already mounted horses and were fighting, scattered. Others were in the willows fighting. I joined to save the tepees.

I came against the soldiers on side opposite the other warriors. Those warriors—not more than ten—were scattered, shooting from sheltered places.

From all sides we mixed them up. I made an advance against some soldiers. Got close enough to take good aimed shots. Three of those same enemies went down. I only know I shot fast and saw each time a soldier fall. I rushed in. Took guns and cartridge belts from those three soldiers. That is the custom of war. Those guns afterwards were used by other Indians.

We now mixed those soldiers badly. We could hit each other with our guns. It was for the lives of women and children we were fighting. If whipped, better to die than go in bondage with freedom gone.

Those soldiers did not last long. Only about thirty at that place were left standing. Scared, they ran back across the river. We could not well count how many dead soldiers, but we killed a good few. They acted as if drinking. We thought some got killed by being drunk. I saw four killed before getting this far up. I had not time to see what others were doing at this place.

I am telling you true! Those soldiers hurried back across the river. Too many of them falling, and they ran.

We followed the soldiers across the stream. I waded it just below that old pole bridge. Of course there was no bridge then. Reaching that open space among the willows, I saw a soldier only a few steps ahead of me. Stepping cautiously, stooping, looking among the willows with gun ready (Yellow Wolf was pantomiming his story), he did not see me approach. I got within four steps of him. I would touch him while he lived. He must have felt me back of him. Whirling, he brought his gun around. But I was too quick. My bullet went through his breast. He fell and did not move.

A young man, this soldier wore a uniform. I took his gun, cartridge belt, and trench-digging knife. I quickly gave the gun and ammunition to a warrior who had none.

The soldiers were now running to the hill. Desperate fighting in the brush, among the willows, and in open places. Close pressed, the soldiers hurried up the bluff. On the flat they stopped to barricade themselves. Had all the warriors had guns, not many soldiers would have reached the bluff.

Up to this time not twenty Indians had rifles. Every gun taken was quickly used. When they could, soldiers spoiled those of partners who were killed. They broke a few Indian guns as well.

McWhorter's Comment:

Casually passing along the river where it turns suddenly in a great sweep towards the western mountain, Yellow Wolf paused. Studying its eroded bank, he spoke half musingly: "Looks some change in this bank." And then:

It is a wonderful story I am telling you. When I reached here, desperate fighting was being done. I saw a soldier standing like this:

McWhorter's Comment:

Yellow Wolf, stepping down the bank, stood motionless at the water's edge, facing east, with his head turned north toward where Wahlitits and his wife were killed—more of which later.

Like this that soldier stood, the lower part of his body hidden by the bank. Some kind of marks or stripes were on his upper arms or shoulders, as if an officer. I thought he was alive, and brought my gun to shoot. He could see me, but did not move. Then I understood.

That soldier was dead!

When I saw him so facing where Wahlitits and his wife lay, I was convinced one of them had shot him. There seemed no other way he was killed. He was the only dead man I ever saw standing.

McWhorter's Comment:

The narrator paused meditatively. As if comprehending that his story would be discredited, he added earnestly:

While I am talking, I am convinced of this. My chiefs were here then. Now I am alone, succeeding them. No witnesses, this is why I feel to tell only truth of what I saw in battle, of what I myself did. You must know I am speaking true. What I, Yellow Wolf, saw and did, only.

A tepee stood above that of Wahlitits. It belonged to Wetyetmas Likleinen (Circling Swan), a large man. He died here, fighting at his tepee home. Never went anywhere. He did not run. His wife was killed here. Their tepee stood close to White Bird's, to Tulhulhutsut's and to that of Chuslum Moxmox (Yellow Bull).

Now I speak of another of the best warriors. He was killed there at the next tepee downstream. Only a few steps from Wetyetmas Likleinen. His name was Tewit Toitoi.

Here by his tepee sat smoking, Wahnistas Aswetesk, a very old man. He was shot many times! As he sat on his buffalo robe, one soldier shot him. He did not get up. Others shot him. Still he sat there. Others shot him. He did not move. Just sat there smoking as if only raindrops struck him! Must have been twenty bullets entered his body. He did not feel the shots! After the battle, he rode horseback out from there. He grew well, but died of sickness in the Eeikish Pah where he was sent after the surrender. The wounds did not seem to grow. It was just as you see mist, see fog coming out from rain. We saw it like smoke from boiling water (steam), coming out of his wounded body. He was not shot in the head.

Several dead soldiers lay scattered around here. More were killed farther up the village.

Proceeding thirty-two steps upstream, Yellow Wolf continued:

I saw here a dead Indian lying under the riverbank, his leg in the water. His name was Lazzykoon, as pronounced by the whites, but we called him Allezyahkon—an old-time name with meaning known only to the oldest Indians. His age about sixty snows, he was not classed as a fighter. His son was Lahpeealoot (Two Flocks on Water; later known as Phillip Williams). Lazzykoon had often said to his son: "If the Nez Perce go to war with the whites, we will not go. Our family will not join them."

Fifty steps farther upstream, he went on:

I saw another Indian lying here dead under the bank. He was about thirty years old and died fighting. His name was Wookawkaw (Woodpecker).

Besides the three soldiers I saw fall as I shot, I saw four others killed a little below here. I do not know how many were killed all counted, but more were killed above here.

In meantime there was hard fighting among the brush. I will show you where some bad struggles took place.

McWhorter's Comment:

Yellow Wolf now piloted us to the west side of the stream and, passing directly by the place where he had been victor in the rifle duel with the young soldier, he headed across the open bottom land over which Colonel Gibbon's most unobstructed charge had been launched. Yellow Wolf pointed out, near the west bank of the river, where it bends towards the mountain in a great sweeping curve, a well-preserved buffalo wallow which the troops passed in their morning onslaught against the sleeping village. Without a hesitating step, our guide proceeded some hundreds of yards and stopped near a large circular clump of willows flanked by a much smaller clump. After his usual moments of reverie before speech, he told the following:

I have told you that Wahchumyus (Rainbow) was killed early in the fight, before sunrise. What happened here I did not see. But it is true as told me by witnesses. They have also told it to you. I was here after the fight. I saw the dead in the same positions as when they fell.

At this place a tall soldier—must have been near seven feet—and a short Indian met. The Indian, Wahchumyus, stepped from behind that small bunch of willows. The soldier came from back of this big cluster. About four steps apart, both raised guns at same time. The Indian was the quickest, but his gun snapped. The tall soldier shot him through the heart. He fell backwards, dead.

Wahchumyus was a great warrior, brave in all fighting. He had whipped in many battles in the buffalo country. All the tribes knew and feared him. His name was strong over all the land. That big soldier had killed one of our best warriors.

When Wahchumyus fell, the tall soldier turned and ran south. He passed Wahchumyus on his left. He sprang behind those bushes (about fifty feet to the south). Other soldiers were passing close, hurrying to the hill. Hohots Elotoht (Bad Boy Grizzly Bear) was back of those willows. Both their guns were empty. They clubbed with their guns, then grabbed each other. They wrestled. The big soldier was too much for the short Indian and threw him. Both struggled for their lives. The big soldier was on top. The Indian called twice to his *Wyakin* for help. He was heard and was given strength to break from his enemy.

The two stood up. Not equally matched, again Elotoht was thrown. His arm doubled under the tall soldier who was now choking him. Elotoht could no longer free himself.

A brave warrior, Lakochets Kunnin, came running. He shot the tall soldier and killed him. The bullet broke one bone in Elotoht's arm above his wrist.

A few Indians hiding from the fighting witnessed the killing of Wahchumyus. Saw the fight between Elotoht and the big soldier. But none offered help. Towassis (Bowstring) was there. He did nothing—was not a fighting man. Owhi, standing away back like a looker-on, saw it all. From the Yakimas, he was not a Nez Perce. He did no real fighting, always keeping out of it.

Pahkatos, killed a few hours later than Wahchumyus, approached the closest of any of the warriors to the soldier trenches. He got killed purposely. Wahchumyus and Pahkatos had been partners fighting the Sioux (Assiniboins) in the buffalo country. These two war mates had agreed that both should die the same day. In the same battle, as had their fathers. The death of these two mighty warriors was a great loss to our fighting strength. They were strong in planning battle.

Lakochets Kunnin was a fine young man, a brave warrior. He knew not fear. Scared at nothing! While driving the soldiers to the timbered flat, it was at foot of bluff, right by the trail, it happened. Lakochets there, where I showed you, mixed a soldier in a hand to hand fight. The soldier had a gun and was getting the best of Lakochets. Peopeo Tholekt rushed in and wrenched the gun from the soldier, and Lakochets then killed him. It was hard struggling and the soldier would have come out best had Peo not been quick.

At the Big Hole: Savagery of the Whites

AFTER THE MORNING BATTLE, after the soldiers ran to the woods, I started back with others to our camp. I wanted to see what had been done. At this place I came to a dead soldier (feigning death). A knife was in his hand. He lay as he had fixed his position—rifle at right side. When I stooped to get the gun the soldier almost stabbed me. His knife grazed my nose. I jumped five, maybe seven, feet getting away from that knife. Approaching, I struck him with my *kopluts.** He did not raise up. I took his gun and cartridge belt.

Taking those guns made me a chief. I killed a few soldiers. I took some guns and became a chief. It is the custom of the tribe.

We saw another soldier. Wounded, he was afraid or knew not what he was about. One warrior took his gun from him, and afterwards, I went back and got his cartridge belt. Something was tied to the belt. I opened it. There was hardtack and a little bacon. Later I ate that lunch. I did not bother the soldier. He could not live.

From then until now, all the tribes know that I have full right to take food from anybody, no difference who. When an act is done at the risk of a warrior's life, it is thereafter known that he is entitled to take food wherever he happens to be.

Here, we recrossed the creek to our camp. It was not good to see women and children lying dead and wounded. A few

---

* War club.

soldiers and warriors lay as they had fallen—some almost together. Wounded children screaming with pain. Women and men crying, wailing for their scattered dead! The air was heavy with sorrow. I would not want to hear, I would not want to see, again. About ten warriors had been killed when the tepees were fired on before anyone was armed. All this was seen. The chiefs now called to the warriors to renew the fighting where the soldiers had hidden themselves.

In the meantime after the soldiers had been driven back, a citizen soldier was captured. It was over among those biggest willows. He threw his gun away, but someone who helped capture him found it. I heard a voice call out, "Kill him!"

"No! He will tell us some news!"

That was what I heard one man reply. They brought him close to a tepee. Lakochets Kunnin, a young warrior, was leading the prisoner. I did not see from which side of the tepee one man came stepping and joined the group. The man who came from back of the tepee said commandingly, "Do not waste time! Kill him!"

While Lakochets Kunnin stood holding the prisoner, the new man with gun ready without more words shot him. Killed him dead. He then spoke, "No use! The difference is, had he been a woman, we would have saved him. Sent him home unhurt! Are not *warriors* to be fought? Look around! These babies, these children killed! Were *they* warriors? These young girls, these young women you see dead! Were *they* warriors? These young boys, these old men! Were *they* warriors?

"*We* are the warriors! Coming on us while we slept, no arms ready, the soldiers were brave. Then, when we have only a few rifles in our hands, like cowardly coyotes they run away.

"These citizen soldiers! Good friends in Bitterroot Valley! Traded with us for our gold! Their Lolo peace treaty was a lie! Our words were good. They had two tongues. Why should we waste time saving his life?"

This warrior, Otskai, was my brother (first cousin). No reply was made to his talk. All were convinced to his side. He had spoken right. A brave warrior, a good fighter, but at times his head did not act right. Would do things at a wrong time. But nobody could say Otskai was afraid, that he ever hid from the fighting!

The citizen soldier was a young man. We afterwards learned he was prominent in the Bitterroot country. He was wearing poor clothes. At the surrender the Nez Perce were asked, "Who killed the young man prisoner at the Big Hole?"

When asked this by those United States soldiers, nobody answered. Otskai and I were not there. We had escaped, going to the Sioux in Canada. Lakochets Kunnin had also escaped, but he was killed by enemy Indians. Chapman, interpreter in the Indian Territory, asked who killed the citizen soldier, a prominent man. Nobody knew. Nobody would tell. Up to this day, this time, nobody has ever told who killed that citizen soldier.

McWhorter's Comment:

During the foregoing depiction, we had traversed the entire length of the original camp, and now, guided by Yellow Wolf, we doubled back some distance to learn of other tragic happenings. He designated a spot fifteen paces out from the west line of tepees, and towards the river in the direction from where the charge was made on the camp. After a few moments of silent meditation, the old warrior told the following ghastly story:

Here, alone, stood a small tepee, what you call a hospital, erected for a purpose. In this tepee during the night before the attack, the wife of Weyatanatoo Latpat (Sun Tied) gave birth to a baby. Wetahlatpat's sister, Tissaikpee (Granite [Crystal]), an oldlike woman, was with her as nurse. What I am telling you are facts; as I, Yellow Wolf, saw with my own eyes.

As I have already told, we came back from driving the soldiers to the hill to find part of our village in ruins. This tepee here was standing and silent. Inside we found the two women lying in their blankets dead. Both had been shot. The mother had her newborn baby in her arms. Its head was smashed, as by a gun breech or boot heel. The mother had two other children, both killed, in another tepee. Some soldiers acted with crazy minds.

Wetahlatpat was a brave warrior. But we saw him no more in that fight. After helping drive the soldiers to the hill, he came back here. Finding all his family killed, he spent the rest of the day burying them. His sister, a widow woman, he also buried.

I did not see the burying of our dead. The fighting, the scouting, had to be done. In each family, the nearest relations did the burying. If a warrior lost a child or his wife, he quit the fight to bury his dead. If any of his family were bad wounded, he quit fighting to take care of them. Because of this, some of our bravest warriors were not in the fighting after driving the soldiers to the timbered flat. But Alokut, whose wife was wounded, did not go with the camp. Relations took care of her.

McWhorter's Comment:

Yellow Wolf proceeded south to a very slight depression in the ground a few feet in diameter. Designating the scarcely noticeable "sink," he said:

Here Wahlitits was killed early in the fight. It happened immediately after I passed on my way to where the soldiers were mixing the Indians up. His tepee stood just south of here, in the main village line. Like all the warriors, he was bothered to get moccasins and rifle. He sprang out and ran to this place. He dropped flat in the sink behind a log thick as a man's leg. Across this log, his rifle pointed at the willows over there where the soldiers would be first seen. He killed a soldier who stepped from the willows. I do not know how, but Wahlitits was then killed by another soldier. When hit, he must have raised up, for he was found lying on his back.

Wahlitits' wife, a brave woman, was with him. When he fell, she grabbed his gun and fired at a near soldier. I do not know if more shots than one. Some said she killed the soldier who had killed Wahlitits, and then was quickly killed herself.

We found her lying across her husband's body as if protecting him. I heard she had been wounded before Wahlitits was killed. She was the only woman who did fighting in that battle that I knew about.

Wahlitits lay with face to the sky. A brave warrior, he did not turn back from death.

Closing Scenes at the Big Hole

I WILL TELL HOW we got this gun.* Six of us were mounted and this side (southwest) of the entrenched soldiers. They were my uncle, Old Yellow Wolf, brother to my mother, Tenahtahkah Weyun (Dropping from a Cliff), Weyatanatoo Latpat (Sun Tied), Pitpillooheen (Calf of Leg), Ketalkpoosmin (Stripes Turned Down), and I, Yellow Wolf.

We were scouts on the lookout. Scouts everywhere that enemies might be coming. From across the valley south of us, I heard a voice—a Nez Perce voice—call a warning, "Look this way!"

Looking, we saw three scouts riding fast toward us. Drawing near, one of them yelled, "Two white men riding on trail towards you!"

We ran our horses in that direction. Soon we saw them! We chased those two white men back the way they came. We fired at them. Up there we found the cannon. We saw the big gun on a wagon with men. Four, maybe six, mules hitched to that gun wagon. While we charged this cannon, the men having it in keeping fired it twice. But some distance away, we scattered, and nobody hurt. I saw a warrior off his horse running afoot towards this cannon from the opposite side. This was Seeyakoon

* Field piece.

Ilppilp (Red Spy), a brave man, a good fighter. He came running, dodging, getting closer and closer to the main cannonman. That soldier did not see him. Then Seeyakoon, still at good distance, shot him in the back, killing him. At the same time Tenahtahkah dropped the right-hand lead mule. The cannon was completely stopped. Some other soldiers with it skipped to the brush, escaping with their lives. But the main warrior in its capture was Ketalkpoosmin, a young man afraid of nothing.

This little fight over, we again heard one scout across the creek calling, "Coming down this way leading one pack horse, about ten soldiers!"

We mounted in a hurry and went to meet these new enemies. As far as to our camp (600 yards) one of the soldiers was leading the pack horse. My uncle, Espowyes (Light in the Mountain), was some distance ahead of us. I saw him head this soldier off and take the pack horse. That soldier put up no fight. He skipped for his life. We fired at him, but did not stop him. Espowyes was brother (relation) to Chief Joseph. Those ten or eleven soldiers ran their horses fast back up the trail. When we got to that pack horse, we cut the rope holding the packs, dropping them to the ground. With rocks the boxes were broken open. It was ammunition, more than two thousand cartridges.

I paid no attention, but about thirty Indians were there by this time. We all piled after that ammunition. Some got only few cartridges. Some got more. Later it was divided evenly by the chiefs. Just one kind of rifles it fit—those we took from the soldiers.

Most of the warriors now went back to fight the soldiers in their trenches, while several scouted the woods above us, the mountainside. Might be soldiers coming through that way.

Only my uncle and I rode up the trail where the ten soldiers had fled. We went quite a way and decided those soldiers had left for the Bitterroot Valley. We turned back. Had we found them, one would have watched them, while the other returned to bring warriors for the fight.

While we chased those soldiers and captured the ammunition, other Indians knocked out whatever was used in firing the cannon. Took off the wheels and rolled them down a steep place to the swamp or creek brush. We could have fought the soldiers with that gun had we known how to use it. I understood Peopeo Tholekt shallow-buried it, digging with his hunting knife. He came there as the fight ended. Poker Joe afterwards rolled it down the bluff to thick brush. I knew Poker Joe very well. He was a great leader—a brave warrior.

I am telling the facts. What I saw, and what was told me about the big gun hiding. I am telling to hurt nobody. The true history must be given.

With my uncle I now rode up the open mountainside to timber where other scouts were watching. They were guarding against any new enemies who might come. Hiding up there, we would be ready to head off any soldiers coming along the trail below. The fighting at the soldiers' trenches was going on. The gun reports did not grow less.

McWhorter's Comment:

From the scene of the capture of the howitzer, Yellow Wolf led us northwest up the open hillside to the timber. He passed over the shoulder of the ridge point with unerring accuracy, and proceeded to a small parklike opening on a slightly sloping flat facing the northeast.

This place was headquarters on this side of the creek for the scouts and guards who were watching for any new enemies who might be approaching over the trail. A good bunch of men were standing here, I, Yellow Wolf, among them. Our horses were tied just back of us.

Word came that Sarpsis Illppilp (Red Moccasin Tops) had been killed. He was lying dead near the soldier trenches. Chuslum Moxmox (Yellow Bull), his father, made announcement, "We do not want to leave him there. We do not want to leave him for crazy white people who might cut him in pieces to make fun of brave warrior. Who will go bring his body away, bring him to this place?"

Then the word went around, "We are bringing Sarpsis Illppilp away from there!"

Seven or eight of us started down that way (northeast). We had to keep away from the soldiers' aim, stay hidden in the timber. Tipyahlanah Kapskaps (Strong Eagle), cousin of Sarpsis, was our leader. I cannot recognize every place as then. Young trees have grown up, changing looks of woods and land. But I will explain best I can.

When we came down above where the ranger station now stands, we tried avoiding shots from the soldier trenches. Weweetsa (Log), who had been wounded in the right side earlier in the fight, was the rear man. He became exposed and was killed (wounded) by a bullet from the trenches. It struck at the collarbone and came out at left shoulder. Weweetsa soon regained life and remained with us two weeks. Then, with three other wounded men, he went to the Flathead Reservation. He got well of the shot but was killed soon afterwards by Flatheads in a quarrel.

Hardly three minutes after Weweetsa was shot, Quiloishkish had his right elbow shattered. His name is Flathead language. At Bearpaw Mountain fight he escaped to the Sioux. Never did surrender. Finally returned to Lapwai where he died. At the wounding of Quiloishkish, we all returned to this place.

We thought to try again. Six or seven of us went this time. A shallow draw led down where Sarpsis lay. We worked down it quite a ways, within about twenty steps of where he lay. Then Tipyahlanah sprang forward and caught up Sarpsis, who was still breathing. Only ran with him a few steps when he was shot through right side just below short rib. Wounded, he carried his brother (cousin) part way to safety, then fell. Sarpsis there died. Tipyahlanah crawled back up to the benchland. We came back up here, our hearts feeling bad. After another council, we said we would try again.

A third time we were ready to go. My uncle Yellow Wolf told me he would go in my place. As I have told you, he was my mother's full brother and first cousin to Chief Joseph. This is why I stayed in Joseph's teepee, by his campfire. Relations always stay together.

They went down. The dead man had a white wolfskin over his shoulders. His father, Yellow Bull, kept shouting from the wooded bench, "Who saves the body can have the wolfskin!" That wolfskin was strong medicine.

I do not know only as they told when they came back. While the other warriors kept firing at the trenches from hiding places, Tahwis Tokaitat (Bighorn Bow), a strong man, crawled down to the body and pulled it away. The soldiers did not see him. As he brought the body behind a tree, Yellow Bull called to him, "You have done what you wanted! Come away!"

They brought the body of Sarpsis Ilppilp up here and buried it secretly. I saw the bullet mark. He was shot in the throat. The bullet cut one strand of his wampum beads.

Yellow Bull did not keep his promise to give the white wolfskin for bringing away the body of Sarpsis .The mother, a magician, got the skin. It was taken from her by Tahomchits Humkon, a medicine man. At the last battle, wearing this wolfskin, Tahomchits was shot across the back of neck. He always shook afterwards—hands shaking.

Not many warriors stayed at the fighting. A very few could hold the soldiers, while if any new enemies came, warriors must be to hold them back. Where the soldiers buried themselves, one warrior, going from tree to tree while shooting, could be as three, maybe as five or seven, rifles.

That same afternoon of the attack on our camp, all women, children, old men, and wounded left, going forward on the trail. Chief Joseph, White Bird, and fighting men also went. Many had wounded friends and relations to care for. The families must be protected if new enemies appeared.

It was the women and children we must fight for. So, in the evening all warriors, all but thirty, left to join the camp, to be there before darkness came, to watch for soldiers through the night. We remaining would fight as we could, and bring news if other soldiers came.

Night drew on. We then went after the fighting strong. Scattered among trees, lying close to the ground. In low places hard to see, we crawled close to those trenches. We heard the soldiers talking, swearing, crying.

Late in the fore part of the night, we heard noise in the willows under the bluff below the trenches. We heard one talking loud in the trenches. Then we heard him crying! When we heard this, we understood. Must be some young man (a volunteer) escaped us to the willows, and the old man (his father) could not go. Probably he was wounded. Then the escaping soldiers seemed all returned to the trenches. That was what we thought, hearing such noises.

The night grew old, and the firing faded away. Soldiers would not shoot. Would not lift head nor hand above their hiding. We believed they had but little ammunition. Of course, they must have some few cartridges, but shots slowed. Then they stopped entirely. We knew then they were holding cartridges for maybe a charge by us. We did not charge. If we killed one soldier, a thousand would take his place. If we lost one warrior, there was none to take his place.

We then held council to know what best to do. The older warriors always decided. They talked this way:

"Those soldiers can no longer be dangerous to the families. They are afoot, all badly scared. Our best warriors are gone. No use that more of us get killed fighting so far from families. A few young men will stay and watch these soldiers. See if others come. They will follow the camp later. Must now be near middle of night."

The camp then packed and left. Only eight or nine of us young men who had swift horses remained behind. Only a few of us, we did not try rushing the soldiers. Why get killed? The soldiers were safely corralled. Families good distance away.

We just settled down to watch those soldiers.

Late in after part of night we heard a white man's voice. He shouted up on the mountain. Might be some soldier lost! Maybe guiding in other soldiers? We did not know what might be doing up there.

It was almost dawn when we heard the sound of a running horse. Soon a white man came loping through the timber. He was heading for the trenches. We did not try to kill him. Had they wished, some warriors where he passed could have shot him. They said, "Let him go in! We will then know what news he brings the soldiers!"

When that rider reached the trenches, the soldiers made loud cheering. We understood! Ammunition had arrived or more soldiers were coming. Maybe pack horse of cartridges left in the woods with soldiers guarding? Some of us went back over the trail looking for any horse there. We found none. Had we gone two hundred steps farther, we would have captured their cavalry horses. All their supply train! We did not look in a gulch where concealed. This we learned after the war was quit.

I was watching from south side of hill. When all returned from hunting for pack horses, we assembled south of trenches. There was a short council. Chief Alokut was our leader. It was thought to quit the watching, and follow after the families. Soldiers must be coming. They might overtake the camp. Might capture or kill the rest of the old people, women, and children. Our camp was only a half-sun's travel ahead. Our business was now to warn them. If fighting was to be done, we would all be there.

We gave those trenched soldiers two volleys as a "Good-by!" Then we mounted and rode swiftly away. No use staying. Those soldiers buried, hiding from further war. We quit the fight. They were brave when attacking our sleeping village, firing into our tepees! Eight women had been killed, eight more wounded. One of these died next morning. Another died still later. That was ten women to lose their life at the Big Hole. Many children and old men were killed. Killed in their tepees or when running for shelter places. A few bad wounded were buried on the trail.

Only twelve real fighting men were lost in that battle. But our best were left there.

Traveling was hard on the wounded. So bad that when we reached more safe places, several of them stopped. Remained scattered and hidden away. A few of these were never afterwards heard of.

McWhorter's Comment:

When Yellow Wolf was informed that Colonel Gibbon states that the Nez Perces were seen throughout the day following the first day's battle, and that the parting shots from the warriors came about eleven o'clock that night ["Report of the General of the Army," 1877, p. 71] the usually impassive narrator smiled, but earnestly protested:

Not true! Badly scared, that commander and his soldiers maybe saw ghost Indians in the woods. They were brave when killing women and children, crushing new born babies' heads while in the mothers' arms. Shooting men who had no guns! Afraid of armed warriors, they lay too close in dirtholes to know when we left!

No Nez Perce were there after those good-by morning shots. We were not there to see the new soldiers you say came. They must have arrived after we followed the camp. In all the war, General Howard never came where we could see him.

5 NIGHT ATTACK

By August 13th Howard had brought together in the Big Hole Basin the various elements of his command including infantry and baggage wagons. He knew that he should be well equipped because the trail he must follow would be through rough country and over rocky hills and mountains. Because he did not know where the trail would lead, the procurement of food and ammunition would always be a problem. Remounts for the cavalry and draft animals to replace worn out horses to haul the baggage wagons and artillery might or might not be available for purchase. He could not, as the Wallamwatkins were now doing, appropriate the cattle from the settlers and pioneers as he passed them—and still hold his job.

Joseph led his people southward through Stevenson and Lemhi canyons back into Idaho. There Chief White Bird held a council with the hereditary enemies of the Nez Perce, the Shoshone. White Bird asked the numerous and warlike Shoshone to assist the Wallamwatkins in surrounding and destroying Howard and his entire battalion.

The Wallamwatkins wanted vengeance. The Shoshone understood. They had no love for white people, perhaps less than the Nez Perce. In their minds they did not question the outcome of a combined attack on Howard, but there would be no way of keeping secret the destruction of Howard's forces. More soldiers would come and more and more. There would be artillery and gatling guns aplenty. The Nez Perce and the Shoshone would be blown to pieces. Any who might escape would be tracked down, run into stockades and held there until they died. The Shoshone were not contented with their lot, but it was better than confinement in a stockade with only the comforting thought that they had wiped out Howard and his forces. The Shoshone gave the Wallamwatkins presents of dried meat, buffalo robes, ammunition and ponies, and wished them well.

The Wallamwatkins turned northward. They came to a ranch at Horse Prairie Creek. Eight white men took refuge in the house and started shooting through the windows. The warriors surrounded the house, rushed it, killed every white man and rode off with their horses. Continuing down the Lemhi Valley along the Salmon River the warriors overtook a wagon train hauling supplies for Colonel Shoup. Included among the supplies was a keg of whiskey which the teamsters gave the Indians. Their plan was to wait until the Indians were howling drunk and then try to escape. The charity was misapplied. The whiskey put the Indians in a sportive mood. The fleeing teamsters furnished the sport. The warriors on horseback chased them and stuck them with spears, like pig-sticking.

General Howard guessed that Joseph's swing back into Idaho was a feint and that he would soon return to Montana riding obliquely toward Camas Meadows and that from there they would ride through Tacher's Pass two miles east of Henry's Lake into Yellowstone Park. Howard was wrong about Joseph's motive in turning westward, but he correctly anticipated Joseph's plan of march. Accordingly Howard sent Lieutenant George Bacon with forty cavalry to occupy Tacher's Pass. Obviously Howard expected Bacon to turn Joseph back when Joseph tried to enter the pass. Howard also expected to be following so closely on Joseph's heels that when Joseph did turn back he would find himself boxed in.

Howard must have lived by the military manual; otherwise he would have had the common sense to know that Bacon with forty or one hundred and forty couldn't have turned back Joseph, if Joseph had wished to go through.

At Pleasant Valley Howard's chances of success in the boxing-in plan were somewhat improved by the augmentation of a band of volunteers from Virginia City led by Captain Calloway and a company of cavalry from Fort Ellis led by Captain Norwood.

Howard waited until his scouts told him that Joseph had crossed the stage road at Dry Creek Station and gone on toward Camas Meadows. Then he closed in behind. The plan was functioning.

Joseph entered Camas Meadows and went eighteen miles toward Henry's Lake before camping. Howard camped well behind him near the edge. He took an elevated position near a trout brook. The meadows were lush with grass. Because of the rising ground, the water and the forage Howard's position seemed impregnable, but Howard while hoping for the best prepared for the worst. He posted his cavalry in line of battle to protect his camp. Captain Wells with forty infantry was ordered to bivouac near the brook in reserve formation. The Virginia City Volunteers camped a hundred yards away on a knoll between two arms of the willow bordered brook.

At nightfall Howard ordered the horses and mules to be brought within the line, the cavalry mounts to be tied to picket ropes, the draft horses to be tied to their wagons and the bell mares which led the pack-mule trains to be hobbled. With effectives of one hundred cavalry and fifty infantry Howard and his officers felt so safe from a night attack that before rolling up in their blankets they took off their boots, belts and pants. Cavalry pants were very tight and not condusive to relaxed slumber. However before drifting off to sleep Howard had a lurking feeling that somehow he was still not out of the woods. He remembered that in the twilight he had seen two or three Indians fooling around a few hundred yards from camp, but he gave them no further thought. He should have.

Actually there were two or three Indians erect and forty-one others and their ponies prone in the grass and therefore not visible from Howard's camp. By nightfall the two or three Indians had slipped between Howard's sentinels and were cutting the mules' hobbles and removing the bells from the mares. Meanwhile the forty-one Indians concealed by the grass had gotten their ponies up, mounted them, and forming a column of fours rode at a walk to Howard's line. In the starlight the sentinels, knowing that Lieutenant Bacon led forty cavalry men, assumed that the column of Indians walking their horses was indeed Lieutenant Bacon's troop returning from Tacher's Pass and therefore permitted the column to come very close before challenging. The sentinels had no way of knowing that Joseph's scouts had counted the men in Bacon's detachment at Tacher's Pass and that that was why there were exactly forty-one mounted men approaching. Of course the Indians did not know the countersign, so the nearest sentinel fired.

The Indians whooped and rode into the mule herd. In the past Howard hadn't ordered that the cavalry mounts be picketed at night, but those were the nights when he slept with his pants on. Joseph never suspected that on this particular night he would catch Howard not only with his pants down, but entirely off and that as a consequence the horses would be tied. He expected that as usual both the mules and the horses would be merely bunched under guard. Indeed he hoped by one stroke to convert Howard's command into one hundred per cent infantry. Had Joseph succeeded, Howard with no trenches or fortifications would have been in a precarious condition. He would have been immobilized in a remote district. Organized aid could hardly have reached him in time. And there was now no mercy in Joseph's heart.

Joseph's timing had not allowed a sufficient interval for the two or three warriors to cut loose the horses, but they were able to cut all of the bells off of the mares and gallop away with them followed by the entire mule herd while the forty-one warriors created a diversion by shooting at every soldier who reached for his pants—and gun and cartridge belt.

Note—Howard's military baggage was carried in pack saddles on the backs of two or three hundred mules. There was no practical way to drive or guide so many mules, but because of a peculiar quirk of mule nature driving was unnecessary. Mules will slavishly follow a bell-mare (a mare with a bell hung round her neck). Three or four bell mares each guided by a mounted man with a lead rope will lead the entire train of pack mules wherever the cavalry may go. In this case, the Indians rang the bells.

Anyone who has tried to shoot rabbits on snow in the moonlight knows that without daylight aim is uncertain. No one was hit except the bugler who was blowing "Boots and Saddles," and he was killed. A dream come true for almost every private in any army.

When the thudding hooves of the galloping mule herd passed Howard, he suddenly sat up, his whiskers bristling with astonishment. As soon as his stubborn illusion of the cold impossibility of a stampede had been dispelled into the warm reality of a cloud of stinging dust, he shouted an order to three troops of cavalry to follow, recapture and bring back the mules. The captains of the three troops, Carr, Norwood and Jackson, knew that the mules did not know where they were going, but they had an idea that wherever it might be it wasn't any good. They also knew that mules lacked imagination. So why follow in the pitch dark an animal like that? The captains took their time about finding their pants, extending their searching almost to the point of discovery. The enlisted men copied the captains. It was chill dawn before they were wearing their boots, pants and cartridge belts. Then they galloped furiously forth. They could see the Indians with the mule herd about five miles away, close to the rocks of a lava bed.

The three cavalry troops raced each other across the rippling prairie grass straight into an ambush for which the mules were being held as bait. It was then that the cavalry captains could see how prudent they had been in not finding their pants until dawn. If they had ridden into that ambush during darkness, the massacre of Indian women and children at Big Hole would have been in part avenged.

Captain's Carr's troop recovered the mules, but had to abandon them right away to effect their own escape. Captain Jackson also managed to extricate his men. Captain Norwood ordered his men to dismount and the horses to be led to a cottonwood grove in a small natural depression a quarter of a mile away. The dismounted cavalry hid behind rocks and alternately fired and dodged bullets until Joseph's warriors by executing a double flank movement got behind them. Cavalry boots are not recommended for men about to run a fast quarter mile over rough ground, but bloodthirsty Indians provided an incentive. The warriors wore moccasins. They were fleet of foot and in good condition. They wanted very much to catch one of Norwood's men, but all of the cavalrymen had reached the cottonwoods and were down on the rim of the depression and shooting before the Indians could come within tomahawk-throwing distance.

The Indians crept through the tall grass close to the rim and wounded eight soldiers, two mortally and one inconveniently. The latter was shot sideways through the seat of his pants and had to eat his meals for weeks standing up. A sergeant climbed a tree. From that height he could see the Indians in the grass. By directing the fire of his comrades he assisted in holding back the Indians until General Howard with the infantry and artillery came close enough to drive off the Indians. Indians have coped with artillery, but they don't like it, especially a howitzer loaded with grape.

Howard and all of his troops returned to camp for breakfast. On the way they picked up twenty mules which the Indians had abandoned as worthless. The Indians had been right about those twenty mules.

YELLOW WOLF'S STORY
OF
THE NIGHT ATTACK

From the Big Hole to Camas Meadows

THAT ENDED THE BIG HOLE BATTLE—a hard, desperate fight. Had some of the chiefs not thought all war ended for sure at Lolo peace treaty, we would not have been caught as we were. Looking Glass made us believe we were safe.

After bidding those soldiers a rifle "Good-by," we left, following on the trail of the families. Riding hard, we overtook them that same morning at their first camp from the battle. But some had already left, and other were packed to start.

The name of this camp place is Takseen (Willows). The people had been a long half-sun reaching there. Could not travel too fast with some bad wounded on travois. They had gone scattering from the Big Hole.

At this camp died Aihits Palojami (Fair Land), wife of Alokut. Died of wounds, leaving a boy baby. Of course she was buried secretly.

We now kept moving for three suns, watching always for horses. While we had many horses, it was good to have fresh ones. Best, too, that none be left for soldiers. It was aimed that no horses could be found by soldiers anywhere we passed.

We took many horses at places I do not know by white names. Some fighting and a few white people killed where horses were captured. Of course citizens did not like to lose their horses, many of them good horses.

It was during this time, the second sun from the Big Hole, that what I now tell you took place. Came morning, and the families moved, a guard of warriors following at a distance in the rear. I held back of the guard to be a scout, a lookout, for pursuing enemies. It was a sure fact that in those times I was as a watching eye, missing nothing that was danger.

All the people knew what I could do. That I could smell white people, the soldiers, a long distance away. I would then tell the boys: "Get ready your arms!" My guardian Spirit instructed that I scout mostly alone.

As I now look back, I was lucky to come through that great war. I thought that I might die in a war somehow, but not by the bullet. I knew from the promise given, no gun would ever kill me. I am now getting old, and I think that I will die from sickness sometime. But I am still well and in good condition.

It was just mid-sun when I mounted my horse and followed after the camp. None of the enemies had appeared coming on our last sun's trail. Alone, I loped along, not too fast! I watched everywhere. If antelope acted curious, it might be danger. If prairie birds flew up in distance, it might be buffaloes stampeding, getting away from something—maybe soldiers!

I looked ahead about a quarter mile. Something must be there? I checked my horse to a trot, then to a walk. I took a good look. The sun pictured something against a big rock. I thought it must be the shadow of a man. I did not stop my horse, but I made a strong look.

Yes—a white man!

I did not act differently—did not show surprise. I looked another way and turned my horse slightly. Watching me, that shadow-man saw and raised up from his hiding. *Eeh!* Eight of them! They began firing at me. I was on good ground, and ran my horse at his fastest. I did not return their fire. Too far to shoot with horse running. Quartering away, I thought to save my cartridges. I did not look back what they were doing. I laughed at those men. Eight white men—maybe citizen scouts—waiting for one Indian to ride close and be killed. That shadow was not a lie.

Those white men did not follow me. They were afoot. The warriors had gathered up all their horses.

It was dark when I reached camp. I reported to the chiefs what I had seen, what I knew. If soldiers following, they were far behind.

I walked through part of the camp. Some people had lain down, others were fixing blankets for sleeping. One woman lay on a buffalo robe, moaning, with many around her. Badly shot through the stomach at the last battle. They told me she could not live. Next morning the woman on the robe was dead.

We continued traveling. During this time a train of eight wagons was captured. I was back as a scout but came up as camp was being made. Those wagons formed three teams, drawn by mules and horses. Loaded with different kinds of goods, and lots of whisky. That whisky was mostly in barrels. That whisky was soon opened up. Some Indians got bottles and rode away; but many began getting drunk there at the wagons. In the meantime three of the white men were killed in a fight. Two Chinamen with the wagons were not hurt. They cried, and were left to go see their grandmother (Yellow Wolf here evinced unusual amusement)!

The Indians were getting bad. Ketalkpoosmin called out: "If soldiers come they will kill us all!"

He and all the sober warriors were then appointed by the chiefs to spill the whisky on the ground. Peopeo Tholekt was one who helped, and I, Yellow Wolf, helped.

Two drunk Indians shot at each other, one getting head grazed by bullet. Itsiyiyi Opseen (Coyote with Flints) stabbed Heyoom Pishkish, an oversized man later known by whites as Lame John, under the right arm. Heyoom did not grunt, did not lie down. He had a strong Power and became well.

Ketalkpoosmin was shot by Pahka Alyanakt (Five Snows [Years]), who was mad drunk. Of course, drinking Indians did not want the whisky spilled. Ketalkpoosmin after two, maybe three, suns' travel, was left at camp to die. He asked to be left.

He could not hold to life. A good warrior, he had much in capturing the cannon-gun at Big Hole fight. Pahka Alyanakt was killed at last battle.

It was about the tenth sun from Big Hole that a report came. Perhaps ten o'clock in the morning, and camp had not broken. We heard the shouting, "Soldiers close! Soldiers right upon us!"

Then came call from the chiefs, "Come, all you warriors!"

When the warriors gathered, the chiefs gave orders, "Get horses!"

Horses ready, the chiefs said, "We are going to meet the soldiers! All warriors will go!"

A scout came riding and reported, "Soldiers making camp!"

The chiefs now made arrangements to arrive at the soldier camp in darkness of after part of night. Warriors now staked their horses to graze, while scouts closely watched the soldiers.

After sundown, and darkness growing, we started, riding slow. The chiefs said, "If we get to where the soldiers have stopped, and it is afterpart of night, we will take their horses."

We traveled slowly. No talking loud, no smoking. The match must not be seen. We went a good distance and then divided into two parties—one on each side the creek. I was on right side of this creek, called Wewaltolklit Pah. Its name is because it flows some distance, and then drysinks—disappears. I do not know the white men's name for this creek. It is not large.

Chiefs Alokut and Tulhulhutsut were the outstanding leaders of my company. These men were always in lead of every fight. Teeweeyownah and Espowyes led the other company. Brave men with swiftest horses were always at the front in war movements.

We rode on through the night darkness. Before reaching the soldier camp, all stopped, and the leaders held council. How make attack? The older men did this planning. Some wanted to leave the horses and enter the soldier camp afoot. Chief Looking Glass and others thought the horses must not be left out. This last plan was chosen—to go mounted.

Chief Joseph was not along.

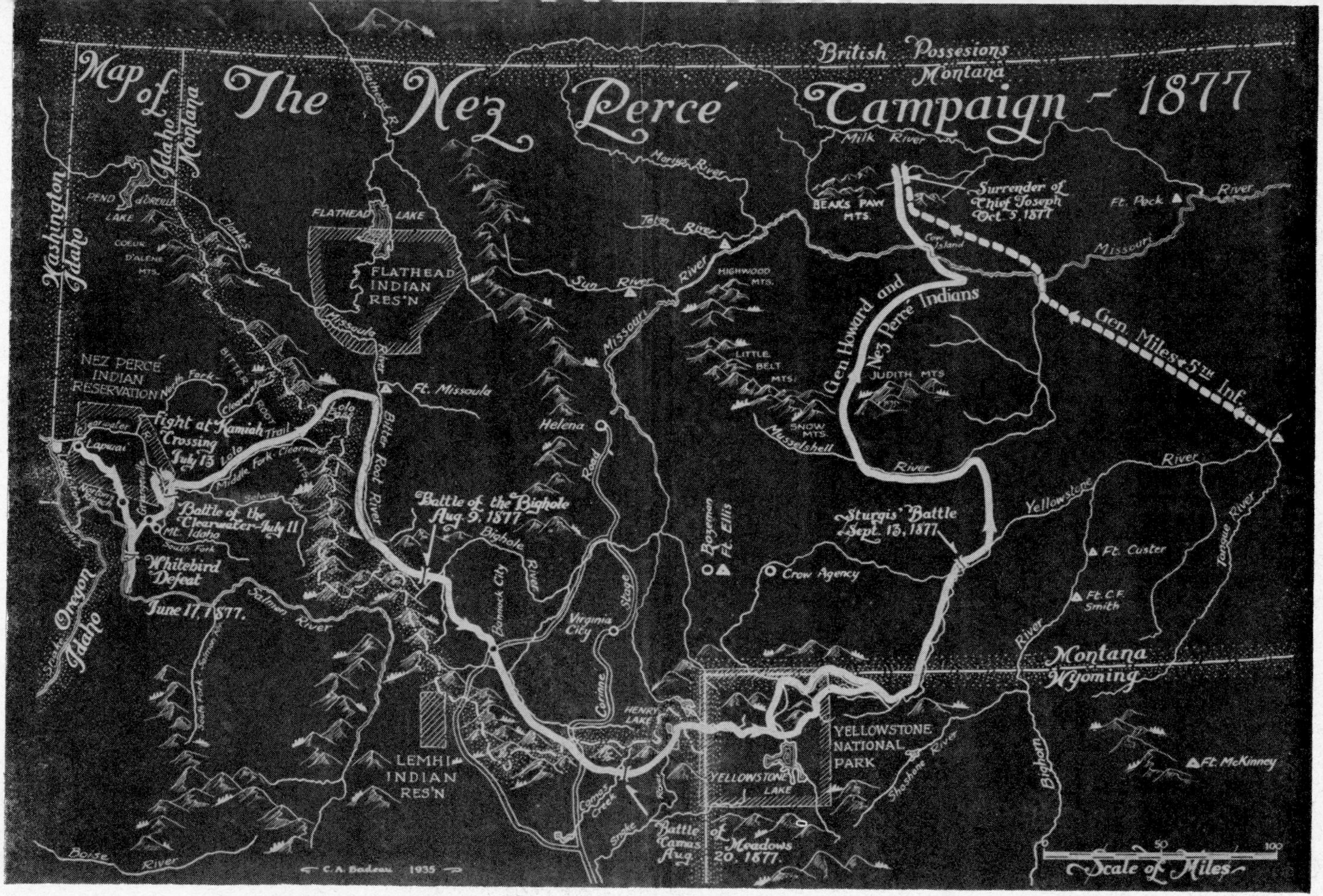

Courtesy American Heritage Publishing Co., Inc.

Map of the Nez Perce campaign of 1877.

Courtesy of Washington State University.

Chief Yellow Wolf, Chief Joseph's nephew. The war club and gun shown in the photograph were carried by him in the War.

Courtesy The Historical Society of Montana and American Heritage Publishing Co., Inc.

Chief Yellow Wolf, the last survivor of the battles of Big Hole and Bear's Paw, shortly before his death in 1936.

Courtesy Lewiston Tribune, Lewiston, Idaho.

War Chief Joseph, from an original ambrotype.

Courtesy of "Montana," The Historical Society of Montana and The American Heritage Book of Indians.

Chief Joseph in 1903, shortly before his death.

Courtesy Lewiston Tribune, Lewiston, Idaho.

Chief Whitebird, taken July 12, 1879, at Lapwai, Idaho.

Courtesy Smithsonian Institution.

Chief Looking Glass, who was killed at Bear's Paw.

Courtesy Smithsonian Institution and American Heritage Publishing Co., Inc.

Peopeo Tholekt, cousin of Chief Joseph.

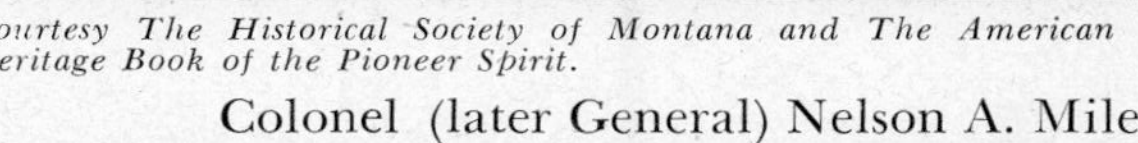

Major-General O. O. Howard.

Courtesy The Historical Society of Montana and The American Heritage Book of the Pioneer Spirit.

Colonel (later General) Nelson A. Miles of the Fifth United States Infantry at Fort Keogh, Montana Territory.

Brigadier-General David Perry.

Courtesy The Historical Society of Montana and American Heritage Publishing Co., Inc.

General Samuel D. Sturgis of the Seventh Cavalry.

Courtesy Washington State University Archives.

Whitebird Canyon. "Looking down into the Whitebird cañon where on June 17th, 1877 occurred the battle of Whitebird. At the extreme left centre Colonel Perry and 90 troopers and eleven volunteers came upon the Nez Perces and suffered one of the most crushing defeats an army ever suffered. Leaving 35 men upon the field, men to whom life was sweet, men who being soldiers were forced to do what they were told regardless of right or wrong." Text and photo by Emil Kopac.

Clearwater River.

Courtesy Mrs. Betty Raymer, Washington State University Archives.

Camas Prairie.

Courtesy of the National Park Service

Meadow along the north fork of the Big Hole River where the Nez Perce camp was located. Gibbon deployed the Seventh Infantry and civilian volunteers along the base of the hill during the night. The attack on the camp was made through the willows and across the river. The retreat route was similar to the attack, going back to the left of a wooded knoll, which is just out of the picture.

Courtesy of the National Park Service.

The wooded knoll where Colonel Gibbon was forced to retreat and dig in after the dawn attack on the Nez Perce camp at Big Hole.

Courtesy Dr. C. M. Drury and The American Heritage Book of Indians.

A group of Nez Perce, flanked by the agent and the agency clerk, after their defeat in 1877.

Then we went. It was not yet daylight when we ran into soldiers. They must have been the guard soldiers. I heard a white man's voice call, "Who are you there?"

Then a gun sounded back of us. It was one of the guards who called, and after that first gun, we fired at where the voice came from. Then we heard guard-soldiers speaking, calling to their headman. Some were crying. They ran, and one voice called loudly for them to come back to their guns. But those guard-soldiers did not mind him.

McWhorter's Query:

Where were the guns of those soldiers who were standing on guard?" I interposed.

Their guns were stacked.

McWhorter's Query:

You did not really hear the soldiers crying, did you?" I asked.

I heard them cry like babies. They were bad scared.

The soldier camp was alarmed. The bugles sounded quickly. The warriors were yelling and shooting fast. They had circled the soldiers' horses, stampeding them. The soldiers were now also firing in every direction. Some young men had gone in to cut loose the horses tied, and I, Yellow Wolf, was one of them. I found three horses staked on long ropes. I cut them loose. At this time the Indians were driving the horse herd rapidly away. I could see no Indians. Mounting, I followed silently as I could with my three captured horses. When I got out from the soldier camp, I turned the horses free. Lashing them, I fired my six-shooter, yelling loud. Frightened, those horses ran into the herd the Indians were driving. We kept going, did not stop.

After traveling a little way, driving our captured horses, sun broke. We could begin to see our prize. Getting more light, we looked. *Eeh!* Nothing but mules—all mules! Only my three horses among them. I did not know, did not understand why the Indians could not know the mules. Why they did not get the cavalry horses. That was the object the chiefs had in mind—why the raid was made. The place where we took General Howard's mules is called Kamisnim Takin (Camas Meadows).

We looked back. Soldiers were coming! Some foot-running, others mounted. Then we divided our company. Some went ahead with the mules; others of us waited for the soldiers. Then we fought, shooting from anywhere we found hiding. A few warriors made a flank move, and from a low hill did good shooting. Peopeo Tholekt was one of those flankers. Soon those soldiers ran for a bunch of small timber not far away. They went fast. It was then we crept close and shot whenever we saw a soldier. What I saw of soldiers falling, I do not know. Earlier in the fight, a soldier with a bugle was shot from his horse at foot of a small bluff and killed, Indians were on that bluff, protected behind rocks. It was a sharp fight for some time. After a while I heard the warriors calling to each other, "Chiefs say do no more fighting!"

Then we quit the fight. Of dead soldiers I saw I know not how many. No Indian was bad hurt, only one or two just grazed by bullets. We followed after the mule herd to camp. When we all reached there, the Indians made for those mules. Some took two or three, others took three or five. I did not know how many mules we got. All were kept for packing and riding, but the warriors did not ride them.

General Howard could not take those mules from us.

We stayed the rest of that sun and all night at the same camp. Not until next morning did we move to another place. Scouts watching General Howard, we kept moving every day. The soldiers did not hurry to follow us. They slowed after losing their pack mules.

6 THE FLIGHT THROUGH THE YELLOWSTONE PARK

HOWARD REMAINED IN CAMP FOR SEVERAL DAYS WHILE HE SECURED a replacement of mules from Virginia City seventy miles away. Lieutenant Bacon, after waiting vainly at Tacher's Pass for two days, rejoined Howard. As soon as Bacon had gone Joseph and his people rode through the Pass and on into Yellowstone Park.

As the Wallamwatkins rode into the Park at one point, General William T. Sherman, General of the Army, the man who so infamously marched through Georgia, rode out of the Park at another point. Neither knew of the other's presence. Sherman was making a personal inspection of western forts. If Joseph had known, his warriors would surely have taken Sherman prisoner. President Grant held Sherman in high esteem. He might have given the Nez Perce the Wallowa Valley in exchange.

On August 27th Howard resumed his pursuit of the Wallamwatkins. They were already passing through Yellowstone Park. They had never been there before. They didn't know the way, so they impressed into their service two small groups of white people who were enjoying a summer vacation exploring the Park. Most of the captured white people escaped, but the Indians retained a Frank Carpenter until he got them back on the trail. Without lingering Joseph led his people across the Yellowstone River, around the lake and up Pelican Creek in the direction of Stinking Water.

To follow their trail Howard attempted to build a wagon road through the Park, but after hauling wagons through forests and canyons and over mountains where the wagons had to be lowered two hundred feet from perpendicular cliffs by ropes and after that across fallen timber, he sent the wagons back to the nearest post, Fort Ellis, and strapped the necessary baggage to pack-mules.

Of the two exploring parties captured in the Park one party resisted. Two of its members were killed. The other party was surprised while they were cooking breakfast. One of the men (believed to be Carpenter) walked up to Yellow Bull and shook hands. The Indians asked for some flour, sugar and bacon. The leader of the party, Mr. Cowan, with ill-starred parsimony refused. Offended, the Indians took all the food and equipment and made the party prisoners. They shot one member, a Mr. Oldham, in the leg and let him escape on the other leg. Oldham later said that it was very painful. Then they shot Mr. Cowan several times. He had to crawl away through the bushes. He was unable to crawl the more than one hundred miles to civilization. Fortunately for him some of Howard's scouts tripped over him. Both men survived, but they learned about hospitality the hard way. Had Mr. Cowan made the Indians welcome and given them all of their food, rifles and ammunition, and offered them Carpenter as a guide and keepsake (if they wished) he could have saved the whole party much inconvenience. It would have been Indian nature to have turned the party loose and to have released Carpenter when they had no more use for him. They should also have learned from their experiences that when meeting Indians, if a person shows fear, the Indians immediately lose all respect for him. That person is then in danger.

Twice during the flight of the Wallamwatkins a white man who could see that he was about to be shot made the sign of the cross and thereby saved his own life. An Indian primitive will not shoot at anyone "making medicine." He believes that the act of "making medicine" invokes the aid of spirits which may be good or bad. Who knows? If the Indian should shoot the white man anyway, the spirits having been aroused from their usual dormant condition by the white man's invocation might descend with fury upon the Indian.

Joseph led his people out of the northeast corner of Yellowstone Park by crossing the outlet of Yellowstone Lake, the Yellowstone River, on the Baronet bridge. His rear guard warriors set fire to the east end of the bridge because the wind was blowing from the east. But their medicine was weak. After they had gone the Wind Spirit who did not wish to see the bridge destroyed crossed the river and blew from the west until he had blown out the fire. At least that is the way the Indians accounted for it.

Three sunsets later, on September 6th, Howard arrived, examined the ruined bridge and ordered his soldiers to tear down the house of Mr. Baronet, the man who had built the bridge, bring the planks and bore holes in them. By boring corresponding holes in remaining bridge timbers, they were able by pegging to repair the bridge to an extent. Howard ordered his troops to cross.

The bridge swayed and rocked under their tread until it creaked like a smashed calliope. The torrent of the Yellowstone roared fifty feet beneath. The men were doubtful that the bridge would hold. The horses were sure that it wouldn't and tried to go back but the soldiers spanked them and made them go ahead. They all got over safely, went into camp, and that night had nightmares about it. Mr. Baronet when he returned home may also have had nightmares.

The next day Howard, ○ "wound along the sharply marked valleys which here run at right angles to the yawning river." ○ On the nearby hill tops he saw mounted gunmen and rovers. Howard coaxed them down, assured them that he wouldn't try to draft them into the service and asked them where Joseph had gone. They said that Joseph's people were only thirty miles away, trying to reach the Clark's Fork River, the only practicable crossing through the mountains to the level country farther down the Yellowstone River. The short cut to the Clark's Fork was through Soda-Butte Canyon. The rovers added that the Wallamwatkins had avoided Soda-Butte Canyon and were making their way over mountains and through forests apparently to achieve concealment.

Near the back entrance of Soda-Butte Howard saw the Soda-Butte silver mine. The miners offered Howard their services. He accepted and sent them ahead as scouts. The explanation of their enthusiasm was that the Wallamwatkins had surprised four miners, killed three and seriously wounded one.

Between the silver mines and the foot of Clark's Mountain three scouts sent out by Colonel Sturgis* to find Joseph found Howard. Sturgis had sent out several scouts at various times to contact Captain Cushing and General Howard, but none had ever returned. For the first time Howard now learned that Sturgis was only fifty miles away and that Joseph was somewhere between them trying to reach the prairie to the north by way of Clark's Fork River.

While his scouts were probing the mountains between the Clark's Fork and the Shoshone River, both of which flowed irregularly northeastward into the Yellowstone River, Howard dispatched Captain Cushing with three partial companies of cavalry down the Clark's Fork Valley to the Yellowstone River. At the confluence of the Clark's Fork and the Yellowstone where the country was level, Cushing's orders required him to turn left and follow up the Yellowstone to the new Crow Agency. From that base Cushing was supposed to give warning if Joseph should come down the Yellowstone Valley. Cushing was also expected to establish contact with Colonel Sturgis at the Old Crow Agency on the Bighorn River, about fifty miles above its confluence with the Yellowstone. Like the upper Yellowstone and the Clark's Fork the Bighorn flows northeastward. About sixty miles upstream the Bighorn receives the Shoshone River. Some forty miles above its confluence with the Bighorn the Shoshone flows near the base of Heart Mountain. That was where the Wallamwatkins were hiding. The scouts sent out by Cushing, Howard and Sturgis to find them did find them, but that was the last thing they ever found. The Sturgis scouts who found Howard when they were looking for Joseph did not realize, nor did Howard realize, that they found Howard because Joseph wanted them to do so. Otherwise they would have met the common fate.

---

* Colonel Sturgis, commanding officer of the Seventh Cavalry based at Old Crow Agency on the Bighorn River, had been ordered by telegraph by Colonel Gibbon to contact General Howard who was approaching from the southwest.

YELLOW WOLF'S STORY
OF
THE FLIGHT THROUGH THE YELLOWSTONE PARK

Into Yellowstone National Park

IT WAS, I think, twelve suns from the Big Hole that we camped on the southwest side of a fine lake (Henry's Lake). Camped for about one sun. Then we went through a gap (Targhee Pass) into the Yellowstone Park. We did not follow the usual Nez Perce trail. We traveled over a hunting trail instead.

We were troubled about direction for a short half-sun, but soon found the right way. No help from Crow Indians! No help from anybody but one white man. He acted as guide once. It was like this:

One noon camp while the families were getting ready to go, I took my horse and went ahead quite a way—five, maybe six, miles. The sun was about there (four to five P.M.). I heard someone coming behind me. I looked back. It was my brother (cousin) Otskai. I told him, "I am glad you have come."

We traveled on. We heard chopping. Maybe it was soldiers? We went there where we heard the chopping. It was a white man doing cooking. We went up to him, one on each side, in back of him. We grabbed him! He was armed but did not offer fight. Otskai understood a little English and talked with him. We stayed there quite a while, and then a lot of Indians came—just to be friendly with him.

We did not want to do him harm. Only if he had horses or things needed, we might take them for ourselves. One warrior, supposed to be bad, came up. He was Teeweeyownah (Over Point of Hill). He asked, "Can any one talk to him?"

They found Heinmot Tosinlikt. Henry Tabador was another name he had. A half blood, he was bad, but could interpret. This white man was asked if he knew the way to the head of Yellowstone Park, toward the Crow Indian lands above Elk Water, as the Crows call it. He said he did and would go with us. Said his horses were lost, and he was on hunt for them. The warrior told him he would give him a horse to ride, and that it would be a gift for him to return on.

Then I said to my brother, Otskai, "Take him down to the chiefs. They will make him tell about this trail, where this trail will take us." Then I left.

The Indians were partly lost for a short time. Not sure of their way. This man who was oldlike, this white prisoner, was all the guiding they had. Showed them for half of one sun. He was kept for a few suns, but we did not try holding him longer.

In meantime I kept going. I did not tell anyone where I was going. It was to watch ahead, and this half blood, Henry Tabador, overtook me. He asked where I was going. I told him I was watching for more white men, and he said, "I will go with you."

We did not go far until a horse was heard coming behind us. Another fellow came up. He was Tiskusia Kowiakowia. He asked where we were going, and Tabador said, "Heinmot Hihhih is out looking for white men. I am going with him."

Tiskusia Kowiakowia said he would go, and he came with us. Soon another young fellow, Towassis (Bowstring) overtook us. He was followed by Nosnakuhet Moxmox (Yellow Long Nose). We now were five, and the four said to me, "You are supposed to be our leader."

We rode on, always watching for enemies. We went up a meadow, and our scouting took us to a swampy place about three miles long. The sun had gone down, and darkness was coming on. I told the men we were going to stay there all night. They already were staking their horses. I was going to stake mine when one of them said, "Let me stake your horse. I will do that for you."

He took my horse, and as I turned back, I saw a light at some distance, a small light. I called the others to come. Pointing, I said, "Look that way!"

Nosnakuhet Moxmox said, "That is fire burning!"

"Yes," I answered. "It may be soldiers or other white people. We will go see why it is."

But one boy thought different. He warned, "We better not go there. It is a swampy place. Our horses might mire down, for we cannot see good."

I replied, "We will lie right here till morning. Then we are going to have a fight with them."

All agreeing, we took our blankets, but built no fire. No fire when scouting. I did not know if they meant true when they answered, "All right," to what I said about fighting. Some of them were afraid, I was sure. Only two, Tabador and Towassis, were brave. The others were not fighters. I knew not why they had come with me.

Early, at breaking light, I awoke the boys. All got ready. We saddled horses and rode on a swift gallop along a draw. It was quite a ways to where we had seen the light.

When we got there, we saw four persons lying close to the fire. Then we saw two more not so close, and a little apart was a small tent. These people were not soldiers, but all white people seemed our enemies. We talked what to do with them. I said we would kill them. But the half blood, Heinmot Tosinlikt, said, "No! We will capture them. Take them to the chiefs. Whatever they say will go."

Then some of us, not all, went close to the fire. Two boys stayed back. The white men were getting up. Henry, our interpreter, told them we would not hurt them. The leader was a fine looking man. He shook hands with us. He asked, "Who is the leader of this bunch? I see five of you."

Heinmot Tosinlikt pointed to me. He said, "There is our leader!"

Because I shook hands with him put me in mind not to kill him. He looked at me and said, "I am going to ask you. Why you come here? I hear a little about you."

I answered by the interpreter. "Yes, I am one of the warriors."

Then these white men got afraid. The leader asked, "Would you kill us?"

"They are double-minded," I told him.

It was hard work, this talking to the white man. Not understanding many words of his language made hard work. At the end he asked, "Can we see Chief Joseph? Will you take us to him?"

"Yes, but some boys are very bad," I told him. "They might kill you." That is what I told the good-looking white man. I wanted to be a friend to him.

Then he said, "Will the chiefs do anything to us?"

I answered, "I guess not."

"All right," said the white man. "We want to see Chief Joseph. We will go." That was the white man's answer.

I stepped to the tent doorway. I threw back the flap. A white man was standing there. He spoke. What he said, I did not understand. Two women had been in the tent, but they had run away. The white man called them, but they did not answer. Six times he called, then the two women, one smaller than the other, came from the brush.

While we were there, the leading white man gave us sugar, flour, and two good pieces of bacon. The food made our hearts friendly. Heinmot Tosinlikt said, "Take it. I will put it on my horse and pack it for us."

But the white man from the tent showed mad. He said something to the leader, who then stopped giving the food.

The white men harnessed their team and saddled their horses. They had eight head, and I saw one good roan among them. Two men and the women rode on the wagon, the other men rode horseback. When they were ready, we mounted our horses. We took the lead, white people following.

Whatever now happened to their lives, I could not help. I

did not tell them go see the chiefs. It was their own mind—their own work—that they were going. They heard me say the Indians were double-minded in what they can do.

At last, after we traveled part of that sun, I heard a great noise ahead of us. The other Indians had seen us. Not the chiefs, only the warriors. Quickly they made for us. The warriors mixed us up. They did not listen to anybody. Mad, those warriors took the white people from us. Going on, I saw them no more for a time. But I saw their wagon where left by the trail. When we camped for noon, I saw those prisoners. They were all alive. Wattes Kunnin (Earth Blanket) was first to grab the good roan horse.

After dinner the chiefs called, "We will move! All get ready!"

Those nine (there were ten) prisoners the warriors bothered. The chiefs took the two women away from them. One was full grown, the other young and small. Both good looking. I saw everybody making to travel. Soon all were ready, some already gone. I did not see the white people at this time, but heard they were being treated right. Then, soon, I heard some gun reports.

It was the bad boys killing some of the white men.

But one they did not kill, and two escaped into the brush.

McWhorter's Query:

When asked why they were shot, Yellow Wolf replied:

Some ran into the brush. It was for trying to escape.

The man Otskai and I captured the day before was on ahead as guide. He knew the trail. The other man and two women came up with the families.

That night camp was made late. There was some rain, but not hard. Next morning we traveled on, and at noon the chiefs said, "We will camp." Place of this camp was Koos Kapwelwen (Swift Water), which joins the Yellowstone River. At this camp I saw the chiefs turn loose the young man and the two women, the three together. The chiefs had agreed and said, "We free these white people to go home."

The women were given horses, the man was made to go afoot.

They must not travel too fast. Food was given for their living while going to some town or wherever they lived.

We did not want to kill those women. Ten of our women had been killed at the Big Hole, and many others wounded. But the Indians did not think of that at all. We let them go without hurt to find their own people. The man captured by Otskai and me, the one who had guided the families, went later. None of them were hurt. Only those who tried to escape.

There were two other small scouting bands in the Yellowstone Park country besides mine. One was headed by Kosooyeen, the other by Lakochets Kunnin. I do not know which of these made attack on some hunters or visitors, but I have heard they killed one man. Each party did scouting every sun.

It was a few suns after the chiefs turned the white man and women loose that what I am telling you happened. It was coming towards sundown when we saw a white man standing in the doorway of a house. We stopped not far from him but did not dismount. We sat on our horses, six or seven of us, thinking. Chuslum Hahlap Kanoot (Naked-footed Bull) said to me, "My two young brothers and next younger brother were not warriors. They and a sister were killed at Big Hole. It was just like this man did that killing of my brothers and sister. He is nothing but a killer to become a soldier sometime. We are going to kill him now. I am a man! I am going to shoot him! When I fire, you shoot after me."

Chuslum Hahlap Kanoot then fired and clipped his arm. As he made to run, another warrior, Yettahtapnat Alwun (Shooting Thunder) shot him through the belly.

McWhorter's Comment:

At this point I interposed. "You know General Scott? He was a lieutenant in the Seventh Cavalry at that time, and says that with ten men he chased eighteen of you Nez Perce so closely that he recovered nineteen head of horses abandoned by you, which you had stolen. In that chasing he found the man you killed at the house while the body was yet warm."

Yellow Wolf smiled grimly as he replied:

These soldiers did not let us know they were chasing us. We would have been glad to see them! Only six, maybe seven in our band. We had no captured horses.

We rode into the woods looking for anybody getting away. Finding no one, we decided to remain concealed there until after dark. When came the dusk, we went back to the house, all going inside but two men. With matches we looked around, taking arms or anything wanted. Soon somebody outside called, "Soldiers attacking us!"

All ran out as crazy. I was last to get out the door. My horse near by was rearing on the rope. I could not get him loose, I jerked up my gun and fired twice toward the soldiers. I heard horsefeet to my left. Hemene Moxmox, my uncle, called to me, "My son, do not lose your head. Have clear mind. Do not miss any of them. Shoot straight!"

I heard another noise coming. I glanced that way, and saw Watyahtsakon. The three of us made for those soldiers. I went around the house where lots of willows grew. The soldiers went through those willows. One was wounded on a white horse. He and Watyahtsakon both drew up their guns. The Indian beat him, and he fell from his horse. This warrior was a great hero with a strong Power. Nobody could get him. I do not know if the soldier was killed. We found his gun and ammunition. The horse we did not get.

We chased the soldiers, or whoever they were, into the brush. My uncle said we would not go in after them. They might be too many for the few of us.

We now started for home. But I thought to get horses from white men where I knew. The others did not agree to this. A little council was held, and they said, "No! We are all alive after the fight. We better go home. Not try taking any horses."

I did not listen. I went back toward where some white men were staying. I did not hurry. Just breaking day, I started the horses, bunched together, the way I wanted to go. I saw about five or six white men in the house watching me from the windows. When they saw the horses going, they fired two or three times. The guns scared the four horses I was driving, and they ran away. There were two bays, one buckskin, and a roan. The gun reports helped me get away with their own horses.

I was glad to take four horses from six men. I looked back and saw there were no more horses. They could not follow me.

Driving my captured horses, I started over a hill toward the river. In time I overtook my friends. They had camped where I left them and were riding slowly, holding back for me. About one-fourth mile off we saw a bunch of Indians breaking camp. They were Crows and Bannacks, packing up to leave. Scared of us, they were hurrying fast to get away. We did not try catching up with those coward Indians.

In the distance were several horsemen approaching, bringing many horses. We had no glass. Some boys thought they were soldiers. But I knew differently. The wind was from them, and I could smell. I said, "No! I know our people. No soldiers there."

It was true. Our camp was on the move. No enemy in sight, but in wartime we are like children—afraid of the whip!

We halted and when the camp came up, the others of our party fell in. All soon passed over a small hill.

I remained behind. Obeying my Spirit Power, I watched for any pursuing enemies. I saw none, and reached camp soon after dark.

7 CHIEF JOSEPH'S ESCAPE

The Counter-March at Clark's Fork

COLONEL STURGIS COMMANDED THE SEVENTH CAVALRY. IN 1876 the entire regiment including its commanding officer, General Custer, had been killed by the Sioux. The regiment had since been recruited by replacements and staffed by young and inexperienced officers. They were encamped at the Old Crow Agency on the Bighorn awaiting orders. On August 27th Sturgis received them from Colonel Gibbon. He was "to push up to the head of Clark's Fork." That would have sidetracked Sturgis for good so far as Joseph was concerned. It was a typical Gibbon order. Fortunately for Howard, Sturgis remained at the Old Crow Agency until August 31st. Meanwhile he sent out two scouts and an Indian boy. When it had become painfully apparent that there was no point in keeping the scouts' names on the payroll any longer, Sturgis led the Seventh Cavalry up the Bighorn River and its tributary, the Shoshone, to the eastern end of Clark's Fork Canyon which begins at Bridger on the Clark's Fork River and cuts through the hills to Cowley on the Shoshone, a distance of about thirty-five miles.

Sturgis knew nothing of the topography of this part of the country. He had no maps. The Indians had captured his guides. There was no visible trail through Clark's Fork Canyon. He was about to leave his wagon train and artillery at present Cowley and pass through Clark's Fork Canyon to Clark's Fork River and turn left upstream toward the north fork of Clark's Fork River to reach Soda-Butte Pass, never dreaming that Howard had come through Soda-Butte Pass and was presently encamped at the base of Clark's Mountain practically across his path.

Sturgis sent out three more scouts to travel his intended route and warn the miners at Soda-Butte silver mines that Joseph and his warriors were on the war path in that region and that they had better watch out. Sturgis did this out of the goodness of his heart.

It was not from charitable motives, however, that Joseph saw to it that those three scouts, less skilled than the others, arrived in Howard's camp and informed Howard that Sturgis had by that time sent his wagon train and artillery back to the Old Crow Agency on the Bighorn River and had gone on up the Shoshone River to Heart Mountain. That was the information that Joseph wanted Howard to have.

Howard instantly jumped to the conclusion that Joseph must be on the ridge above him about midway between himself and Sturgis. He assumed that Joseph was at that very moment watching Sturgis chasing a will-o'-the-wisp up the Shoshone River leaving the way wide open for Joseph to come down the hill and follow the Shoshone River down to the Bighorn and thence to the Yellowstone River and open country.

Naturally Joseph would have done just that, had it not been for the people of the Crow Tribe living in the vicinity of the Old Crow Agency. They were known as the River Crows in contrast to the Mountain Crows. The Mountain Crows were friendly to the Nez Perce. The River Crows were loyal to the Army. Chief Looking Glass had made a special trip down the left bank of the Bighorn to the Council Lodge of the River Crows. He had asked them for permission to pass eastward through their country. Permission had been denied.

After his return the Wallamwatkins had held a council on the subject. It had been resolved that they would abandon the idea of going eastward. Instead they would travel northward to the Old Woman's Country (Canada).* It might be supposed that they reached this decision because they respected the territorial rights of the Crows. It is more likely that they had little fear of the U. S. Cavalry, but were very concerned about their

* A reference to Queen Victoria.

chances of crossing Crow Territory without losing about a thousand of their ponies. In the light of later events they had cause for such concern.

So instead of riding downstream along the bank of the Shoshone, Joseph rode upstream and high on the shoulder of the hill among the trees where Sturgis couldn't see him. He even passed Sturgis' right flank traveling in a reverse direction, and still Sturgis didn't see him.

When Joseph became convinced that Sturgis was heading toward Heart Mountain, Joseph sent some of his young warriors equipped with lariats farther up the Shoshone Valley. His scouts had just told him that Howard was coming straight up the other side of the ridge from Clark's Fork Valley with all of his forces. Howard's horses were practically on their knees clawing and pawing for footholds. Sometimes the men were up-hill hauling the horses and again the horses were hauling the men. Men and animals alike seemed determined to reach the top.

They did reach the top. The view was magnificent. To the southward Heart Mountain, rising in solitary grandeur over twelve thousand feet above sea level, stuck up like a sore thumb. Howard's signal men waved flag signals and flashed mirrors to let Sturgis know where they were. Sturgis by this time should have been on Heart Mountain, but he wasn't. The few young warriors with lariats whom Joseph had sent southward had cut a lot of bushes, bound them into bundles and tied the bundles to their lariats. They were galloping around the base of Heart Mountain a couple of miles ahead of Sturgis, dragging the bundles of bushes after them and kicking up such clouds of dust that Sturgis and the Seventh Cavalry were clapping spurs to their horses in the firm conviction that the Wallamwatkins were almost within their grasp.

While that festive chase went snorting off to the southward Joseph reversed his direction and rode back to an old dry watercourse which bisected the ridge. It was about twenty feet wide and rose on either side in sheer rock straight up to a great height. Indeed it somewhat resembled a roofless tunnel which ended near the bottom of Clark's Fork Valley. The floor of the water-course was uneven and strewn with boulders, but water had smoothed them somewhat. The Indians' ponies negotiated them successfully.

At about the time that Joseph was leading his people down the valley of Clark's Fork, Howard's scouts picked up Joseph's trail on the east side of the mountainous ridge. They even found the terminal of the dry water course where Joseph had entered. Then Howard, like the grand old Duke of York, having marched his men up a hill, marched them down again using that same watercourse. Sliding down the declivity the fur wore off of their horses' rumps and the hair departed from their tails. By the time they had reached the bottom, their knees were so sprung that they were incapable of much speed even on a smooth road.

Meanwhile the gay young warriors having divested themselves of the bundles of bushes, and the Seventh Cavalry having returned along the west side of the ridge, the young warriors descended on the other side, about where Howard had climbed up. Before the Wallamwatkins had left the Clark's Fork Valley the young warriors had rejoined them.

Riding day and night over perilously rough and hilly country Sturgis finally overtook Howard's limping column pretty well down the Clark's Fork Valley. When they rode out into the prairie at the confluence of Clark's Fork and the Yellowstone they met Captain Cushing with his small command and wagons bearing much needed supplies from the Crow Agency. Had Cushing arrived earlier, as he should have done, the warriors would have gobbled up both Cushing and the supplies.

For the cavalry it had been a pursuit marked by futility and frustration. Indeed as the warriors followed Joseph across the moderately placid Yellowstone northward toward the Musselshell River, they were talking not about the cavalry but about what ailed those Crows.

But Colonel Sturgis, now in the Clark's Fork Valley miles behind them, was talking to General Howard about what in the world ailed himself. He explained graphically and in detail over and over again, until it seemed as though he couldn't stop explaining, how Joseph had bamboozled him.

He said that as the dust had settled and the evidences of Indians riding just ahead of him had become fewer and finally vanished altogether, he began to suspect that he was "being made a donkey of." Turning about he had led his command back along the hillside and on September 10th had picked up the trail of the Wallamwatkins. At first he could hardly believe his eyes, but when it became plain that he might as well believe them, since everyone else was seeing what he saw and talking about it besides, there could be no question. Joseph had bamboozled him.

One of his troopers, Theodore Goldin, was so impressed with Sturgis' powers of self-expression that he noted in a narrative of the campaign:

□ "We knew our old Colonel was hopping mad that the savages had outwitted him. As we returned to camp we heard the old ——— declare with many an explosive adjective that he would overtake those Indians before they crossed the Missouri river, if he had to go afoot—and alone. He wound up his oration with an order for reveille at half-past three and an advance at five o'clock." □

Howard repressed his own annoyance and watched with quiet amusement Sturgis' frustration. He was intelligent enough to perceive that the interests of the Service would be best served by supplying a colonel in that state of mind with reinforcements, and instead of giving him orders turn him loose and let him do it in his own way. Accordingly Howard loaned him Lieutenant Otis of the Artillery with howitzers on pack mules and fifty of Sanford's cavalry led by Captain Bendire. Howard also dispatched a messenger to Colonel Miles at Fort Keogh near the confluence of the Tongue and Yellowstone apprising him of the situation so that he could head off the Indians, if Sturgis failed to stop them. Then Howard who was inwardly grinning gave Sturgis a slap on the back and said "Don't worry any longer Colonel. You still have a chance. Go and get 'em."

Sturgis in a state approaching frenzy cursed at each little delay until he had reorganized the Seventh Cavalry and was again on the trail of the Wallamwatkins on the north bank of the Yellowstone and moving downstream. On September 13th at the present site of Billings, Montana, Sturgis had called a halt to await word from his scouts. Suddenly Pawnee Tom rode up yelling "Indians!" Sturgis howled the order to mount and ride. They trotted along the bank of the Yellowstone and then, on topping a rise, they saw Joseph's people cooking a meal at the mouth of Canyon Creek. Sturgis ordered his troops to dismount and attack. He had three hundred and fifty men. Joseph's warriors were outnumbered, but superior in fighting qualities.

Through Canyon Creek

WHILE THE INDIAN MOTHERS and their children mounted and rode up Canyon Creek, a narrow ravine with banks from ten to twenty feet high, with here and there a small pool of stagnant alkaline water, the young warriors rode to meet Sturgis. The charge of the dismounted cavalry drove them back. The cavalry could afford wasteful, chance shots because they had plenty of ammunition. The warriors had to make every shot count. Their instructions from the chiefs were to retard the soldiers until the women and children had gotten a good start up Canyon Creek, even if it came to a hand-to-hand encounter.

The canyon, though narrow at the mouth, became even narrower as it tapered over a four mile course toward its head. In places there were protective overhanging ledges. Also there were little side ravines like deep trenches. What the Indians had already discovered soon became obvious to the soldiers. Whoever occupied the ravine first would have the advantage. Sturgis immediately ordered the troops commanded by Captain Benteen and by Major Merrill to remount and try to head off the Indians and particularly the pony herd, which with tails in the air was making for the canyon without urging.

The race for possession of the canyon was described by Goldin in his narrative as: □ "We went at a mad gallop" and "on we galloped" and "For a few moments it was doubtful which would win." □

Inferentially Goldin thought that the cavalry were beating the Indians by a whisker when suddenly Indians with rifles arose in the canyon mouth and spoiled a good race by letting the cavalry have it.

Afterward there was a running fight up the ravine and along the sides. Every time the soldiers could crawl to the edge of the canyon, and upon parting the grass look down upon a huddle of Indians in the bottom, they made a flock shot and laid Indians down flopping. When the soldiers stood up and roared with laughter, the bushes on the opposite side of the canyon parted, Indian heads appeared over the sights of rifles and the laughing soldiers received the ground rake.

The rest of the day was devoted to playing hide and seek in and near the canyon to the accompaniment of sniping by both sides. Twenty-one Indians were killed. The soldiers' loss was three killed and eleven wounded. In the chill dusk the soldiers retreated to the mouth of the canyon, ate hardtack, tried to find a dry place to sit, wrapped their blankets around them and listened to the moaning of the wind.

The Wallamwatkins withdrawing up the canyon in the cold darkness listened to sounds far more disturbing, the warriors of the River Crows signaling each other with coyote howls and owl hoots as they moved into position for a dawn attack. When the soldiers had attacked some twelve hours before at the canyon mouth the Wallamwatkins had tried desperately to crowd their pony herd into the ravine. Most of the ponies did get in, but Benteen pushed the Indian rear guard so hard that they had to abandon about four hundred of the less vigorous animals to save the others. In the running fight with the Crows, after leaving the head of the Canyon the next morning, Joseph's warriors lost five hundred more ponies. With these the Crows were satisfied and abandoned the pursuit.

At dawn of the following day Sturgis resumed his relentless pursuit of Joseph with an ardor worthy of fugitives more deserving of being harried. The fugitives were a few proud Indian families guilty of nothing more atrocious than trying to avoid white people and of defending themselves when the cavalry officers thought that they weren't moving fast enough.

Sturgis' column covered thirty-seven miles that day. Some rode. Some walked, leading their horses. The troop was strung out over ten miles. This leading was not an act of kindness to a faithful but exhausted animal. The horses being led had developed hoof disease and were unable to carry a rider. So the cavalry-men made their crippled horses walk the entire distance to the evening camp-fire. Then they shot the horses and roasted the diseased meat over the fire. After that they ate the meat.

The following day Sturgis reached the Musselshell River. The traces and signs showed that the Indians had passed more than twenty-four hours previously. With a fair portion of the Seventh Cavalry converted by failing horse power to the Seventh Infantry, and not at all pleased about it either, it seemed to Sturgis that his best course would be to wait for Howard. After Howard's arrival, with remounts, their united troops rode on northward toward the Missouri River.

Weeks previously Howard had sent Miles with his infantry and artillery to Fort Keogh to stop Joseph in case he turned eastward. Now when Howard's messenger reached Miles at Fort Keogh with an order to march northward parallel to Joseph, but at an intervening distance of thirty to forty miles, Colonel Nelson Miles* was ready. He marched the next morning.

Despite being set upon by white men and men of their own race on two succeeding days, the Wallamwatkins exhibited no self-pity. On the contrary they showed as they rode northward that they had retained their sense of humor. Trotting along a road they saw a stage coach ahead. There was no movie camera to record what followed, but they acted it out in what later be-

* Miles had been promoted from Captain to Colonel.

came known as the spirit of the old west. The coachman whipped the horses to ever increasing effort. The heads of bewhiskered young men popped out of the coach windows, took in the situation and then were hastily withdrawn. Still in the lead the coach arrived at the relay station. Having no script director to manage the scene, no attempt was made to defend the station. The attendant followed the passengers into the bushes.

The young warriors dismantled the stage, burned the mails and the station and rode away leading all of the horses. A lot of muddy coffee and poor food badly cooked went up in flames. Hundreds of the bedbugs, fleas and chiggers usually resident in coach relay stations perished amid the ashes.

Just before dismantling the coach the young warriors put on a wild west show of their own. They climbed into the stage and over the stage until it was so crowded that it somewhat resembled an open Brooklyn horse-car going to a Hibernian picnic. Then they drove off at a gallop. Other young warriors, playing the role of robbers, ambushed the stage, tipped it over and pretended to kill the passengers. During the procedure the stage was demolished. The rest of the Wallamwatkins, as the audience, laughed and applauded Indian fashion. That tiny bit of fun gave them much needed emotional relief. Perhaps it was just as well that they were unaware that Colonel Miles was creeping up on their right flank.

YELLOW WOLF'S STORY
OF
CHIEF JOSEPH'S ESCAPE

The Canyon Creek Fight

MORNING CAME, and soon the families were on the move. After starting, one of the chief's told some of us to go ahead about one sun to see if soldiers were in the way. All knew General Howard was good distance behind. No danger there, so a few of us went ahead as the chief ordered. We traveled, keeping a strong lookout for enemies. None were seen. No signs discovered, and night drawing on, camp was made.

Next morning early, we were riding. More must be seen of what was in that wild country. Our party was slightly scattered. Soon we saw it—a fire! Just a short distance, and we started to go there. Then he was seen—a man—leading a buckskin horse. He saw us, and sprang to his saddle. A tall fellow, wearing a buckskin suit. He went! After him came another man, leading a gray horse. He, too, jumped on his horse and went; but he proved a fearless man.

The fellow on the buckskin was shot and fell to the ground. The man on the gray ran swiftly ahead. Otskai and I went after him. I had a fast horse, and soon Otskai said to me, "My horse is giving out. Go on, brother! Grab that fellow's neck! Jerk him off his horse!"

I kept running my horse to his best. But just beyond my reach, this fellow jumped to the ground. His horse knocked him over, and I, going fast, passed him a few steps. I was off my horse as the man regained his feet. We both drew up rifles and fired. I did not know if I hit him. His bullet glanced my head, shaving through my hair. I was brought to my knees, blinded. Nearly knocked out, but did not know I was hit. I was partly out of sense. The enemy was trying to work his gun when Otskai killed him. Then was seen why his gun would not work. The hammer had been knocked off by a bullet—my bullet, for the other warriors were a good distance away. Had this not been done, he must have killed some of us. He was a brave man.

I know not why the big rifleshot did not go through my head. It only put me out of sense a short time. It must have been some help saved me from death. But no bullet was to kill me.

When I came back to sense, I heard Heinmot Tosinlikt say, "That other white fellow is not dead!"

We both went down to him, and Heinmot said, "I am going to finish him!"

I told him, "Do not do that! His wound is bad. He will soon die. It is not good to waste ammunition."

There was no more fighting that sun.

I guess maybe the soldiers heard our shots. They came afterward—not that sun—but missed us. We had gone down the creek while they came along the hillside. That is why they found that wounded fellow. He had not died.

In the meantime, we had gone up the hill. Looking around, we saw their camp. We saw them taking that wounded fellow back, traveling along the hillside. We could see the Crows and the Bannacks together.

All bunches going back to camp. We did not make ourselves seen to the enemy.

That night we stayed close to the main families' camp, guarding during all the darkness.

Next morning all soldiers went north over the hill, not seeing us. We saw five citizen men start back with the wounded fellow toward the Crow Indian Agency. We watched and followed them. It was about noon, when they stopped for food, that we charged them. But they saw us coming, and the five men mounted and skipped for their lives. They might have escaped from us, for they had good start in the race. But other Indians were crossing below. They were the ones to head them off. Siyikowkown (Lying in Water) shot one fellow from his horse; the bullet cracking his head. It was Otskai again to do the finishing.

The other four men got away. Of course, that first wounded fellow on the travois was killed after the four men escaped. It was Peetomyanon Teemenah (Hawk Heart) who killed him. Every white man in those mountains could be counted our enemy.

We had no more fighting that sun.

Three suns after I was scalp-wounded, there came a close call for my life. I went for my horses and while letting them drink, I sat down on the creek bank. Scouting and night guarding, I must have gone a little asleep. I must not have been full awake when I heard, as dreaming, "Look out for *hohots!* Look out for *hohots!*" Still I was sleeping. I did not understand with good sense. I heard again, away off like dreaming, "Look out for *hohots! Hohots* coming close to you!"

I was partly awake now. I turned my head where was a noise. *Eeh!* I saw it—a big *hohots* (grizzly bear). My rifle was in my hand. I sprang up as I threw back the hammer. That *hohots* made for me, a bad sound coming from his mouth. As he stood up, I held my rifle ready. That bear came stepping to the muzzle of my gun. Just touched it when I pulled the trigger. He fell, and I finished him with my war club. Struck him on the ear.

You ask if I was afraid? No, I was not scared. The bear had no gun. Did my heart travel fast after it was all over? (Laughing) No! I could not save myself by running. I must hold my ground. Must stand face to face with that *hohots.* After I had killed him, why, I thought about it. I had been close to death.

From fighting the grizzly, I drove my horses and that night camped with the families. Next morning everybody got their horses ready. They packed up. I saddled my horse. I was to go one way, alone. I traveled only a little distance when I saw a blanket signal. I understood that warning. It meant, "Soldiers coming close!"

I ran my horse to where the blanket was calling. When I reached that warrior who was riding in short circles, I saw soldiers near, and across the valley from us.

The traveling camp had nearly been surprised. Soldiers afoot—hundreds of them. I whipped my horse to his best, getting away from that danger. No more warriors to signal, the blanket waver also left. His signal had been mostly for me.

But we did not go together from there. We had our warrior ways. We did not line up like soldiers. We went by ones, just here and there, entering the canyon.

I came to one place at the mouth of the canyon. Only one warrior there doing the fighting. His horse hidden, he was behind rocks, holding a line of dismounted soldiers back. He was shooting regularly, not too fast. As I approached, he called to me, "My boy, run back from here! Soldiers too close. They might kill you. Do not stay here with your horse!"

When I heard those words spoken, I knew the voice. I was convinced that this brave warrior, Teeto Hoonod, was right. I was drawing the soldiers' fire. I made no answer, but turned my horse from there. Only a few jumps, when I noticed my saddle cinch dangerously loose. Saddle slipping back on my horse. I stopped and got off. There was a big noise in my head. I did not hear anything separate. It was the sound of many guns all roaring at once.

I did not turn, I did not look around anywhere! I was fixing tight my cinch. I knew not how close the soldiers were approaching. When I had fixed my saddle, I mounted. I turned my horse and went. Then I looked back. Soldiers still lined up moving forward slowly. Must be fifty of them I could still see. I was not scared because of their shots. I remembered the promise that bullets would never kill me. I made escape from those soldiers and came to where the warriors were protecting the families as they drove the horse herd into the canyon.

Other soldiers horseback, like cavalry, were off to one side. Away ahead of the walking soldiers. They tried to get the women and children. But some warriors, not many, were too quick. Firing from a bluff, they killed and crippled a few of them, turning them back.

In the fighting here a little later, some soldiers got on higher ground. Firing down, they killed two horses and wounded Silooyelam in the left ankle. Two other men were wounded but not at this time. They were Eeahlokoon, shot through the right leg below the knee, flesh wound. The other warrior, Elaskolatat (Animal Entering a Hole), was hit from the rear. Bullet entered left hip and came out front left thigh.

We stayed hidden among the rocks and timber. Watching the soldiers who soon went into camp. Then we left for home, barricading the upper canyon as we went. It was after dark when we reached camp. Staking our horses, we had supper, then lay down to sleep.

Next morning the families moved early. We were on Elk River, and some of us stayed back to watch the enemies. I looked one way and saw strange Indians. I looked good! Then I thought, "They must be either Walk-round Sioux or Snakes. I will go see."

I rode closer. *Eeh!* Crows! A new tribe fighting Chief Joseph. Many snows the Crows had been our friends. But now, like the Bitterroot Salish, turned enemies.

My heart was just like fire.

Chief Alokut, my uncle, was not far away. He dismounted and I, too, got down from my horse. We both fought from the ground. In short time, Alokut sprang up, leaped on his horse and galloped away. He hurried with others to drive Crows now fixing to flank the moving families.

Left alone, Crow Indians tried to surround me. To cut me off from all my people. I was not afraid. I brought myself to be brave. I mounted my horse and went. I did not hurry. Just loped along. I paid no attention to the enemies. Distant soldiers and nearer Crows were firing at me.

I looked back. Two Indians were overtaking me. One came as close as that (twelve feet), riding hard. We both fired at same time. It was just like one gun. He missed me, and I did not know if I hit him. As I whirled my horse the better to fight, both Indians rode swiftly away. I thought I must have wounded him.

I now brought my horse facing another way. Other Crows were firing at me as they raced past at a distance. They could not hit me from horseback.

I dismounted to do better shooting. Then came both Crow and Snake Indians. There must have been a hundred. They rode, hanging low on side of horses, doing underneck shooting. They got my right thigh—a hide-graze.

Then I took shots lying flat on the ground, but it was hard to hit fast running horses at distance. A bullet struck my saddle. One went through top of my horse's neck, just within his mane. He went sort of wild. I was holding him with rope around his jaw.

Then I thought: "If my horse is killed, they will get me sure!" I was up! Springing to the saddle, I went rapidly away. Those Crows and Snakes did not follow me.

McWhorter's Interpolation:

In order to bring out the Nez Perce reply to the charge that the Crows double-crossed the Government forces by giving secret aid to the enemy, I interposed, "General Howard claimed that the Crows helped you to get out of that country by directing you which way to go." Yellow Wolf's reply was emphatic:

Not true! The Crows fought us. They killed one warrior and two old, unarmed men. They did not act as guides for us. We had men who knew the country, who scouted far ahead all the time. They found each day the way to go.

McWhorter's Interpolation:

"History states," I added, "that the Crows only wanted your horses, and that they cut out about three hundred from your herd and drove them back to their reservation." To this, Yellow Wolf replied:

I never heard that story before. If they took horses, it was those we left along the trail. Too lame with sick (tender) feet to travel fast as we were going. We lost maybe thirty or forty horses not too lame. I know not if anybody got them, or if just lost.

Some Crows told Chief Looking Glass not to travel too fast. Said they would join and help us. But Looking Glass paid no attention. He now knew they were against us. He knew the

Crows were lying, that they wanted the soldiers to catch up with us. Although we had helped them in battles, we all knew not to trust the Crows.

Leaving those Indians, I overtook some Nez Perce warriors far back of the moving families. They then knew I was alive. Not killed as they had thought. I joined with these warriors who were acting as guards. They must fight off enemy Indians, also pursuing soldiers, should they overtake us. But when I rode among them, my horse would not be still, kept stepping about, pawing and plunging. He made a great dust. Chuslum Hihhih (White Bull) got mad and began whipping my horse. A brother of Charley Moses ordered Chuslum to stop with the whip. He said: "You see the horse has been shot?" My uncle, then noticing the wound, said to me, "Do not stay here. You better go to camp."

I believed him and went. I tried to catch the moving families, but it grew dark before I got halfway. I became lost! My wounded horse made poor travel at night.

After two days without eating, I thought to camp. Nobody to be seen anywhere, I looked for a good camping place. There was a great row of rocks—what you call a "slide." You could see farthest from its top. I went there, lay down watching. I could hear—could see all around—everywhere. No blanket, but must not build fire.

I had left my saddle with my uncle. My wounded horse might go down on me, and I did not want to lose my saddle. With saddle and its blanket, camping not bad, but I was just as I had stripped for fighting.

Came about sunrise. I was looking away off. Watching what might be seen as light grew wider. I happened to drop my eyes. *Eeh!* It was there—a *takialakin!* What you call antelope. I shot that *takialakin,* killed it!

I sat down and turned towards the west. As far as I could see to a rising ground, was an Indian. Of course that Indian had heard the gun report and was coming straight to me. I did not know the kind of Indian. Maybe a Flathead, Snake, Crow, or Sioux. That would be good. I would kill that Indian! He was coming fast, about as far away as that tepee (600 yards). Then I recognized him. He was of our tribe, my cousin Hekkik Takkawkaakon (Charging Hawk). He came up and said: "I was little afraid to come to you. What you shoot?"

I killed *takialakin!*" I answered.

"That is good! Come my friend, we will now start fire and have roast meat breakfast," was what he told me.

We soon had a fire and roasted all the meat we wanted. When done eating, I said to him, "Where is the camp? I was lost last night."

"You are off from the place," he told me. "Off about half-hour ride away. West of here. What made you go this way?"

"I have wounded horse. It got dark. I could not see direction I was traveling," I told him.

"We will go now," he said, and I got on my horse. We went, carrying the rest of meat with us. My cousin now asked me, "Were you cold last night?"

"No!" That was my answer. "I had company. I had blanket over me. Of course I was not freezing last night."

When I said that, the warrior laughed. He replied, "You are telling the truth!"

McWhorter's Query:

Mystified, I inquired of interpreter Hart what Yellow Wolf meant by saying he had a blanket over him, when he was really practically naked and had no covering. Evincing amusement, Hart replied:

"Why, Yellow Wolf was mad! His heart was big and sweatin' with mad! That kept him warm."

"Could he sleep under such conditions?" I asked.

"Yes, he says he slept. Night is for the sleeping."

Hekkik Takkawkaakon, now my partner, knew where the people were, and we went there. We came first among the women who had the camp packed ready to move. The Crows were watching to attack the horse herd and my partner hurried away to help the warriors on guard.

I saw the women were scared at the Crows and the Snakes,

with all the best warriors off guarding the horse herd. It came to me strong, how General Howard took many different tribes to help him in the war. I thought this wrong! But of those Indians on his side I was not afraid. When we met them they ran from us. General Howard's warriors were afraid. Only when we were moving would they come after us. I was told later that two hundred Indians helped the soldiers at that time.

A bunch of Bannack Indians, and maybe some Crows, came closer to the women. This bothered them. I could not find time to change my wounded horse. That horse could run strong though shot in top his neck. Teeweeyownah (Over the Point) joined me and we rode for those Bannacks. But his horse, a racer and not trained for battle, ran away with him. We were both then alone. When I drew near those Bannacks, they jumped from their slower horses and ran to hiding. I got from my horse and took one of theirs. Then I took another horse. They did not fire at me from the bushes. I did not follow after them. I had horses and rode back to camp. Left the enemies afoot. These Bannacks, I understood later, were of General Howard's scouts.

We were two, but I have told you how my partner's horse ran away with him. After I took those horses, I heard a shot—several shots—of about half a mile, in the direction he went. Then my partner's horse came running by me. I thought, "They have killed him!"

It was true! I do not know which killed him. Bannacks or Crows. He was the only Nez Pece warrior killed in all the Canyon Creek and trail fighting. I do not know if he killed any of the enemies. He was brave and strong, but the Crows were too many. With a trained horse he would not have been killed.

I do not think any Crows or Bannacks were killed. They were many and we only a few. Our warriors could not chase far to fight them. The moving families must be guarded.

No soldiers were seen in this running fight. They must have been back where the yesterday's fight was, burying one another. I could not tell how many Bannacks. They kept too far away. No more came close to trouble the women after we chased them.

McWhorter's Query:

At this point I asked the narrator if he thought General Howard wanted his Indians to attack women and children. He answered vehemently in the affirmative.

I am tell you, my friend! It is so, what I have seen, what I have done. They are facts, my words! I do not want anything not true.

I do not like the lie. If I lie, I will know it when I come to my death. I am telling you what I tell all the people at our celebrations. General Howard had those Bannacks, those Crows, to come against us.

Two old men—not warriors—were killed by the Crows. Tookleiks (Fish Trap), and Wetyetmas Hapima (Surrounded Goose) became separated from the families and were caught by the once friendly Crows. Tookleiks turned back looking for a missing horse, and was seen no more. Maybe Wetyetmas Hapima was on like business. I do not know. Both were too old to do fighting. General Howard's Indians killed all our old people they found. The two were not killed by soldiers. No soldiers caught up with us from where we left them at Canyon Creek.

None of the three were buried. We had no time, no chance to do the burying. The killed were too far scattered.

I do not understand how the Crows could think to help the soldiers.* They were fighting against their best friends! Some Nez Perces in our band had helped them whip the Sioux who came against them only a few snows before. This was why Chief Looking Glass had advised going to the Crows, to the buffalo country. He thought Crows would help us, if there was more fighting.

* Tribes hostile to the allied bands of the Lower Nez Perce during their flight toward the Canadian border were Crows, Bannacks, Blackfeet, Snakes, Cheyennes, Assiniboines (the Walk-Around Sioux) and a portion of the Christianized Upper Nez Perce on the Lapwai Reservation.

8 THE FLIGHT FROM THE BIG SNOWY MOUNTAINS TO THE BEARPAWS

RIDING NORTHWARD FROM CANYON CREEK THE WALLAMWATKINS were in a flat dusty country of cactus, sagebrush, prickly pear, bunch grass and alkaline water. Joseph crossed the Musselshell River and saw the blue bulk of the Big Snowy Mountains against the northern horizon. Having crossed the plain, he ascended the Big Snowy, descended and bore to the left around Judith Mountain. Slightly to the northeast in a bend of the Missouri River on Cow Island there was a ferry and freight depot at the terminal of steamboat navigation during the autumn. Joseph needed desperately to replenish his supplies. The steamboat *Benton* on its last trip of the season had just discharged fifty tons of freight, partly government and partly private. Twelve soldiers commanded by Sergeant Molchert guarded the freight. They took cover as the warriors swam the river.

While the main band of the Wallamwatkins was ransacking and destroying the freight and throwing a few shots now and then at Molchert's small fortification, a detachment of warriors rode westward into the mouth of the Judith Basin where they surprised a wagon train driven by nine teamsters. They had great fun chasing the teamsters into the hills, shooting at their britches as they ran. They accidentally hit two and killed them. Returning, the warriors burned the wagons.

Major Ilges, commanding at Fort Benton about eighty miles up the Missouri River from Cow Island, upon learning of the tumultuous passage of the Wallamwatkins, put his troops in boats and pushed them out into the current of the Missouri. Then he rounded up thirty-six casual cowboys and rode cross country toward Cow Island. He arrived on September 25th and at once followed the trail of the Indians up Cow Creek Canyon. He didn't have to follow very far. Seventy-five mounted warriors came whooping and screaming down the canyon to meet him.

While the warriors were more than a half mile up the canyon Ilges heard them coming and ordered his cowboys to dismount and find cover. The Indians also dismounted, separated into small parties and tried to outflank the cowboys. The usual sniping followed. It lasted all day. Two Indians were wounded. One cowboy and a horse were killed. The American taxpayer met the ammunition bill for both sides.

At sundown Ilges and the cowboys who had been overjoyed at contacting the warriors were just as happy to escape from them and return to Cow Island. The warriors had completed their assignment by holding back the pursuing white men until the Wallamwatkins had started up a stream bed which had worn a low pass through the Little Rocky Mountains. During darkness the warriors rejoined the main band.

Meanwhile General Howard led his command by short marches from the Musselshell River to the Big Snowy Mountains. As he skirted Judith Mountain, he made a note for his report: ○ "Then in this broad and open country trails began to diverge, multiply and grow dim. Between Houston and the mouth of Judith River where it flows into the Missouri thousands of acres of the prairie were on fire and so on reaching it the new trails were annihilated. Great uncertainty for the want of information began to press upon me, but I had resolved to go at least as far as the Missouri and carry out my orders to chase the Indians to the British lines.

"I had in my heart earnestly petitioned for God's help, expressing a sentiment that I hope was sincere 'If thou wilt grant my request, do so, I beseech Thee, even at the expense of another's receiving the credit of the expedition.'" ○

In other words Howard was trying to make a little trade with God. In a polite way, of course. In his further account of the campaign he said: ○ "We knew from a long experience that the Indians watched well to the rear and moved very much as we did, keeping one, two and sometimes three marches ahead. When we stopped to rest they did so. When we moved short distances they shortened their journeys. Therefore we planned for the same operation to continue. Meanwhile I endeavored through our numerous scouts to keep informed of where the Indians actually were." ○

One ponders upon how God should react when one of His sons beseeches Him for assistance in capturing several of his brothers with the intent of reducing them to a condition of restricted movement bordering on bondage. God must have been touched by that selfless willingness to yield all credit for the glorious act. And yet General Howard, a devout and pious man, not only prayed to God "in his heart" for such a boon, but soon afterward saw his prayer answered, according to his own account:

○ "I said to Mason as my spirits grew lighter 'Colonel, I believe we shall capture these Indians yet.'

"Alexander (doctor) asked with a hearty laugh 'What is more hopeless? There isn't one chance in a million for Miles. I cannot see General where you found your hope.'

" 'All right' I answered. 'Mark my words and see if I am not right.'

"Mason hoped with a slight despondency of tone that my prediction might prove true. It was not long after this conversation before some message bearers hove in sight. We had not met horse or man for several days. A manifest excitement quickened the motion of the entire command as two horsemen were discerned coming on at a steady gallop and every moment approaching nearer.

"The courier dismounted and handed me a note. It informed me that the Indians had burned a freight-train of wagons and had crossed the Missouri at Cow Island and gone. Miles crossed the Missouri there and is still in pursuit." ○

So Miles, the million-to-one shot was paying off! That was God's answer to Howard's prayer. It should be kept in mind that when Howard offered Joseph and his people a part of the Lapwai Reservation he stipulated that the U.S. Government would provide them with schools and churches and that the Wallamwatkins must accept, even though they might not want them. This was necessary in order that the Wallamwatkins might become civilized. From the text of Howard's account it seems that he had stood up for God and now God was standing up for him.

Meanwhile instead of depending on God, Colonel Miles was depending on his scouts. He had selected them carefully. He did little sleeping himself, therefore saw no reason why the scouts should sleep. When Joseph was passing three miles west of Carroll, Colonel Miles crossed the Missouri River twelve miles to the eastward. As Joseph's people were destroying freight at Cow Island, Miles was forging northward toward the Little Rockies, a distance of twenty miles. From the crests of the Little Rockies Miles' scouts watched the Wallamwatkins cross the prairie to the Bearpaw Mountains and disappear among the ravines.

Miles' command included artillery, complete with howitzers and gatling guns (forerunner of machine guns), infantry, cavalry and baggage wagons carrying ammunition, food, tents and blankets. It was now late in September. Cold winds were whirling snow across hill and prairie. Relentless as a wolf pack, Miles' troops traversed the Little Rockies going due north. Descending to level ground at the northern extremity of the hills, they crossed Snake Creek, a tributary of the Milk River. While the Wallamwatkins were riding in a northwesterly direction over the Bearpaw Mountains, Miles was following the north fork of Snake Creek toward its source in the northern foothills of the Bearpaws. He was then about fifty miles northeast of the Wallamwatkins. Thenceforward victory or failure became entirely a question of his success in stalking his prey. All unsuspecting, Joseph led his people down the northern foothills of the Bearpaws, within an easy day's ride of the Canadian border and camped in the head of the Snake Creek ravine.

When Miles' Cheyenne scouts informed him that the Wallamwatkins were crossing laterally the northwest slopes of the Bearpaws in a due northerly direction, Miles immediately left the north fork of Snake Creek and marched directly south across the Bearpaws. At the crest of the ridge he crossed Joseph's trail, then making an arc to the north, returned to it. At that point Miles threw off his mask. There was no longer need of concealment. It now became a question of haste, for Joseph had gone to earth just south of the border in open country. If Miles could rush his troops to that ravine while Joseph was still in there, he might be able to hold him until General Howard could come up with reenforcements. After that Joseph's people would be so hopelessly outnumbered that they would eventually be forced to surrender. Miles didn't care whether his soldiers or horses ate or slept at all. They had to keep going day and night until Miles was ready to pounce. They could eat and sleep after that.

YELLOW WOLF'S STORY
OF
THE FLIGHT FROM THE BIG SNOWY MOUNTAINS TO THE BEARPAWS

Northward Across the Missouri

NEXT MORNING after this last fight with General Howard's Bannack Indian scouts, we moved camp early. For five suns we moved, meeting only little trouble. The Crow tribe was left fai behind. It came morning of that fifth night, and the families made packs for moving.

There is a little story. I have said that I was scout to keep watch on the back trail. But this sun I was sent early ahead of the families. I took the lead. I brought myself to be a scout. In the fore part of the morning I ran onto a band of *heyets*, the mountain sheep, the big-horn. I thought to kill one of them. My rifle was swung in case alongside my saddle. I drew the gun, but before I got it clear, it went off. My horse was shot through hind leg. Not broken, but bad flesh wound.

I was half a sun ahead of other Indians. I threw my saddle down for them to pick up, and went on afoot. It was toward evening. I came to a small creek. I heard a horse nicker. It was not too far to a small, open place. I saw four white men. I thought, "I will go to them!"

I started, and one said not to come. I did not understand very well, but I knew he wanted me to stop. I did not mind him. I kept on, and those four men grabbed their guns. I jerked my rifle up, but not fast enough. They all fired. I was shot right across the left arm. I nearly dropped my gun! I yelled, and went after them. One made toward me, and I shot him. I know not which fired first, but he missed me. I was too mad to know where the bullet struck him. The three of them ran. They ran fast, and about sixty steps away I downed one. The two went into the brush, and I hurried to the four staked horses.

I led those horses to where they had a tent. It was about five o'clock. I said to myself, "Where will I find my food?" Then I found it.

I thought of my horses. These white men had a saddle, and I put a packsaddle on one horse. There was a sack and a half of flour. I packed up and went on. I did not know where the other Indians were. I was just going any way.

It grew dark. I was taking all the horses and traveling was slow. About nine o'clock I heard Indians shouting. I said to myself, "Now I am getting to my friends alive!"

I answered them and when I got to camp, my mother gave me some food. They then asked me, "Where have you been?"

"On ahead!"

When I answered that, they told me, "You lie down and rest."

I lay down with my blanket on a buffalo robe and slept until morning. We ate breakfast, and my uncle asked me, "Where you get your horses?"

"Four white men made war on me," I answered.

"Were you afraid?"

"No! The whites are just like those little flies. Sometimes they light on your hand. You can kill them!"

"The gun is danger?"

"No! I think they have those play guns. Just like children."

"Not soldiers? Not scouts?"

When he asked me that I answered, "No, just citizen dress. All was easy for me."

McWhorter's Query:

Yellow Wolf laughed softly at the recollection, and when asked why he wanted to go to the white men when they told him not to do so, he answered quickly:

All white men were spies. Enemies to be killed. Those four white men with horses would quickly have brought soldiers. Furthermore, I will tell you. Those men spoke war when they drew their guns. I understood that meaning.

We moved on. It was the sixth sun from fighting the Crows and Bannacks when we came to a large river. Its name at the crossing we struck is Seloselo Wejanwais, a kind of colored paint. There were a few buildings there. The chiefs said, "We will cross this river!"

We were just waiting for one another, for all the families to come up. I heard the voice of a man talking. I understood soldiers were camped across the river. It was the only place to ford. The water was deep elsewhere.

Each of the five chiefs called to his own men. When through with this, they all came together. There were not as many as a hundred warriors. We thought those soldiers might shoot at us crossing, so about twenty warriors went first. The others remained close to the river shore, where we would have more chance to return their fire. But there were no shots, so the rest of the warriors started across to the soldiers' side. Of course I did not remain behind. I heard some Indians say, "If the soldiers do not fire on us, we will do no shooting."

We reached an island. We could not see the soldiers. We went a good way and got on shore. The pack outfit came across, the whole train and the horse herd. To let all this and the families pass, the warriors stopped a short distance from the soldiers. One chief instructed me to take the families about two miles and make camp. It was near one hour from sunset. No tepee poles, camp making was not hard for the women. While this was doing, I heard one man say, "Some warriors now riding towards the soldiers."

I hurried to join in the fight. I heard the guns popping. The fighting had started. I soon reached there. The soldiers had a bank protection. We could not get to them and, darkness falling, we slowed up firing.

No warrior was killed. Only one, Husis Owyeen (Wounded

Head), had his scalp cut by bullet-splintered wood. In Big Hole battle his head was bullet-glanced, which gave him his good name. He was a brave warrior.

The soldiers had everything fixed up. I saw food piled high as this house (one story) where the steamboats landed. Lots of other goods as well.

Before night came, we took food as wanted. Each family took maybe two sacks flour, one sack rice, one sack beans, plenty coffee, sugar, hardtack. Some took bacon. Everything to eat.

All this we captured from the soldiers. We did not starve that sun, that night. Whoever wanted them, took pans, cooking pots, cups, buckets. Women all helped themselves. When everybody had what they wanted, some bad boys set fire to the remaining. It was a big fire!

We warriors stayed there all night, watching and exchanging shots with the soldiers. The chiefs who made rulings were at camp. They said, "Let's quit! Soldiers are under bank. We can do nothing. Nobody killed and we have plenty of food."

A man was sent who told us what the chiefs said. The older warriors got together and minded the order. We turned from those soldiers, ending the shooting. It had been nearly like play.

When I reached camp, my pack was already done up. The families and warriors were leaving, and I changed horses. I was staying behind. One hour passed, but those soldiers did not go anywhere.

My horse was loose-saddled. I waited about another hour, keeping good lookout. Then, tightening the saddle cinch, I mounted and followed after the camp. It must have been three miles I went. Coming to a narrow canyon, I looked ahead and saw that the wagon road crossed a creek. Then I thought I saw signs of a man. I pretended not to see anything. I got down to fix my stirrup. It needed no fixing. I only played working at it. But all the time I watched the spot where the man-sign had moved.

Then I saw a white face peering out of the brush. In maybe five minutes another face came in sight. Then two more. Yes, they were looking toward me. After taking a good look, I knew.

They were white men waiting. Four white men waiting to shoot one Indian riding by!

There was but that one way. I could not go around them. I took my heart and said, "I must take this road!" Approaching the enemies, I still kept as if I had seen nothing. My stirrup fixed, I made my mind what to do. I thought how to get by those men.

Mounting, I walked my horse in a circle. I bent over as if looking for lost horse tracks. In the meantime I rolled one blanket-cloth legging below the knee. I tied it strong and fast. Then I turned my horse to circle a different way while I rolled and tied the other legging. Of course the enemies did not see what I was doing, working from blind side of horse.

Rolling the leggings was a custom I always followed when going into battle. I will not have clothing on my body. No leggings, no shirt, only the breechcloth, moccasins, and feathers, or whatever I happen to have with me for obtaining power in battle. For this reason did I strip down for the enemies.

I kept my rifle ready but still pretended I knew not of danger. Heading my horse the right way, I kicked him with my heel. Trained, he sprang to a swift gallop down toward the brush-hidden enemies. I passed from their sight a short moment. *Eeh!* There *was* another way—a small trail. I sent my horse up a sandy place where this trail led. I reached the top—not far—and looked down. I saw those men holding ready to shoot. Waiting for me! I was not coming their way. Had some of them been at the gulch, they would have caught me sure. They must not have known the leading-off trail. Maybe they were just scouts watching the wagon road?

I laughed while circling away.

When I got abreast of them, one looked up and saw me. He pointed and all began firing. But I was now about a quarter mile away. They could not hit me. I did not return their fire. I did not stop. I waved my rifle a "Good-by," and just kept loping along. They did not try following me.

I now hurried along to report what I had seen. I came up

with rear warrior guards about noon. They told me "We thought you would be killed! We left some white men horseless back there."

"No! I am alive," I told them. "It was not dangerous passing those men. Had they not looked around when I was so far away, had they lain low, they would have got me. They showed themselves hiding to shoot me."

The warriors laughed. I did not know until then those white men had been placed afoot by our warriors taking their horses. It stopped them carrying to the soldiers news where to find us.

It was early afternoon when we came to a wagon train hauled by many ox teams. The Indians charged. Three white men were killed, and several got away. Then the warriors went for those wagons. They were loaded with supplies—must have been for stores somewhere. There was lots of whisky. But before Indians got at it, soldiers appeared. Not too close, but approaching, and wagons were set afire. There was some shooting, but no Indian was hurt. We thought we killed one or two soldiers. Those soldiers stopped before getting very near us. No oxen were killed. We traveled on a ways, and made early night camp.

9 THE SURRENDER

YEARS AFTERWARD INDIAN INSPECTOR JAMES MCLAUGHLIN ASKED Joseph why he didn't go right on across the Canadian Border the next day. Obviously had he done so, he and his people would have been safe.

Indians are extremely reticent when talking to white men about other Indians. In his reply Joseph only hinted at his real reason and then not until the end of his speech. He said:

"I knew that I had made a mistake by not crossing into the country of the Red Coats, also in not keeping the country scouted in my rear." *

In other words mistake number two was in not knowing about the proximity of Miles. Joseph went on to explain that his people and their horses were exhausted and needed a rest. The wounded needed a chance to recuperate. There was game in the vicinity. They needed meat. Joseph continued:

□ "I sat down in a fat and beautiful country. I had won my freedom and the freedom of my people. There were many empty places in the lodges and in the council but we were in a land where we would not be forced to live in a place we did not want. I believed that if I could remain safe at a distance (Canada) and talk straight to the man that would be sent by the Great Father, I could get back the Wallowa Valley and return in peace. That is why I did not allow my young men to kill and destroy the white settlers after I began to fight. I wanted to leave a clean trail. I had sent out runners to find Sitting Bull to tell him that another band of red men had been forced to run from the soldiers of the Great White Father and to propose that we join forces if we were attacked." □

* *Hear Me My Chiefs!* Edited by Ruth Bordin, Caxton, 1952.

Joseph had not forgotten that a few days previously he had carried on a running fight with Colonel Sturgis and a band from the River Crow Tribe at practically the same time. He knew that the Sioux, after wiping out Custer and his command, had hastily crossed the Canadian border and had camped just north of the frontier. Following the Crow incident he naturally wondered what would happen if he should cross the line without warning and barge into the Sioux camps. He had reason to believe that they might drive him back into Montana and the arms of General Howard. So he sent out runners to discover Sitting Bull's views on the subject. Unfortunately the messengers stopped at a village of Assiniboines.* The Assiniboines promptly murdered all of them for their fine rifles.

Joseph sent more messengers. They got through to Sitting Bull, but they had to ride forty miles north of the border to find the Sioux. They learned that the Sioux were not at all interested in helping Joseph, but they were very much interested in keeping well out of the way of the U. S. Army. Therefore Joseph was prudent in contacting them. He could not have entered the country in which they were living without having received their permission. Not unless he was willing to fight out in the open on two fronts at the same time. He remembered the Crows.

Sitting Bull and his band of two thousand Sioux should not be regarded as totally lacking in sympathy for Joseph and his unfortunate band of Nez Perce. It was afterwards discovered that the Sioux had pretty well hunted out the game in the country just north of the Montana border. At the time of Joseph's arrival in the vicinity the Sioux were not getting enough to eat to keep them from feeling hungry much of the time. That winter there would not have been enough to feed the Sioux and the Nez Perce. There was enough game at the northern tip of the Bear Paw Mountains to feed the Nez Perce that winter. This was the true reason why Joseph elected to stay just south of the border.

---

* The Assiniboines were a part of the Sioux.

Joseph's camp, eight miles from the base of the northern extremity of the Bearpaw range, was described by Lieutenant Henry Romeyn of the Fifth Infantry of Miles' Troops:

□ "The camp was located on a small stream called Snake Creek in a kidney-shaped depression covering about six acres of ground. Along the western side the stream ran in a tortuous course, while through it from the steep bluffs, forming its eastern and southern sides, ran steep-banked stream beds* from two to six feet deep with enough sage brush to hide the heads of the Indians." □

The 30th of September at 4 A.M. Miles broke camp. Four hours later his cavalry galloped up to the stream bed at the southwestern end of the camp. The Wallamwatkins were taken by surprise, but so was the cavalry when a line of warriors appeared above the sagebrush and let them have it at close range. When the cavalry galloped over the rise with pounding hoofs and jingling bits they had no idea that they were about to be mowed off of their horses like that. They didn't wait for someone to tell them what to do. They knew what to do. They galloped back over that rise before the Indians could reload. The retreat was more rapid than the advance. Only forty per cent returned to safety. They were all enlisted men, no officers. Another battalion of cavalry, perceiving in a split second what was about to happen, veered to the left and managed to stampede nearly, but not quite, all of the Indians' horses and ponies. There were about a thousand. That battalion also returned to safety in great haste minus fifty-three of the one hundred and fifteen who had ridden so gaily forth.

While the cavalry were herding the ponies within the army line a few warriors followed and tried to stampede the ponies in another direction. For a few minutes it was touch and go as to whether the Indians or the cavalry would win possession. The ponies were bewildered having had no similar experience. While the ponies were milling and trying to decide, about one hundred ponies carrying Indian families and packs suddenly dashed out

* In the early fall the stream beds were dry.

of the camp and headed for Canada. They were escorted by sixty warriors.

The Indians' attempt to regain the pony herd had been sincere, but it had mostly served to mask a dash for freedom. And the dash was successful. That small band did enter Canada. The warriors failed to recover the herd, but they returned safely to their camp.

When Miles first attacked, Joseph happened to be across the creek opposite the tepees. He had to get back to be in the fight. His own account of it was:

□ "We had no knowledge of General Miles' army until a short time before he made a charge upon us, cutting our camp in two and capturing nearly all of our horses. About seventy men (warriors), myself among them, were cut off. My little daughter, twelve years of age, was with me. I gave her a rope and told her to catch a horse and join the others who were cut off from the camp. I have not seen her since, but I have learned that she is alive and well.

"I thought of my wife and children who were now surrounded by soldiers and I resolved to go to them or die. I dashed unarmed through the line of soldiers. It seemed to me that there were guns on every side, before and behind me. My clothes were cut to pieces and my horse was wounded, but I was not hurt. As I reached the door of my lodge my wife handed me my rifle, saying 'Here's your gun. Fight!'

"The soldiers kept up a continuous fire. Six of my men were killed in one spot near me. Ten or twelve soldiers charged into our camp and got possession of two lodges, killing three Nez Perce and losing three of their men who fell inside our lines. I called my men to drive them back. We fought at close range, not more than twenty steps apart and drove the soldiers back upon their main line, leaving their dead in our hands. We secured their arms and ammunition. We lost, the first day and night, eighteen men and three women." □

Watching the fiasco, Colonel Miles pulled at his big moustache and wondered what to do next. It occurred to him that everyone needs water, even people as indestructible as Indians. Drive them out of that stream bed and they'd take refuge in neighboring dry ravines. After that, if he could keep them there, thirst would win the battle for him. Miles' lips parted in a cruel smile as he ordered elements from the Second and Seventh Cavalry to attack on the north and east fronts of the Indian position. He also ordered a detachment of the Fifth Infantry to attack simultaneously, as nearly as they could, by the southwest.

By this time the cavalry had learned from heavy losses in action that the smart way to charge the entrenched Nez Perce was to gallop up to the Indian line, fire a pistol at a bush, a rock or an Indian if one was visible, wheel sharply to right or left and really gallop until out of range. The Fifth Infantry detachment, being less experienced, obeyed their order literally. They: □ "charged down the slope, along the open valley of the creek and reached the west end of the Indian village. The deadly fire of the Indians with magazine guns disabled thirty five per cent of the detachment and rendered it impossible for them to take the remainder of the village." □ Miles so stated in his report to the Secretary of War.

Observing that it was no use, Miles ordered a bugler to sound retreat. Some of the infantry returned. Others sneaked back after dark. At the next roll call only two men out of three responded with "Here." The rest were listed as missing in action.

During darkness the Wallamwatkins, both men and women, dug with knives, frying pans and their hands a system of trenches and dug-outs. Miles extended his effectives in a thin circle clear around the Indian position. Then he sat down in his tent and pulled both ends of his moustache. He had cause. If Sitting Bull and the Sioux should come and catch him thus extended, they would wipe out his entire force like the fox snapping up the gingerbread man.

Outside it was snowing hard. A rising wind soon developed into a blizzard. The soldiers, including the wounded, had to sit on the hills and take it. Nor could they safely light fires because of the Indian sharpshooters. There were no tents for them. Some of the soldiers may have recalled General Braddock's words just before they buried him, following the battle of Mononghahela, "We shall know better next time."

While the enlisted men shivered, hungry and exhausted in the freezing wind, Miles continued to pull his moustache and muse. Finally the moustache came up with an idea. Send a messenger to Colonel Sturgis and ask for reenforcements. Miles knew Sturgis as a conscientious but impulsive officer who meant well, but was forever getting lost. Miles might have thought of Sturgis as a relative of the Hodag, the bird who flies backward because he doesn't care about where he is going, but does wish to find out where he has been.

Howard and Sturgis had both had opportunities to corner Joseph, but Joseph had eluded them easily. Not until the last moment had Howard ordered Miles to participate. At last, given a chance, Miles by superb trailing and timing had nailed down Joseph near the border. Miles had by some earlier trailing and timing married the niece of General William Tecumseh Sherman, General of the Army. Still he was only Colonel Miles not Brigadier General Miles. And now here was a chance to distinguish himself by making prisoner Joseph and his band after Howard and Sturgis had failed. Had Miles sent a messenger to General Howard, it would have been an admission of failure. Howard would come and, as superior officer, would be entitled to all of the credit. As for Sturgis—Miles felt that he could handle Sturgis, who was, after all, just another colonel. The main thing was to call up reenforcements. The messenger would probably find Sturgis fooling around the Missouri River, wondering how to get across.

It is doubtful that Miles for one instant considered that a strong, happy and unoffending people must be butchered so that he could wear a star on each shoulder-strap. Joseph was fighting to preserve his people and their way of life. It was a good way of life. It was attuned to nature. And there was music in it. Miles was fighting for Miles.

Next morning, October 1st, Miles dispatched a messenger

with a note to Sturgis. Then, using the information about the distribution of Joseph's camp which he had gleaned from the survivors of the preceding day's attack, he placed his field artillery where it could do the most good. The shelling began.

Well placed artillery fire against a defensive position is very convincing. Joseph had great courage, but he couldn't endure shell bursts above the heads of Indian women and children. After giving Joseph a sample of what he could expect, Miles ordered a cease fire and sent a messenger with a white flag into the Indian camp. Joseph asked Yellow Bull to receive the messenger. Joseph afterward described the interview.

□ "Yellow Bull understood the messenger to say that Colonel Miles wished me to consider the situation; that he did not want to kill my people unnecessarily. Yellow Bull understood this to be a demand for me to surrender and save blood. Upon reporting this message to me Yellow Bull said he wondered whether Colonel Miles was in earnest. I sent him back with my answer that I had not made up my mind but would think about it and send word soon. A little later Miles sent some Cheyenne scouts with another message. I went out to meet them. They said they believed Colonel Miles was sincere and really wanted peace. I walked on to Colonel Miles' tent. He met me and we shook hands. He said 'Come let us sit down and talk this matter over.'" □

In his report to the Secretary of War Miles said that Joseph was accompanied by several warriors. They seemed to be in a mood to surrender until they became suspicious "from some remarks that were made in English in their hearing."

By permitting enlisted men or even officers of his staff to come close enough to the Indians to satisfy their curiosity Miles made a mistake. Miles should have fed Joseph and his warriors well, given them blankets to sit on, hot coffee to drink and a present apiece of tobacco. He should have held his staff in sight but out of earshot and talked with Joseph through his interpreter. Then he should have asked Joseph to go and bring out his people so that they could all be fed and made warm. After that they could return to their camp and talk it over among themselves. Later they could let him know their decision. Meanwhile they could retain their rifles and other weapons. There would have been no difficulty. Joseph would have surrendered quietly and with good grace.

But that is not what Miles did. Instead he: □ "detained Joseph overnight," □ military parlance for "he held Joseph prisoner." That was his second mistake. Miles' third mistake was to send Lieutenant Jerome to □ "reconnoiter" □ the Indian village; that is to spy on the Indian camp. Miles may have believed that in Joseph's absence the Indians would stand in awe not knowing what to do while Lieutenant Jerome snooped around their defenses. If so, Miles was never more wrong in his appraisal of Indian reaction.

Yellow Bull hauled Jerome off of his horse. The young warriors fought each other like boys yelling "I saw him first." Each wanted to give Jerome the first whack. Yellow Bull restrained them by explaining to them that Jerome as a hostage would help in Joseph's safe return, whereas if they killed Jerome, Miles might retaliate on Joseph. The young warriors saw the light.

To make sure that Jerome would not be hit by a shell fragment or a stray bullet they hustled him into an underground passage where the temperature was about 48°. It was also penetratingly damp, but the warriors were indifferent. It mattered only that Jerome be kept alive until Joseph's return.

In the cold darkness Jerome may have thought that Miles wasn't very bright. But Miles had a better opinion of himself. Having Joseph in his hold, perhaps a bit sooner than he had anticipated, he now dispatched a messenger to Howard with word that he had corralled Joseph's band (the Wallamwatkins) of the Nez Perce.

While that messenger was riding southward, the first messenger reached Colonel Sturgis the evening of October 2nd at Cow Island. In Miles' calculation his second messenger would find Howard puttering along the Missouri River near Fort Hawley, out of contact with pretty much everybody, particularly the

Indians. Actually Howard had gone farther up the Missouri. At Carroll, on October 1st, he had found the steamboat *Benton* tied up to the shore. With an artillery battalion, two aides and a few scouts Howard went aboard leaving Sturgis in command with orders to follow with the troops. In his account of the incident he said:

○ "We steamed up the river as rapidly as possible. The Missouri is shallow at this season and our vessel often ran aground. I was curious to see how the river could be navigated with so little water. Soon I noticed that when the steamer struck a sand bar, as it often did, it put out immense wooden arms which are vitalized by a steam windlass and lifted itself little by little over into deeper water." ○

On October 2nd the steamboat vaulted over a last sand bar and bumped against the north bank opposite Cow Island. Howard and his men disembarked and rode north. They experienced no difficulty in picking up the wide trail of the Wallamwatkins. On the same day the messenger from Miles reached Sturgis leading the troops upstream along the south bank of the Missouri.

Comprehending the note at a glance, Sturgis told one and all in military terminology to get a move on. The response was so enthusiastic that the entire outfit reached a point opposite Cow Island only a few hours after Howard had disembarked and ridden north. Sturgis got the troops, equipment and baggage across the Missouri by using the *Benton* as a ferry. Then he followed Howard's trail to within two hours' march from the battlefield and camped.

Meanwhile Miles' second messenger had caught up with the first. Together they reversed their direction and tried to catch up with Howard. Almost in sight of Miles' camp they did overtake Howard. For the first time, and yet the last one to know, Howard, the commanding officer in charge of the campaign, was made acquainted with the state of affairs. Without pausing to reflect upon such informal procedure, Howard rode on.

It was after dark and snowing on October 4th when Howard

rode into Miles' camp. The only illumination was the flashes of intermittent rifle fire from the pits on both sides. When he met Miles, Howard characteristically greeted him heartily saying:

□ "Hello, Miles! I'm glad to see you. I thought you might have met Gibbon's fate. Why didn't you let me know?" □

Well, of course Miles had let him know, but he had bypassed Howard and had let Sturgis know first. He was expecting Sturgis with the troops when who should ride up but Howard with the staff. Had arrivals been according to Miles' plan, Sturgis would have come with such a weight of men, ammunition and artillery that before daylight the Indians would have been dead or coming over with their hands up. Then let Howard and the staff arrive. Miles would have had victory in the bag and plenty of witnesses to prove it. That star was hovering right over Miles' shoulder strap when Howard's snow-matted whiskers punched through the gloom.

Instead of attempting to answer Howard's question with another question "Where, oh where is Sturgis?" Miles saluted formally and gave him a cold greeting. As a junior officer he offered Howard the comfort of his tent while another was being prepared.

Howard asked that his aides be cared for, then followed Miles to the tent. At the entrance Miles stepped aside and stood rigidly at attention until Howard had entered. Inside the tent Howard put a hand on Miles' shoulder, gave him a quizzical smile of understanding and assured him that he would see that Miles received full credit for capturing the Indians and would not take over command until after the surrender. In other words Joseph would surrender to Miles, not to Howard.

By inference, had their stations been reversed, Miles would probably not have made such a generous gesture. Had he attempted such a thing he would have been out of character and probably would not have gone through with it. For example three days earlier when Yellow Bull came into Miles' camp to learn what had become of Joseph, Joseph in telling about it later said:

□ "General Miles would not let me leave the tent to see my friend alone.

"Yellow Bull said to me 'They have got you in their power, and I am afraid they will never let you go again. I have an officer in our camp and I will hold him until they let you go free.'

"I said 'I do not know what they mean to do with me. But if they kill me, you must not kill the officer. It will do no good to avenge my death by killing him.' " □

Of course there was an interpreter present who repeated this dialogue to Miles. Two pulls at the moustache told Miles that the capture of Joseph by sacrificing the life of a junior officer (and there were men in Congress who might say that it was premeditated) would place among the fixed stars in the sky the star he desired for his shoulder strap. There was also a matter of a note from Lieutenant Jerome which Red Wolf's son had just brought him from the Indian camp. Long afterward Yellow Bull told about that note. He said:

□"After we kept Jerome in our camp for a day and a night he wanted something to eat. I and Tom Hill told him we had nothing he could eat, that he had better write a note to Colonel Miles and ask him for something to eat. He wrote a note to Colonel Miles. Red Wolf's son took the message to Colonel Miles. And we made an exchange of prisoners." □

Rather! A twirl of the moustache told Miles that if the Wallamwatkins should not kill Jerome, if Jerome should manage to escape to civilization and tell the true story, whether Joseph were killed or not, the star would prove to be an eight ball. Naturally Miles released Joseph.

Upon Joseph's return the chiefs held a council on the subject of surrendering. The report made afterward by Joseph was: □ "We could have escaped from Bear Paw Mountain if we had left our wounded, old women and children behind. We were unwilling to do this. We had never heard of a wounded Indian recovering while in the hands of white men." □ It was agreed however that any who wished to make a break for the border had the consent of the council. As soon as Jerome was back in his own lines firing was resumed by both sides.

It was still going on, but fitfully like the night of July 4th when nearly all of the fire-crackers have been exploded. However the weather that night of October 4th was not much like July 4th. The wind shook the tent in which Howard and Miles were sitting until the frost particles which had accumulated on the tent lining came loose in a shower which sparkled in the flickering candlelight.

Having made Miles easy about receiving credit for a successful campaign, Howard went on to reassure him about the threat of Sitting Bull and the large band of Sioux camped just across the border. He explained that by mid-morning Sturgis with all of the troops, artillery, entrenching tools and baggage wagons would be camped two hours' ride to the southward in a direct line with the supposed site of Sitting Bull's camp. The combined forces of Miles and Sturgis were much too powerful for the remnant of the Wallamwatkins and the Sioux. For one thing the Sioux would need all of their ammunition for the winter's hunting. A drawn battle with the army might exhaust their supply and the season was so far advanced that it was doubtful if they could get any more. Howard also suggested that Sturgis' arrival in the vicinity the next day might put Joseph in a mood to talk surrender.

About noon the next day white flags were passing back and forth between the two camps. Joseph could see that there was no hope of aid from Sitting Bull. His own people had passed the limit of their endurance. Further resistance would be futile. As Joseph later explained it, probably to a military board of investigation:

□ "I could not bear to see my wounded men and women suffer any longer. We had lost enough already. Colonel Miles had promised that we might return to our country with what stock we had left. I thought we could start again. I believed Colonel Miles or I never would have surrendered. I have heard that he has been censured for making the promise to return us to Lapwai. He could not have made any other terms with me at that time. I would have held him in check until my friends came to my assistance. Then none of the soldiers would have left Bear Paw Mountain alive." □

Through the years which followed Miles worked his way up to the maximum number of shoulder-strap stars. Inevitably he ran into criticism from the War Department at various times. On one such occasion Miles' campaign against Joseph was brought into the limelight and given a second look. In the above quoted speech Joseph's arm was extended in fierce protection for the man who had conquered him and his people. That's how an Indian really carries a grudge. That's the true Indian.

On October 5th at two-twenty P.M. all firing ceased. At four P.M. Joseph rode out of his camp accompanied by a guard of five warriors and ascended a hill where Howard, Miles, three junior officers and an interpreter were waiting. One of the officers, acting adjutant Lieutenant Wood had provided himself with writing materials so that he could take down verbatim Joseph's speech of surrender.

As Joseph rode up, his head was bowed, but he straightened when he swung off the saddle. Flinging out his arm to full length he offered his rifle to Howard. Howard smiled and motioned to him to give it to Miles. Joseph complied. Turning to the interpreter he said:

□ "Tell General Howard I know what is in his heart. What he told me before, I have in my heart. I am tired of fighting. Our chiefs are killed. Looking Glass is dead. Tulhulhutsut is dead. The old men are all dead. It is the young men who say yes or no. He* who led on the young men is dead. It is cold and we have no blankets. The little children are freezing to death. My people, some of them, have run away to the hills, and have no blankets, no food; no one knows where they are—perhaps freezing to death. I want to have time to look for my children and see how many of them I can find. Maybe I shall find them

* Alokut, Joseph's younger brother.

among the dead. Hear me, my chiefs. I am tired; my heart is sick and sad. From where the sun now stands I will fight no more, forever." □

Joseph held out his empty hands. His head and wrists showed cuts made by grazing bullets. He wore a gray woolen shawl pierced by four or five bullet holes. His buckskin shirt and leggings had a dozen more bullet holes. His face between the heavy braids of black hair was expressionless. Then his face lighted with a sad little smile as he shook each proffered hand, turned and entered the tent provided for him.

During the rest of the afternoon a straggling line of Indians with their rifles and the remnant of their wretched ponies struggled through the snow into Miles' camp. That spectacle wrought a change in Miles' hard heart, already weakened by Howard's generosity and confidence where confidence was little deserved. It was like breaking through a prison wall and admitting the light of love. Months later Miles showed this when he took issue with the Secretary of War on behalf of Joseph and the survivors of his band.

That night in the deep dusk White Bird and one hundred and three warriors and women escaped through Miles' picket line, reached the border and joined Sitting Bull. Other fugitives sought refuge with the Gros Ventre and the Assiniboines by whom they were either murdered or driven to the wintry hills. This on a larger scale was what Joseph had feared might happen were he to throw his whole band upon the mercy of Sitting Bull.

In his final report of the campaign to the Secretary of War Miles wrote: □ "The Nez Perce are the boldest men and best marksmen of any Indians I have ever encountered and Chief Joseph is a man of more sagacity and intelligence than any Indian I have ever met. He counseled against the war and against the usual cruelties practiced by Indians. He is far more humane than such Indians as Crazy Horse and Sitting Bull." □

As soon as camp could be broken, travois made and places cleared in the wagons to transport the sick and wounded soldiers and Indians, the march to the Missouri River was begun. It was slow because of halts to bury those who died along the way. At the Missouri the steamer *Benton* ferried the column across. Howard dispersed his various cavalry units to the posts and forts from which they had come to join him. With the disabled and his artillery and infantry battalions he embarked on the *Benton* for St. Louis and eventual return to Fort Vancouver in Washington. To Miles he entrusted the Indians with a formal order:

□

"Col. Nelson A. Miles
Fifth Infantry, Commanding District of the Yellowstone.

COLONEL: On account of the cost of transportation of the Nez Perce prisoners to the Pacific coast, I deem it best to retain them all at some place within your district where they can be kept under military control till next spring. Then UNLESS YOU RECEIVE INSTRUCTIONS FROM A HIGHER AUTHORITY, you are hereby directed to have them sent under proper guard to my department where I will take charge of them and carry out the instructions I have already received.

O. O. Howard"

□

Miles wrote the Secretary of War in part "I acted on what I supposed was the original design of the government—to place these Indians on their reservation. And so informed them. I also sent assurances to the war parties that were out and those who had escaped that they would be taken to Tongue River (Fort Keogh), retained for a time and sent across the mountains as soon as weather permitted in the spring. They cheerfully complied."

YELLOW WOLF'S STORY

OF

THE SURRENDER

Forty-eight Hours from Freedom

It was early dawn next morning when two men left camp to scout ahead. Started long before the families had packs ready to go. It was cold, and a storm looked gathering. I remained after all had gone—after the rear guards had gone—to watch back on the trail. During that day I saw no white man.

But those two warriors scouting ahead, after crossing the mountain, found Walk-around Sioux Indians camping. The scouts took our camp below them a short way.

There was friendly visiting that night.

Next morning (Sept. 29), not early, the camp moved. No white men were seen by scouts ahead. We guarded the back trail, but saw no signs of soldiers. We knew distance to Canadian line. Knew how long it would take to travel there. But there was no hurrying by Chief Looking Glass, leader since crossing the big river (Missouri).

About noon the families came to where camp was to be made. The scouts knew and had several buffalo killed on the campground. The name of this place is Tsanim Alikos Pah (Place of Manure Fire). Only scarce brushwood, but buffalo chips in plenty. There are other places in Montana of same name. With horses' feet mostly sick (tender) and lots of grass, the chiefs ordered, "We camp here until tomorrow forenoon."

It was afternoon when I reached camp. Of course some young warriors were out on buttes and ridges watching if enemies might be near. But we expected none. We knew General Howard was more than two suns back on our trail. It was nothing hard to keep ahead of him.

Next morning (Sept. 30), not too early, while some were still eating breakfast, two scouts came galloping from the south, from the direction we had come. As they drew near, they called loudly. "Stampeding buffaloes! Soldiers! Soldiers!"

Some families had packs partly ready and horses caught. But Chief Looking Glass, now head of camp, mounted his horse and rode around ordering, "Do not hurry! Go slow! Plenty, plenty time. Let children eat all wanted!"

This slowed the people down.

The two Indians who brought the alarm had been visiting at the Walk-around camp. Did not follow the families until next morning. Coming, they saw a herd of buffalo stampeding and knew soldiers must be near. One of these men was Tom Hill.

Because of Chief Looking Glass, we were caught.

It was about one hour later when a scout was seen coming from the same direction. He was running his horse to its best. On the highest bluff he circled about and waved the blanket signal: "Enemies right on us! Soon the attack!"

A wild stir hit the people. Great hurrying everywhere. I was still in my uncle's camp, my home. I saw this uncle, Chief Joseph, leap to the open. His voice was above all the noise as he called, "Horses! Horses! Save the horses!"

I grabbed my rifle and cartridge belts and ran with others for our horses. Warriors were hurrying to the bluffs to meet the soldiers. Soon, from the south came a noise—a rumble like stampeding buffaloes. Reaching the higher ground north of our camp I looked back. Hundreds of soldiers charging in two wide, circling wings. They were surrounding our camp. I saw Sioux or Cheyenne Indians taking lead ahead of soldiers. I ran a short distance, then heard the rifle reports. I stopped. Turning, I saw soldiers firing at everybody. I could get none of the horses. All running from guns.

I grew tired, could run no more. But continuing, I walked

where bullets were flying. Then I came nearer the camp. An Indian called to me he had caught one horse. Indians were not shooting much. Soldiers were firing, hurrying to corral us, to hold us in camp.

Other Indians were out among the horses, not trapped by the circling soldiers. I mounted the horse the man gave me and raced to where those Nez Perce were. Maybe we could still catch a few horses.

I saw an Indian riding a swift horse out where some women were helping catch horses. He looked to be one of General Howard's Lemhi (Bannack) scouts. He was bothering those women, trying to kill them. I grew mad and went after that Indian. I could not catch him, but drove him back among the soldiers.

I well knew the Indian sign language. I can talk to all the tribes. I saw, one hundred steps away, a brave Nez Perce warrior, Heyoom Iklakit (Grizzly Bear Lying Down). He was talking signs with the chief of General Howard's (Mile's) Cheyenne-Sioux scouts. At head of his warriors, that Cheyenne chief rode toward Heyoom Iklakit, who threw him the command, "Stop right there! You are helping the soldiers. You have a red skin, red blood. You must be crazy! You are fighting your friends. We are Indians. We are humans. Do not help the whites!"

The Cheyenne chief stopped as told. He answered by signs: "Do not talk more. Stop right there! I will never shoot you. I will shoot in the air. There are twenty more of us down below here."

Ending the sign talking, Heyoom Iklakit called to the Nez Perce, "He is our friend and will not shoot us. He will shoot in the air!"

All the Nez Perce knew about this. None of us believed the Cheyennes or Sioux would shoot at us.

Heyoom Iklakit left his horse and came up the canyon towards the camp to help fight the soldiers. He knew he was sure to die! The soldiers killed him about fifty steps from where he dismounted. I saw him killed.

The Cheyenne chief lied to Heyoom. He rode south about forty steps from where he had talked, and met a Nez Perce woman mounted. He caught her bridle and with his six-shooter shot and killed the woman. I saw her fall to the ground. We shot at that Cheyenne from where we were. But he was a wise Indian, and we could not hit him.

We now went up toward the butte, past the soldiers who were right below us. There were about twenty of us who took position on a small ridge. We were only a little way from the soldiers. We had a fight. We stood strong in the battle. We met those soldiers bullet for bullet. We held those soldiers from advancing.

We drove them back. One Indian was killed here and a short distance away another Nez Perce was killed.

Then we went out from that hole! We saw that same Cheyenne chief going toward our camp. He had about thirty Indians with him, and we thought he would be killing more women. We held a short council: "We will go back and save our women."

Three of us rode and headed them off. There were several soldiers back of the Cheyennes and Sioux. I was on a bad horse. One I could not manage. He ran away with me, going towards the soldiers. The Cheyennes and soldiers all ran back. The Cheyenne chief who killed the lone woman turned and ran his horse from me. This was the last time I saw him.

Here the narrator paused for a moment, and with a tinge of bitterness, remarked:

In one way I can not see why the calling of the many different tribes to help fight us. We did not call help! We did not ask others to lead us in fight! The way I look at it, we did not make war with any of those tribes. Our war was with the whites. Started by General Howard at our Lapwai council. As I see it, my story can not tell why those Indians were in the battles, why helping the soldiers. Their joining, it became not like war with whites alone. It cannot seem right to me.

This battle continued all that sun, mostly around the camp. I did what I could on the outside with other warriors. But we could not charge close on the soldiers. They were too many for us. The big guns, also, the soldiers had.

A bad mistake was made by Husishusis Kute* during this sun's fighting. Three brave warriors, Koyehkown, Kowwaspo, and Peopeo Ipsewahk (Lone Bird) were in a washout southeast of camp. They were too far toward the enemy line. Husishusis thought them enemy Indians and killed them all. He had a magazine rifle and was a good shot. With every shot he would say, "I got one!" or "I got him!"

Lean Elk (Poker Joe) was also killed by mistake. A Nez Perce saw him across a small canyon, mistook him for one of the enemies, and shot him.

Four good warriors killed by friends through mistake. Four brave men lost the first day.

The Last Stand: Bear's Paw Battlefield

EVENING CAME, and the battle grew less. Darkness settled and mostly the guns died away. Only occasional shots. I went up toward our camp. I did not hurry. Soldiers guarding, sitting down, two and two. Soldiers all about the camp, so that none could escape from there. A long time I watched. It was snowing. The wind was cold! Stripped for battle, I had no blanket. I lay close to the ground, crawling nearer the guard line.

It was past middle of night when I went between those guards. I was not back within the camp circle. I went first and drank some water. I did not look for food.

On the bluffs Indians with knives were digging rifle pits. Some had those broad-bladed knives (trowel bayonets) taken from soldiers at the Big Hole. Down in the main camp women with camas hooks were digging shelter pits. All this for tomorrow's coming.

Shelter pits for the old, the women, the children.

---

* Also spelled Hush-hush-cute.

Rifle pits for the warriors, the fighters.

You have seen hail, sometimes, leveling the grass. Indians were so leveled by the bullet hail. Most of our few warriors left from the Big Hole had been swept as leaves before the storm. Chief Alokut, Lone Bird, and Lean Elk were gone.

Outside the camp I had seen men killed. Soldiers ten, Indians ten. That was not so bad. But now, when I saw our remaining warriors gone, my heart grew choked and heavy. Yet the warriors and no-fighting men killed were not all. I looked around.

Some were burying their dead.

A young warrior, wounded, lay on a buffalo robe dying without complaint. Children crying with cold. No fire. There could be no light. Everywhere the crying, the death wail.

My heart became fire. I joined the warriors digging rifle pits. All the rest of night we worked. Just before dawn, I went down among the shelter pits. I looked around. Children no longer crying. In deep shelter pits they were sleeping. Wrapped in a blanket, a still form lay on the buffalo robe. The young warrior was dead. I went back to my riffe pit, my blood hot for war. I felt not the cold.

Morning came, bringing the battle anew. Bullets from everywhere! A big gun throwing bursting shells. From rifle pits, warriors returned shot for shot. Wild and stormy, the cold wind was thick with snow. Air filled with smoke of powder. Flash of guns through it all. As the hidden sun traveled upward, the war did not weaken.

I felt the coming end. All for which we had suffered lost!

McWhorter's Observation:

Frequent pauses had marked Yellow Wolf's description of the battle thus far, and at this point came a break of several minutes. With no visible emotion, warrior and interpreter sat silent, gazing toward the desert hills beyond the Nez Perce camp at the river's side. When at last Yellow Wolf resumed his story, it was in the same low, evenly modulated tone—generally tinged with sadness, but with an unusual degree of rhetoric:

Thought came of the Wallowa where I grew up. Of my own country when only Indians were there. Of tepees along the bending river. Of the blue, clear lake, wide meadows with horse and cattle herds. From the mountain forests, voices seemed calling. I felt as dreaming. Not my living self.

The war deepened. Grew louder with gun reports. I raised up and looked around. Everything was against us. No hope! Only bondage or death! Something screamed in my ear. A blaze flashed before me. I felt as burning! Then with rifle I stood forth, saying to my heart, "Here I will die, fighting for my people and our homes!"

Soldiers could see me. Bullets hummed by me, but I was untouched. The warriors called, "Heinmot! Come back back to this pit. You will be killed!"

I did not listen. I did not know if I killed any soldiers. To do well in battle you must see what you want to shoot. You glimpse an enemy in hiding and shoot. If no more shots from there, you know you have succeeded.

I felt not afraid. Soldier rifles from shelters kept popping fast. Their big gun boomed often but not dangerous. The warriors lying close in dugout pits could not be hit. I know not why the shells never struck our rifle pits on the bluffs.

The sun drew on, and about noon the soldiers put up the white flag. The Indians said, "That is good! That means, 'Quit the war.' "

But in short minutes we could see no soldiers. Then we understood.

Soldiers quit the fight to eat dinner!

No Indian warrior thought to eat that noon. He never thinks to eat when in battle or dangerous places. But not so the soldier. Those soldiers could not stand the hunger pain. After dinner they pulled down their white flag.

That flag did not count for peace.

The fight was started again by the soldiers after stopping their hunger. There was shooting all the rest of that second sun's battle. Stronger cold, thicker snow came with darkness. No sleeping in warm tepees. No eating warm food. Only at times was there shooting during the night.

It came morning, third sun of battle. The rifle shooting went on just like play. Nobody being hurt. But soon Chief Looking Glass was killed. Some warriors in same pit with him saw at a distance a horseback Indian. Thinking he must be a Sioux from Sitting Bull, one pointed and called to Looking Glass: "Look! A Sioux!"

Looking Glass stepped quickly from the pit. Stood on the bluff unprotected. It must have been a sharpshooter killed him. A bullet struck his left forehead, and he fell back dead.

That horseback Indian was a Nez Perce.

In the afternoon of this sun we saw the white flag again go up in the soldier camp. Then was heard a voice calling in a strange language, "General (Colonel) Miles would like to see Chief Joseph!"

The chiefs held council and Chief Joseph said, "Yes, I would like to see General Miles."

Tom Hill, interpreter, went to see what General Miles wanted, to tell General Miles, "Yes, Joseph would like to see you!" After some time, we saw Tom Hill with General Miles and a few men come halfway. They stopped and Tom Hill called to Chief Joseph. Chief Joseph with two or three warriors went to meet them.

I did not go where they met. I looked around. There was a hollow place off a distance in the ground. I went there and lay down. I could see General Miles where Chief Joseph met him. I could see all plainly where they stood. I was saying to myself, "Whenever they shoot Chief Joseph, *I* will shoot from here!"

There was talk for a while, and Chief Joseph and General Miles made peace. Some guns were given up. Then there was a trick. I saw Chief Joseph taken to the soldier camp a prisoner!

The white flag was pulled down!

That white flag was a lie!

The warriors came back, and right away a soldier officer

(Lieutenant Lovell H. Jerome) rode into our camp. Chief Yellow Bull yelled a warning and grabbed him. I could see them take the officer to the main shelter pit. When I saw all this—Chief Joseph taken away—I ran to where the captured soldier was being held. Held that Chief Joseph might not be hurt. He had on a yellow-colored outside coat to keep off the wet. A strong-looking young man, he did not say much. Looked around, but seemed not much afraid. I do not think he was bad scared.

The chiefs instructed the warriors to guard him. Ordered: "Treat him right! He is one of the commanders."

One man, Chuslum Hihhih (White Bull) got mad at this officer and tried to get the best of him. He said, "I want to kill this soldier!"

The Indians told him, "No, we do not want you to kill him!"

Chuslum Hihhih was mean-minded, had a bad heart. He did no great fighting. Stayed behind where bullets could not reach him. Espowyes, my relation, kept telling him, "Do not hurt the prisoner." Scolding, he said, "Don't you know Chief Joseph is prisoner on other side? We have this officer prisoner here on our side. When they turn Chief Joseph loose, we will turn our prisoner loose at the same time. For this we are holding him, to make the trade. We do not want to kill him. He might be headman of the soldiers. Don't you see soldiers on other side with guns? Why do you not shoot them? Not shoot one who is caught! You see all the warriors who do fighting are not mad at him. Why do you, who do little fighting, want to kill him?"

Chuslum Hihhih made no reply. He walked away.

We all thought Chief Joseph was not killed on the other side, so we let this officer soldier keep his own life. You know we were resting a little. Not after the soldiers, nor soldiers after us. We wanted to remain quiet a few moments.

Two men you already have names of, Wottolen and Yellow Bull, took good care of the prisoner officer. Night drew on, and he was given food. We gave him water and a safe place to sleep in. He was given plenty of blankets.

A buffalo robe for a bed to keep him warm. Nothing was taken from him. Guards watched his shelter pit all night. This, that he might not escape nor be hurt by mad Indians.

But we did not know how our Chief Joseph was being treated over there. He might be alive, or he might be killed.

When morning broke, we did not wake that officer. We let him sleep if he wanted. When he woke, he was brought water to wash hands and face. He was given breakfast and water to drink. As far as that (indicating two hundred feet), that officer could go if he liked. Walk there and back often as he pleased. The chiefs gave strong words that he must not be harmed.

It was about noon of the fourth sun when the officer took paper from his pocket and wrote. I know what he wrote. One Nez Perce understood English very well, and the officer said to him, "You must take my letter to the soldier chief!"

The officer read what he wrote on the paper, and when the Indian interpreted it to the chiefs, they said, "All right!"

This is what the interpreter said the paper told: "I had good supper, good bed. I had plenty of blankets. This morning I had good breakfast. I am treated like I was at home. I hope you officers are treating Chief Joseph as I am treated. I would like to see him treated as I am treated."

But Chief Joseph was not treated right. Chief Joseph was hobbled hands and feet. They took a double blanket. Soldiers rolled him in it like you roll papoose on cradle board. Chief Joseph could not use arms, could not walk about. He was put where there were mules, and not in soldier tent. That was how Chief Joseph was treated all night.

When soldier officers received that letter, they took hobbles off Chief Joseph. He could then walk around a little where they let him. Those officers wrote a letter to our prisoner officer. When he read it, he said, "I have not been treated like Chief Joseph!"

The officer then read from the letter, "You come across to us. When you get here, then Chief Joseph can go."

The chiefs and warriors replied to the officer, "No! If General Miles is speaking true, he will bring Chief Joseph halfway. To same ground we did that other time. It will be that, if he is speaking true words."

This letter was carried to the soldiers by the same interpreter. The soldier officers must have read it, for soon a white flag went up. Then those officers sent a letter to the Indian chiefs. It said, "Yes, we will bring Chief Joseph halfway. You bring the officer to that same place."

The chiefs said, "That is fair enough!"

Then we looked across and saw officers and Chief Joseph. They were coming to halfway ground. A buffalo robe was spread there. The chiefs and a few older warriors took our prisoner to meet them. He shook hands with Joseph and those officers. Then each party returned to its own side, Chief Joseph coming back to our camp.

The soldiers now pulled down their white flag. When the warriors saw that flag come down, they laughed. They said to each other, "Three times those soldiers lie with the white flag. We can not believe them." We younger warriors had not gone to the meeting place marked by buffalo robe.

Chief Joseph now spoke to all headmen: "I was hobbled in the soldier camp. We must fight more. The war is not quit!"

Then the fighting began again. Shot for shot whenever a soldier was seen. All that day we had the way. Those soldiers stayed at long distance. They did not try mixing us up. They did not charge against our rifle pits.

Some warriors talked to charge the soldiers and fight it out. If we whipped them, we would be free. If we could not whip, we would all be killed, and no more trouble. But others said, "No! The soldiers are too strong. There are the big guns, the cannon guns. If we are killed, we leave women and children, old people, and many wounded. We cannot charge the soldiers."

It was slowed-up fighting. Cloudy, snowy, we did not see the sun set. Full darkness coming, the fighting mostly stopped. Some shooting in darkness by soldiers, but less by Indians. The gun sounds died down as night went on.

All night we remained in those pits. The cold grew stronger. The wind was filled with snow. Only a little sleep. There might be a charge by the soldiers. The warriors watched by turns. A long night.

The Last Day: The Surrender

FINALLY THE FIFTH MORNING of the battle drew on, but no sun could be seen. With first light, the battle began again. It was bad that cannon guns should be turned on the shelter pits where were no fighters. Only women and children, old and wounded men in those pits. General Miles and his men handling the big gun surely knew no warriors were in that part of camp. The officer we had held prisoner well knew no fighting warriors were where he sheltered. Of course his business was to carry back all news he could spy out in our camp.

It was towards noon that a bursting shell struck and broke in a shelter pit, burying four women, a little boy, and a girl of about twelve snows. This girl, Atsipeeten, and her grandmother, Intetah, were both killed. The other three women and the boy were rescued. The two dead were left in the caved-in pit.

When a few Indians, mad and wild on white man's whisky, killed mean settlers on Indian lands on the Salmon River, along with one or two women and maybe one child, that was very bad.

Soldiers did not need whisky to kill a great many women and children throughout this war.

This woman and child, and Chief Looking Glass, were only ones killed in this battle after the first sun's fighting. None even wounded. All those not fighting were in the shelter pits. The warriors in rifle pits could not be seen by the soldiers. Indians are not seen in the fighting. They are hid.

The fight went on, but we did not fire continually. We thought the soldiers would get tired, maybe freeze out and charge us. We wanted plenty of ammunition for them if they did.

Darkness again settled down, and only occasional shots were

heard. These came mostly from soldiers, as if afraid we might slip up on them in their dugout forts.

That night, General Howard arrived with two of his scouts, men of our tribe. He did not see much fighting of this battle, and I think maybe he put it wrong in history. Towards noon next day we saw those two Indians coming with a white flag. Heard them calling and I understood. One of them said, "All my brothers, I am glad to see you alive this sun!"

Then the same bad man, Chuslum Hihhih, came and wanted to shoot this Indian messenger from General Howard. Chuslum Hahlap Kanoot (Naked-footed Bull) took his gun from him. Another fellow said, "Let him alone! Let him kill him!"

Hahlap Kanoot asked Chuslum Hihhih, "Why are you mad?" While we were warring, fighting, you lay on the ground, afraid! You are mean! I will take a whip after you!"

Chuslum Hihhih was again ordered to leave. He walked away.

The two Indians he was trying to kill, now speaking again, said, "We have traveled a long ways trying to catch you folks. We are glad to hear you want no more war, do not want to fight. We are all glad. I am glad because all my sons are glad to be alive. Not to go to battle any more. This speaker's name was Chojykies (Lazy). He had a daughter with Chief Joseph's warriors, was why he followed us.

The other man said, "We have come far from home. You now see many soldiers lying down side by side. We see Indians too, lying dead. I am glad today we are shaking hands. We are all not mad. We all think of Chief Joseph and these others as brothers. We see your sons and relations lying dead, but we are glad to shake hands with you today. I am glad to catch up with you and find my daughter, too, alive.

"You, my brothers, have your ears open to me. General Miles and Chief Joseph will make friends and not let each other go today. General Miles is honest-looking man. I have been with General Howard. I was afraid myself. I have been in wars and am no longer a warrior.

"Listen well what I say. I heard General Howard telling, 'When I catch Chief Joseph, I will bring him back to his own home.'

"Do not be afraid! General Miles said, 'Tell Joseph we do not have any more war!' "

Chief Joseph sent those two Indians back where they belonged. Then there was a council. Some of us said to Chief Joseph, "We are afraid if you go with General Howard he will hang you. You know how he destroyed our property, our homes."

Then Espowyes spoke, "I understand every word. If General Howard tries to take us, we will not go with him. All you farmers who had property destroyed feel bad over it. Feel bad because the whites may talk to General Howard, and he will hang us. We should get something out of our destroyed property. Get pay for our homes and lands taken from us."

We heard and believed the words of Espowyes to be true. It must be that we get some pay for our property lost and destroyed.

All feared to trust General Howard and his soldiers.

General Howard we now saw standing, calling loud to know why the Indians were not coming.

All Indians said, "General Howard does not look good. He is mean acting!"

Then came again those two Indians from the soldier camp. They carried a white flag, and General Miles had told them to say to us: "I want to speak to Chief Joseph."

I heard this message, and I heard Chief Joseph make reply, "We will have council over this. We will decide what to do!"

There was a council, and the main messenger talked this way: "Those generals said tell you: 'We will have no more fighting.' Your chiefs and some of your warriors are not seeing the truth. We sent our officer to appear before your Indians—sent all our messengers to say to them, "We will have no more war!"

Then our man, Chief Joseph, spoke, "You see, it is true. I did not say 'Let's quit!'

"General Miles said, 'Let's quit.'

"And now General Howard says, 'Let's quit.'

"You see, it is true enough! I did not say 'Let's quit!' "

When the warriors heard those words from Chief Joseph, they answered, "Yes, we believe you now."

So when General Miles's messengers reported back to him, the answer was, "Yes."

Then Chief Joseph and other chiefs met General Miles on halfway ground. Chief Joseph and General Miles were talking good and friendly when General Howard came speaking loud, commanding words. When General Miles saw this, he held the Indians back from him a little. He said, "I think soon General Howard will forget all this. I will take you to a place for this winter; then you can go to your old home."

Chief Joseph said, "Now we all understand these words, and we will go with General Miles. He is a headman, and we will go with him."

General Miles spoke to Chief Joseph, "No more battles and blood! From this sun, we will have good time on both sides, your band and mine. We will have plenty time for sleep, for good rest. We will drink good water from this time on where the war is stopped."

"Same is here," General Howard said. "I will have time from now on, like you, to rest. The war is all quit." He was in a better humor. General Howard spoke to Chief Joseph, "You have your life. I am living. I have lost my brothers. Many of you have lost brothers, maybe more than on our side. I do not know. Do not worry any more. While you see this many soldiers living from the war, you think of them as your brothers. Many brothers of yours—they are my brothers—living from the war.

"Do not worry about starving. It is plenty of food we have left from this war. Any one who needs a sack of flour, anything the people want, come get it. All is yours."

The chiefs and officers crossed among themselves and shook hands all around. The Indians lifted their hands towards the sky, where the sun was then standing. This said: "No more battles! No more war!"

That was all I saw and heard of chiefs' and generals' ending the war.

General Miles was good to the surrendered Indians with food. The little boys and girls loved him for that. They could now have hot food and fires to warm by.

What I heard those generals and chiefs say, I have always remembered. But those generals soon forgot their promises. Chief Joseph and his people were not permitted to return to their own homes.

We were not captured. It was a draw battle. We did not expect being sent to Eeikish Pah (Hot Place). Had we known this we never would have surrendered. We expected to be returned to our own homes. This was promised us by General Miles. That was how he got our rifles from us. It was the only way he could get them.

The fighting was done. All who wanted to surrender took their guns to General Miles and gave them up. Those who did not want to surrender, kept their guns. The surrender was just for those who did not longer want to fight. Joseph spoke only for his own band, what they wanted to do. Of the other bands, they surrendered who wanted to.

Chief White Bird did not surrender.

When Chief Joseph surrendered, war was quit, everything was quit, for those who surrendered their guns.

One side of war story is that told by the white man.

The story I have given you is the Indian side. You now have it all, as concerned the war.

I did not surrender my rifle.

10 PUNISHMENT IN EEIKISH PAH (HELL)

WITHIN TEN DAYS AFTER THE ARRIVAL OF JOSEPH AND HIS PEOPLE at Fort Keogh orders came from "a higher authority" to send the Indians eight hundred miles by steamer to Fort Lincoln, (near Bismarck) North Dakota. The reason? Subsistence would be cheaper there.

Because the water was too shallow for steamboat travel, and no steamboat was available, Miles ordered that fourteen flat boats be provided for the old people, the women and children. Joseph and the warriors travelled on horseback. All were under guard. Miles saw to it that there was plenty of wholesome food for everybody. Some game was killed along the way.

When the flatboats had reached the Mandan Agency, the officer in charge tied up to the shore for two hours while he requisitioned supplies for the Wallamwatkins. During that period the Nez Perce and the Mandans looked each other over like strange cats in a garret. After they had re-embarked one old Nez Perce said to the officer:

□" 'Those Mandans back there are bad Indians.'

"The officer inquired why.

"The old man replied 'Because they stole two Nez Perce blankets.'

"The officer was sincerely sympathetic. Then on second thought he asked if the Nez Perce had taken anything that belonged to the Mandans. The old man chirped:

" 'Oh yes, we got away with four buffalo robes.' " □

The people of Bismarck received the Wallamwatkins with cordiality and kindness. The Indians responded. For a few days everyone was happy. Then came an order from the Secretary of War directing that Joseph and his people be sent by train to

Fort Leavenworth, Kansas. During November they arrived in the hot, malarial bottomlands at Leavenworth. The Nez Perce were accustomed to the cold dry climate of a mountain plateau and to pure water. At Leavenworth they had to drink the muddy water of the Missouri. It didn't agree with them. Neither did the humid atmosphere. Many of them sickened and died. In vain Joseph protested. Colonel Miles protested to Secretary of War McCrary:

□ "As these people have been hitherto loyal to the government and friends of the white race from the time their country was first explored and in their skilful campaigns have spared hundreds of lives and thousands of dollars worth of property that they might have destroyed; and as they have in my opinion been grossly wronged in years past, have lost most of their warriors, their homes, property and everything except a small amount of clothing, I have the honor to recommend that ample provision be made for their civilization and to enable them to become self-sustaining. They are sufficiently intelligent to appreciate the consideration which in my opinion is justly due them from the government." □

This plea was also in vain. For a Bad Spirit* who lived behind a mask had written to the Secretary of War, "They should never again be allowed to return to Oregon or to Lapwai."

In July of 1878 Joseph and his diminishing band were ordered to the Quapaw Reservation in the Indian Territory reserved for them by Congress. It lay on both banks of the Salt Fork of the Arkansas River. Only four hundred and ten Wallamwatkins had survived. Of them, two hundred and sixty were ill with malaria contracted at Fort Leavenworth. Soon afterward one hundred died. The state of health of the survivors became so desperate that E. A. Hoyt, Commissioner of Indian Affairs, visited Joseph and took him along on a search for a healthier reservation. In his annual report Hoyt stated in part:

---

* The Indian idiom for describing some hostile person whose identity is unknown.

† "The Nez Perce are very much superior to the Osages and Pawnees in the Indian Territory. They are even brighter than the Poncas. Care should be taken to place them where they will thrive." *

Mr. Hoyt had the distinction of being the first white man to perceive that the Nez Perce were a national asset rather than a liability.

Of the reservations visited, Joseph preferred that of the Poncas, although there were no mountains or rivers and the streams were warm. Among the people living there the mortality rate was high. In June of 1879 Joseph's people were removed to the Ponca Reservation and assigned to a portion amounting to over ninety thousand acres. The mortality rate of the Nez Perce soon equalled that of the Poncas. Before that removal, Joseph, with Yellow Bull, made a journey to Washington to plead with President Hayes for justice to his people. The journey was made possible through the intervention of General McNeill. Joseph afterward met a magazine reporter to whom he described his experience with the Washington run-around and brush-off. The reporter gave the story to the *North American Review*. It was published in the April, 1879, issue.

† "At last I was granted permission to go to Washington accompanied by my friend Yellow Bull and our interpreter. I am glad I came. I have shaken hands with a good many friends, but there are some things I want to know which no one seems able to explain. I cannot understand why the Government sends out a man such as General Miles to fight us and then breaks his word. Such a government has something wrong about it. I cannot understand why so many chiefs are allowed to talk so many different ways and promise so many different things.

† "I have seen the Great Father Chief (President Hayes), the Next Great Chief (Secretary of the Interior), the Commissioner of Indian Affairs Chief (Hoyt), the Law Chief (General Butler) and many other law chiefs (Congressmen). They all say that

* The Hoyt Report.

they are my friends and that I shall have justice. But while all of their mouths talk right I do not understand why nothing is done for my people. I have heard talk and talk and nothing is done.

"Good words do not last long unless they amount to something. Words do not pay for my dead people. They do not pay for my country now overrun by white men. They do not protect my father's grave. They do not pay for my horses and cattle. Good words do not give me back my children. Good words will not make good the promise of your war chief, General Miles. Good words will not give my people good health and stop them from dying. Good words will not get my people a home where they can live in peace and take care* of themselves. I am tired of talk that comes to nothing. It makes my heart sick when I remember all the good words and all the broken promises. There has been too much talking by men who had no right to talk.

"Too many misinterpretations have been made. Too many misunderstandings have come up between the white men and the Indians. If the white man wants to live in peace with the Indian, he can live in peace. There need be no trouble. Treat all men alike. Give them the same laws. Give them all an even chance to live and grow.

"All men were made by the same Great Spirit Chief. They are all brothers. The earth is the mother of all people and all people should have equal rights upon it.

"You might as well expect all rivers to run backward as that any man who was born a free man should be contented, penned up and denied the liberty to go where he pleases. If you tie a horse to a stake, do you expect he will grow fat? If you pen an Indian on a small spot of earth and compel him to stay there, he will not be contented. Nor will he grow and prosper. I have asked some of the Great White Chiefs where they get their authority to say to the Indian that he shall stay in one place

* Be self-supporting instead of depending on a handout from the government.

while he sees white men going where they please. They cannot tell me.

"I ask only of the Government to be treated as all other men are treated. If I cannot go to my own home, let me have a home in a country where my people will not die so fast. I would like to go to Bitter Root Valley. There my people would be happy. Where they are now they are dying. Three have died since I left my camp to come to Washington.

"When I think of our condition, my heart is heavy. I see men of my own race treated as outlaws and driven out of the country or shot down like animals. I know that my race must change their way of life. We cannot hold our own with white men as we are. We ask only a chance to live as other men live. We ask to be recognized as men. We ask that the same law shall work alike on all men. If an Indian breaks the law, punish him. If a white man breaks the law, punish him also.

"Let me be a free man, free to travel, free to stop, free to work, free to trade where I choose, free to choose my own teachers, free to follow the religion of my fathers, free to talk, think and act for myself and I will obey every law or submit to the penalty. For this time the Indian race is waiting and praying. I hope no more groans of wounded men and women will go to the ear of the Great Spirit Chief above and that all people may be one people.

"Thunder Rolling in the Mountains has spoken for his people." †

In 1881 Indian agent Jordan reported that the Wallamwatkins numbered three hundred and twenty-eight and that there had been few births.

† "Sunday morning November 17, 1878, Chief Joseph first met Mr. Grover, formerly governor of Oregon. Through his political power Grover had forced President Grant to revoke his order granting Wallowa to the Wallamwatkins as their own reservation. Since that time Grover had been elected U. S. Senator from Oregon. At Washington he had been nominated to chairmanship

of a commission appointed to investigate Joseph's claim that his people could not live on the land in Indian Territory (Oklahoma) to which they had been assigned. They wished to return to Oregon." †

Grover began with: † "Chief Joseph, we are here for the purpose of hearing any complaints you may have in order that we may take them to Washington. We are your friends. We shall try to see that justice is done you. Tell us the truth." †

Joseph nodded, † "I do not like this country. I have seen enough of it since I have been kept in it. I have lost eighty of my people. I am afraid of this country. We must all die if we stay here. When I stopped fighting I surrendered to Howard and Miles. I wished for peace. At that surrender we came to a true understanding. We supposed we were to be sent to our own country, but we were brought down here." †

† "Why do the people in Washington hesitate to carry out their agreements? Our country is very dear to us. We never committed murder. We never did anything to justify you in taking our lands away from us. We gave no trouble in the north until our lands had been taken from us and we had been driven from them." †

† "I can say that all of my people who were lost were lost in a good cause, defending their homes. We ought not to be forced into a country not fitted by climate to our health, a place where we cannot live—where the country will not let us live. Besides this is a poor country. I see nothing here. In a good country I would see my people prosper and multiply. Wherever you see grass growing thickly there you find rich people. Here it does not grow at all and all are poor." †

In the tone of a school master reprimanding a sulky pupil Senator Grover spoke again:

† "Joseph, I come from Oregon. I know the land where you used to live on Snake River. The white people have now settled all over that country. Your father lived there. He refused to give up that land when you were a boy. When the treaty was made, it was made without his assent and without your consent. Your

father refused to leave this land. You refused to leave it. You said 'I will not go away. I will defend my country with my warriors.' The Great Father at Washington said there was the treaty. You said there was no treaty in which you ever joined." †

† "The white men had more warriors than you and here you are. The white men now occupy all your country. You cannot return to that land. Is there any other land in this country which you like better than this? Where do you wish to go? Where do you wish to live?" †

Joseph replied: † "All you have said is true. From the advice I had from my father I could think of no lawful or just way in which our lands could be taken from us, nor by what right the government could order us off of them. That land was the gift of the Great Spirit and sacred to us. If we may not go to our own home, give us a home further north where it is more healthy. Here there is nothing but death day by day. That is all I have to say." †

Grover asked: † " 'Where do you want to go and settle?'

" 'I would like to go up the Sun River on Jappa Reservation on the Upper Columbia River.'

"Senator Grover showed that he knew how to make an election day promise when he declaimed:

" 'We will use our influence to get you settled upon that reservation. Every white person here this morning is your friend. I am sure that everyone here has felt pained by the sad story you have told. The authorities at Washington are your friends. I am sorry that all of the people in the United States could not be here this morning to hear your sad story. You have made friends of us all and we will speak for you. If you have any complaints to make of your agent, you can do so now and we will report it to the government.'

"Joseph considered a moment, 'As soon as I arrived here I began to watch the agent so as to learn his ways and to see what kind of a man he is. It appears that the agent has given me a half of what is due me and has been keeping the other half for himself. I have not made complaints against him because

I have had hopes of getting out of this country and going somewhere else where we could sustain ourselves. When we first arrived here we were supplied regularly, but it is very irregular now. I do not know how much is allowed at Washington. Every two or three days we do not have enough to eat. I never get medicine regularly. I never had a full supply. The people have been dying ever since we have been here. We came without medicine. The people got sick and one by one dropped off into typhoid fever and died. Now we have but three hundred and eighty-three left. The others have died of exposure.' " †

† "In the same official government report there is an explanatory statement appended as follows 'The extinction of Joseph's title to the lands held in Idaho (they were actually in Oregon and Oregon is next to Idaho) will be a matter of great gain to the white settlers in that vicinity and a reasonable compensation should be made to him for their surrender. Joseph and his followers have shown themselves to be brave men and skillful soldiers who with one exception have observed the rules of civilized warfare. These Indians were encroached upon by white settlers on soil they believed to be their own. When these encroachments became intolerable, they were compelled in their own estimation to take up arms.' " †

In this appendage the happy balancing of exultation and melancholy for the sad fate of Joseph's people suggests the fine hand of sympathetic Senator Grover.

† "In 1883 the Rev. A. L. Lindsay made an investigation among the settlers in the Salmon Valley to bring back the scattered Wallamwatkins, some of whom were in Canada. The Attorney General of the United States advised a suspension of all action (against the Indians). The Idaho court complied, but made clear that it was a suspension only. 'The return of those indicted men free will not escape the court.' It was also rumored along the Salmon River that if any of the Wallamwatkins should return, they would be shot on sight by the settlers.

"Lack of unity became the fatal weakness of Indian resistance to the white men's invasions." † Joseph's comment was: □ "The greatest want of the Indians is a system of laws by which controversies between Indians and Indians, and Indians and white men can be settled without appealing to physical force. The want of law is the greatest source of disorder among Indians." □

The recommendations of Indian agents and the pleadings of white friends during the next four years finally stirred Congress to act on behalf of the Wallamwatkins. In the spring of 1885 the remnant of the band, numbering two hundred and sixty eight, were returned to the Northwest by railroad, the Union Pacific and the Oregon Shortline. At Pocatello they were met by Captain Frank Baldwin. He divided them into two parties. One hundred and eighteen were sent under military escort to the Lapwai Reservation in northern Idaho. The remaining one hundred and fifty including Joseph were assigned to Nespelem on the Colville Reservation, State of Washington. This was the last and perhaps the unkindest cut of all. To the Indian the separation forever of a tribal band into two communities many miles apart was comparable to the concomitant deaths of several members of a large, congenial white family.

Joseph ended his days on the Colville Reservation in Nespelem, Washington, on September 21, 1904. It is believed that he died of a broken heart.

YELLOW WOLF'S STORY
OF
PUNISHMENT IN EEIKISH PAH

Flight to the Sioux

You ask me to tell what I know after the war, the things that I have done. It is nothing but the facts—what I have seen, what I have done—that I will tell you. It is of my own hands, my own eyes, that I will tell you.

After Chief Joseph surrendered, all warriors who wanted to go with him gave up their guns, or cached them. Soldiers issued rations. When deep darkness came, Chief White Bird and his people walked out from that camp. They made for Chief Sitting Bull's Camp.

Chief White Bird and his band did not surrender!

Near morning came, and Chief Joseph said to me: "You better go find your mother and my daughter. Bring them here!"

That would be good, I thought, seeing my mother. The first sun of the fighting, my mother and my uncle's (Chief Joseph's) daughter made escape. Yes, I would go find them.

I stood with blanket about me, with rifle inside my legging. Not a long rifle, this that I fought with. I had both cartridge belts under my shirt. I would not stay! I would not go with the people, wherever the soldiers took them. Nor would I hide myself about that battlefield.

During the night soldier guards were all about us. Only the guards; all other soldiers sleeping. I waited until just breaking morning. My mind was made up what to do. I would not hide myself. I would walk out past those guards. They would see me, and if they tried stopping me, that would be good. I would kill them both.

I watched but pretended not seeing them. They did not bother me. Maybe just thought, "Damn Injun going after something. He will be back!" But I went out from everybody. Away from everybody!

There was some inches snow. With my moccasins bad worn, I thought, "This will kill me!" I kept going. Headed for a canyon where one horse was hid. A lot of Nez Perce were somewhere ahead of me. I must find them! I got the horse and went on.

Came full morning, but I saw no one anywhere. Later, I noticed signs of people. I came to the half bloods on Milk River. They treated me fine. Boys watched my horse while he grazed. Knowing I was hungry, they gave me food aplenty. They gave me new moccasins, for my feet were part naked. They directed me how to find my people.

I traveled on, but saw no trace of my friends. If they had passed that way their trail was buried in the blizzard's snow. Came the sunset, but that sun had not been shining. I thought to find some sheltered place to camp. I went on. But my tired horse was slow. Soon I saw Indians in the distance. They were camping! I could not tell if Walk-around Sioux. But those Indians, they knew what kind they were. I got scared! I hid from them!

Then I looked at my magazine rifle. It was loaded. I knew I had two belts well filled with cartridges. One around my waist, one across my shoulder, just as in war. Those cartridges about me, I thought, "I am the same as ten men!" I found myself and came out from hiding. In good view of those Indians I rode towards them. They did nothing. Only watched me, about a quarter mile distant. Then I saw plainly.

They were Nez Perce, my friends! I drew closer and saw women and children among them. I saw my brother (cousin) Lahpeealoot (Two Flocks on Water). There must have been forty, maybe fifty, Nez Perce there.

My mother came to me and said, "Somebody told me you were dead!"

Then I saw my mother, that she had been crying. I answered her, "It is not true! I will sometime get sick and die. The rifle will never kill me. I am saying to you *three times,* I will not die of the gun."

My mother answered me, "When I heard that you lay killed, I had painful feelings about you. My heart grew heavy, but you are alive and with me."

Then my mother laughed. I was happy. Chief Joseph's daughter was also there.

These Nez Perce with horses they could get were headed for Chief Sitting Bull in Canada. Gathered where they were just a few at a time. While catching horses at beginning of battle they had been trapped by soldiers. Cut out from the camp. Many had no blankets. Barefooted, half naked. The Milk River half bloods had helped them out. Gave them moccasins and clothes.

Next morning my mother said to me, "Your horse is here." That raised my feelings. My mother said my horse was tied to a tree, and I went. There was my horse that I took from the soldiers. Chestnut-sorrel horse. I laughed over my horse! I put the bridle on him. I felt just as if flying! My mother told me, "Here is your blanket!" That blanket the half bloods had given her.

We all then went. I would not take my mother and Chief Joseph's daughter back to the soldiers. I said nothing. Traveling that day, we kept scouts back on trail guarding against pursuing soldiers. Night drawing on, we stopped to camp. We hobbled our horses. We built a fire, for it was cold and snowy. We were not through supper, when the horses suddenly stampeded.

All the people jumped and ran from the firelight. I leaped out and lay down in the darkness. I threw a cartridge into the firing chamber of my rifle. I held ready. Whoever showed at that fire would be killed. I heard nothing. Lying still for a while, I called to the people, "Come on! Nothing here!"

Of course it was dark where they were hidden, and after a

little while they returned to the fire. When they reached the light and could see, they laughed at each other. One of the boys said, "This kid is hungry!"

When we ran from the fire, the little supper we had was left there. A boy, maybe of twelve snows, did not leave the fire. Nobody had had anything to eat for about three suns, and that child ate everything up. That was why the people laughed when they saw what he had done. That boy was hungry.

From this place we moved each sun for two suns. Stormy dark, we could not tell direction to go. Often traveled wrong way. It was the second sun, a little past noon, we crossed the border into Canada. In the evening we camped, and next morning, the third sun, we had not gone far when we saw Indians coming. At quite a distance one of those Indians threw a sign:

"What Indians are you?"

"Nez Perce," one of our men answered. Then he signed, "Who are you?"

"Sioux," was the reply.

"Come on," one of our men signed. "We will have smoke ready!"

We knew that some time ago we had trouble with the Sioux, so we must smoke. The Sioux rode up to where we sat on the ground. They got off their horses and sat around as we did. When they sat down, I noticed one to be a woman. Her hair was parted in the center.

All smoked but me. In sign language we asked, "How far to your camp?"

"Must be about one quarter sun ride," was answered.

We got on our horses and followed the Sioux. They rode fast, horses loping all the way. One Sioux rode ahead, fast as his horse would go. He was taking news to the other Sioux. The Sioux came to meet us, maybe halfway. We could see them coming, and we made a mount (line of defense).

But the Sioux mixed us up. They took us one by one. The women and children were separated from the men. I knew we never were friends to the Sioux Indians, and it must be they meant to kill us. This I well understood, and I had my rifle ready.

When we came only a little ways from the camp, we saw smoke from many tepees of the Sioux. For eight or ten miles they seemed strung. I thought to myself, "There is quite a number of Sioux Indians!" Going closer, I could see down the canyon. Nothing But Sioux tepees.

It was yet early morning when they took us scattering, in different tepees. When I was brought to one tepee, I saw Lahpeealoot was there. We sat down. Nice place fixed up! Then I looked at one Sioux. He was making a smoke. He got up with pipe in hand, and I said in sign, 'No!"

He threw a sign at me, "What is the reason you do not want to smoke?"

I answered back, "When I was little, I did not smoke."

"You must have something in you, you do not smoke?"

I answered him, "No! It is bad habit!"

He said to me again, "You must smoke!"

"No!" I answered him.

"What you want, you do not smoke? Maybe you want fight?"

I threw the sign, "Sioux Indian, I will tell you what!"

He answered, "Yes, I know what you going tell me! It is good!"

I signed, "When I was little my mother used to say to me, 'Your father is dead.' Then I would go out in night time, about middle of night, and cry. I would cry until morning! When it grew light, sun was up, I did not know how I came so. I would think to myself, 'Grizzly bear or wolf might kill me.'

"One of the men came to me and said: 'Do not be afraid.'

"I looked at him. A very fine man. He told me, 'It is nothing here dangerous.'

"I felt very good. He instructed me: 'Look at me! I whipped all the tribes around! With what I am giving you, you can do the same things I have done.'

"I do as he instructed me. Everything as directed. I am afraid of nothing in war. One of the things he told me: "Do not smoke! If you smoke, you will find yourself dead!"

"You are a Sioux. I am a Nez Perce. You do not know me. Take a good look at me. I am telling you, Sioux, three times, I will not smoke!"

The Sioux Indian answered me, "I know now the reason you do not smoke. There are many Sioux Indians same way as you."

Quite a number of Sioux were present, and they laughed at him. After a few minutes he again spoke to me, "Nez Perce Indian, you are now my friend. From this time on. What have you, mother or father? You can go hunt them up. Wherever they are, you can stay with them."

Then my heart felt good. I hunted for my mother and found her in one Sioux tepee. They gave me everything I asked, just as if I were one of their children.

In spring, one Sioux made himself as a brother to me. Of course it was the sign language we talked. He said to me, "We will go to the Flatheads!"

"I have no moccasins to go there!"

When I spoke that, he replied, "My brother, I have lots of moccasins. You must go with me!"

My Sioux brother was Yakaussioo (Hawk). After six days, one hundred and thirty-two Sioux, myself, and a smaller cousin of mine, making one hundred and thirty-four, were ready to start. You know the Indians, that they always sing when leaving to go somewhere. We were going through the village camp singing, when I heard someone shouting, "One of our chiefs right now is going to head us off!"

Then I heard the chief calling, "Boys, you better not go! You are not enough!"

He told us many times not to go. Finally one of our leaders agreed, "Well, we better not go!"

We were all afoot. There were two of us always behind, my cousin and I. We saw where they camped, and one of my friends said, "That is good, we are now getting to camp!"

I was dry for water. We came to a draw with a little water showing. I drank from that water. Not long until I felt that I had swallowed something. I could hardly speak. I thought to myself, "I have swallowed an *immel* (black waterbug) in the water!"

Then I said to my cousin, "I think I am going to die."

He answered me, "What is wrong with you? You are not going to die with that little thing!"

"I am going to die!"

When I answered him that, my cousin said, "No, you are not going to die. You have something inside you stronger than that!"

I felt my heart was in my throat. I said to him, "I am going to die, I tell you!"

That was three times I answered him that way.

"No! You will not die!" That was three times he told me "NO!"

I was on the ground. I could not lie still. I heard, off toward the right, something calling, "You know I have told you, nothing will kill you!"

I said to my cousin, "Throw me in the pond!"

He threw me in the pond. I lay there a short while, when the water I had swallowed poured out. About the size of my little finger came some blood. I felt like it was lead or something in my mouth, and blood ran just like bleeding lungs.

Then I felt better. My cousin broke open the roll of blood. The *immel* was inside.

My cousin made fun of me. He said, "You were going to die with that little bug?"

"You were saying true! This little bug, you die with it."

I soon felt very fine and went on to camp. When we got there, my cousin told the Sioux Indians, "A brave man like him dying with a little bug! Very short time ago he was being dead, and now he is alive."

The Sioux laughed.

Turning Back to the Old Home

WE GOT ALONG FINE with the Sioux, who remained camped in the same place all the time we were there. We stayed with them until the first part of June (1878). It was then that one Nez Perce made announcement, "Now is about time we go back to our homeland."

Chief Joseph had sent word from bondage for all of his escaped followers to surrender and come to him. We would obey our leader. It was about thirteen men, some nine women and few children that got ready to travel. We were informed that we would be safe because belonging to Joseph's band. But not all of us were of Joseph's band.

We left the Sioux camp all mounted, and the warriors had guns. A few old men and one or two not quite man age, so only five or six could be counted on to fight. Unarmed, we would soon be killed. Our ammunition was about ten cartridges to each rifle.

We came about three camps when we had first trouble with another tribe of Indians. They were the Walk-arounds. There must have been twenty of them. The women got afraid, but one of the men told them not to be scared. He took my arm and said to them, "Look at this boy! He will be in front of us. I am not afraid!"

We then all dismounted and sat down, ready for a peace smoke. One of the enemy rode toward us a little way. My friends said to me, "That Indian will not bother us!"

I said nothing. Soon I got up and went forward. That Walk-around was armed, and I took my rifle. I came closer to him, and he threw me the sign, "You see that sun? This is your last day!"

I answered him, "I am not a woman. I am a man. I am a warrior!"

He made reply, "Take a good look at the sun!"

I threw him the sign, "You are nothing!" Then one of the Walk-arounds got mad. He threw me the sign, "You are nothing but a woman!"

I answered him, "This is good! I will show you what a woman can do with you. Come on!"

All the Walk-arounds got off their horses. They aimed at me, and I yelled. I was a little afraid, and yelled. I came to myself and made my heart as a brave man. I said, "There is nothing here dangerous!"

Then they fired. One brave Indian ran at me. I met him, and we fired at each other. Both missed, and I said to myself, "I will not kill him with the gun. I will kill him with the war club!"

I ran up against his gun muzzle. He missed me and jumped back. I struck and missed him. He was so far from his friends, he turned and ran back to them, leaving his horse.

I took his horse and led it away. I threw the sign at him, "A little while ago you said I was a woman. See what a woman can do! Woman can take horse away from you! Come on now! We will have a little war of our own. You have bothered me a long time!"

He answered me the sign, "No! You have your life. You better go ahead, the way you are traveling!"

I answered, "Yes, you go on toward your home. You are still alive!"

I thought they would get mad, the way I spoke. They rode on the top of a small butte, and we went on. Those Walk-arounds were afraid. They bothered us no more. My friend took my arm again, saying to the people, "Now look what he has done. I told you we have one boy who can do a little fighting. He is the same as a thousand soldiers!"

We moved for two suns, camping nights. Another tribe of Indians saw us. We saw them coming, where they stopped about a quarter mile away. One man threw the sign, "What tribe are you?"

We answered, "Nez Perce."

He signed, "Come on!"

I went to him, where he came to meet me. When I got there, he signed, "You better come on! We have seven tepees only short ways. You can eat anything you want!"

I told my people, "Let's follow them!"

We followed the direction they went. When we reached the camp, the Nez Perce unpacked and unsaddled. I did not dismount. One of our Indians came and said to me, "Come down to the chief's tepee."

"No," I answered, "go on down!"

The Nez Perce went, and I stayed in the saddle. In a little while my mother came running. She spoke, "One old man told me how one of his people is taking the news to the soldiers!"

"Do not tell me. Go tell them where they are eating bread!" was my reply.

My mother ran. Several Nez Perces came out of the tepees. They said, "We will go see the old man who told your mother." It was true enough, the words of the old man. We packed our things and moved from that place.

They were Lemhi Indians who trapped us.

It was about middle afternoon, and we traveled fast. We all understood signs. We knew what it meant when we saw the buffaloes running, stampeding. One man called out, 'Soldiers meeting us!"

We had come to a washout, a gully. We all dropped in there, and I stood down a ways to one side. One man called to me, "We will die this sun!"

I never answered him. He was a little mad, and called again, "We will now die! Just this sun!"

Then I told him, "Shut up! Do not say a word to me! I am a man, a warrior. I will die. That is good! I will make no council!"

That man said no more to me. I thought that was good. I now cleaned my rifle. Soon an old man, Pauh Wahyakt, spoke, "Now I can see!"

That Nez Perce took his pipe and smoked. A little while and came a fog. All over, just like he was wide smoking. You could not see any distance. Then we went. It was not many steps from the soldiers, where we passed each other. We traveled all night.

We got to a place called Mehtottipmachim (Three Double Mountains) in that country. Coming daylight, sun was up when we reached there. We did not stay long. We went a little ways and saw a buffalo. One man remarked, "We are out of meat. We ought to have meat."

"Yes, we ought to have meat," I answered him.

He was standing on a little bench of the hillside, that buffalo. Three of us went after him. When we got near him, it was not a buffalo. It was a *hohots* (grizzly bear).

When that *hohots* saw us, he made for us. He ran us down the hill a ways. He must have been four feet high standing on all his feet. I did not want to tackle with him.

We split up when running our horses. One man ran straight ahead. The *hohots* took after the other hunter. This man turned his horse and circled towards me. That *hohots* was close after him. He called to me, "Get off your horse! We will fight the *hohots!*"

I jumped off my horse and the man came up to me. He sprang from his horse, for the *hohots* was coming fast. He drew his rifle, and I thought, "He will shoot, but we will never kill him with the gun. I will kill him with my war club."

I drew my club and stepped to meet that *hohots*. When close, he raised up. The man fired, but the aim was not to the right place. The bullet struck that *hohot's* nose. As he dropped down to his front feet, I jumped and struck him behind the ear. That *hohots* dropped. He did not get up. I thought, "We have killed him, but we have no use for him.* He is one of the brave men we have killed."

We moved two suns, and then the same tribe of Lemhi

---

* The grizzly is a scavenger. His meat, although fresh, smells and tastes like rotten flesh. Indians would not eat it unless starving.

Indians surrounded us. It was early morning while we were yet in camp. We were not many. There must have been a hundred of them. They threw us the usual sign, "What tribe are you?"

"Nez Perce," we answered.

They did not believe us. We knew they wanted to kill us. Then the Lemhi spoke the sign, "Follow us! Let us go to camp!"

That was another lie the Lemhi told us. We answered, "Go ahead. We will follow you!"

The Lemhi then went, riding fast. The Nez Perce who saved us the other time said, "I will do the same thing! I will smoke!"

Then came—after the smoking—in the same way, a heavy fog. The Lemhi Indians went one way, we took another direction. Maybe the Lemhis looked for us. I do not know, but they never found us. We left our little food right there where we saw the Lemhi Indians. We packed from that camp in a big hurry.

We now moved three suns without anything to eat. We hunted and hunted. Nothing could we find. No birds to kill! No deer, no rabbits! Nothing anywhere!

The fourth sun came, and no food. Two men went ahead looking for game. I was lying down quite a ways from camp. A man came to me as I lay there. He had a whip, and struck me with it. He said, 'You, a brave man! You are going to starve to death? Stand up! Look for something to eat!"

I stood up and threw my blanket down. I took my rifle and went up the hill. I went about three miles. There was nothing over that way. No game, no white man's stock.

Changing direction, I came to the top of a ridge. Down below must have been fifty cattle. When I saw those cattle, just as fast as I could, I went for camp. I was not the size I am now. I was a slim fellow. I could go swiftly—could go for a long time. When a little way from camp, I heard one man telling the women, "We are going to starve to death!"

He was not one of two men who had hunted for game. I went on where my blanket was and sat down. The same man who whipped me came and asked, "Did you find anything to eat?"

"Yes, I answered him."

"He has found food," this man told the women.

We got our horses, saddled, and went, all of us. We passed the two men who were looking for game. They told the women, "He is lying! There is nothing around close."

The same man who struck me with the whip then asked me, "Did you find anything to eat?"

"Yes," I answered him.

Then we went fast. When we came to where we could see, I said, "Look! What is that? I never tell the lie to anyone. You know yourself we are starving!"

When they saw the cattle they were ashamed. But they were glad for those cattle. We went down near the herd and unpacked. I had found them, so I shot the first steer. Then another man shot one.

That was the time we had meat.

Next morning we left that place. White people do not know the ways of our tribe. We can dry meat in one night. A whole steer, or two. Whatever it is, we can dry it all. Everything was packed up and ready. The camp went on ahead, but I stayed behind as most always. After about one hour I got on my horse and went. I rode fast. When I could see the Nez Perce, they threw a blanket up.

That told me, "Hurry!"

I ran my horse fast. When I reached them they told me some white men were coming, but quite a little distance away. We agreed that we would meet them, but not fight or kill them. They might have a sack of flour to give us. After a council we said, "We will go see them."

We then went to their camp. Nobody around. Those white men had not arrived. One man said, "Let us wait for them."

That would be good, so we dismounted. While we sat around, our horses were eating. In a short while, I saw three white men coming. When they saw us, they called in rough voice, "Get out from there!"

They brought down their guns, working the levers, ready to shoot. I thought to myself, "Well, I guess they want a little trouble!"

They were calling us all names they could think. One of them came close as that (indicating twenty feet). He might shoot, and one Nez Perce said to me, "Grab your gun!"

I took my gun and set it off to one side. I had my war club all the time with me. I stepped to meet the white man, and he yelled something I did not understand at me. I dodged under his gun and knocked him over. He was getting up when I struck him on the head. He fell back and did not move.

One white man cried when he saw his friend not living. He raised his hands, and I told him, speaking Nez Perce, "Yes, my friend, you are alive. When calling me, it was just giving yourself to death. I did not want to kill this man. I do not want to kill you."

I went up to him and took his gun. One Nez Perce boy spoke some English. I said to him, "Tell this white man to give us flour, what he has got."

When this was interpreted to him the man replied, "Yes, lots of flour. Come on!"

He opened the door and asked how much flour we wanted. The sacks weighed one hundred pounds. We told him we would take one sack.

Those men had two soldier saddles, and I thought, "They are soldiers!" When they yelled at me, I noticed the saddles. Then I knew they were soldiers. That was why I struck the man. I asked them, "You soldiers, or just white men?"

They did not answer what they were. After short time I said again, "I am asking you, what? You soldiers? Where is your army?" When I spoke that, one of them replied, "Yes, I have been in the army. I just quit lately. That is the reason for those saddles."

We left the two white men there. It was eight of us came to see them about flour.

Soldiers Against Indians

I DO NOT KNOW who took word to the soldiers. Maybe the soldiers just followed us. This very morning when we were going after beef, they were where we had taken guns from the two men the evening before. Only about two and one-half miles from us.

But we did not know this. We went back on the trail. Tomamo (not Tabador, but another Indian of the same name) was about fifteen steps in the lead. We ran our horses to the creek. We crossed and followed Tomamo through the brush. We could hear his horse running. Then I heard a gun report. I thought someone was killing the beef. Tomamo called, "Where are you boys?"

He came back to us and said, "I just ran my horse through the brush and saw dust. I thought cattle were running. When dust settled, it was a bunch of soldiers. They are close enough to shoot us."

All of us rode through the brush where we could see the house. We watched the soldiers, a troop of cavalry. Tabador said, "Let's have a war right now!"

We missed Tomamo. He had gone aside a way, making a little war of his own. When the soldiers saw us, they fired. I did not dodge, as, putting my rifle by a tree, I fired. Rifles from the soldiers were popping fast. Short of ammunition, we made only a few replies. We did not fight much. It was only a short time of shooting.

One soldier drew near us—ran his horse toward us. He must have gone crazy or something. I stepped to meet him. When only a little ways from me, he jumped from his horse. Afoot, he turned and ran back to the other soldiers. Left his horse there standing. Maybe he was hit by one of our bullets. I took his horse.

What I am telling you are facts. What happened in those days of trouble. I am telling no other than facts, what I saw and did. I think now that soldier could not manage his horse.

Four of us went to have Indian fight. Soldiers began digging the ground, burying themselves. We held council. I said, "If soldiers bury themselves, we can do nothing. We better let them alone."

"No use troubling them! They have trenches. We will get killed," Tabador told us.

We quit. We left the soldiers to finish burying themselves.

A little farther than a rifle shot, we went up a hill. Cattle there feeding in open place. I directed the boys, "Drive the cattle out from that ground. No protection from danger there."

They brought the cattle where it was not quite so open. Those cattle were about two years old. We picked a fat one and killed it. The soldiers were watching us, and we watching them.

Earlier, a soldier who shot at Tabador but missed him, was thrown by his horse, which ran away. Ooyekun now saw this horse on the hillside below us, its foot on the bridle rein. Soldiers were watching the horse and, seeing us looking, one came afoot towards it. He did not get far. A shot sent him running for his dugout shelter.

Tomamo now said, "I am going to get that horse!"

He walked towards the horse. It was just the same. Soldiers fired at him, and he got not near that horse. He ran back from the bullets. Left the horse with foot still on its bridle rein. Tabador now said to everybody, "Whoever wants that horse, go get him!"

Nobody wanted to go. No one cared for that horse. I, too, was scared. Skoloom said, "Brother-in-law, you better get that horse!"

I got ashamed to refuse. I had to go! I stripped my clothes, getting ready. I ran a little, then trotted down the hill slowly. No use hurrying into danger. The soldiers shot at me. I kept going: they kept shooting. I did not get small heart. I became as not afraid. My heart now believed, and I did not get scared. I found my *Wyakin*—just the air. Soldiers could hit nothing of the air. I came to the horse, raised his foot and got the hoof off the bridle. Soldiers did not fire at me after I got there. Maybe they did not like to shoot the horse. I led my prize up where

Indians were butchering. Skoloom said to me, 'Thank you, my brother-in-law. We are going to pack that soldier horse with meat."

We did pack that soldier horse, and we led him away. Soldiers still in their trenches, we left them. Only eight of us, but the soldiers did not try stopping us. They did not leave their shelter to take their horse or fight us. We did not think much of those soldiers.

We went on the trail and came up with the others in about six or seven miles. Before joining them, I told them, "Do not tell the women about seeing soldiers. They will be scared and eat no dinner. After eating, we can tell them our story."

We stopped for dinner. One man not with us for the beef talked to me. I told him, "We did not come till we have a little trouble."

The women got excited. I said to them, "Let us eat first. Then we will talk!"

They did as I said. The women laughed as they cooked the meat. After dinner the order was called, "Pack up!"

Everything was soon packed, ready to ride. The women told me, "We are all ready."

"Soldiers just back of us. We had a little war."

When I told them that, my mother laughed. She said, "I do not get excited if you tell it before dinner. When they claim to get best of you men, and I am alone, then I get scared!"

We moved camp, coming to the summit of a mountain as the sun went down. We could look back on the trail where we had come. We saw one soldier's horse standing on the trail. Only one trail, and he could go nowhere else. We said, "We will wait for him here. If he comes, we will fire on him."

We stayed there, waiting for the soldiers. We listened, if we could hear them coming in the night. I think they were scared. They never came near us.

Morning came, and after breakfast we traveled till noon. We stopped and after eating something, went on. We found a white man who showed us a trail. A very little trail, over a kind of mountain. It was middle of afternoon when we dropped down into a big canyon. Wottolen, the leader, said, "We will camp here. We will stay all afternoon and watch if soldiers come."

The sun went down. No soldiers had come. That night we watched again for soldiers. Next morning, we wanted sleep, so we stayed another night. We waited on the trail for soldiers, if they showed up.

Came another morning, and we went. It was a zigzag trail, and steep for the horses. Tomamo called: "Look back!"

Looking, we saw dust about one mile away. Everybody said, "Soldiers coming!"

Women and men laughed. Nobody got excited. We finished climbing the trail to the top of the mountain. We went down a small creek, heading up on the mountain. From where we saw the dust, we went about two miles and camped at a spring. It was nine or ten o'clock when we stopped there. At noon one old man told us, "Lots of salmon here. We will look for salmon. We will eat!"

Every man, and some women, went looking for salmon. Only six women and seven children left in camp. We did not think well. We forgot that soldiers might be following behind. We acted as not knowing anything. Those women and children in camp! It was just like giving them to the soldiers. All this came to me, and I thought, "No use that I go looking for salmon. Not good that I go fishing. Soldiers may now be in our camp. I will go back to our camp!"

I returned quickly to camp. I found the women in the shade, patching worn moccasins. A good shade, and I lay down to rest. I was not scared at all. I went to sleep. I do not know what the white man calls that sight which came to me. I went into that sleep we call *kahauto weyakakaun* (short life). I slept sound. I was sleeping a good rest! Then something pushed on my shoulder, and I heard a voice calling:

"Wake up! You are dead! Look!"

Then after that voice I saw it! Like a cloudy sun—I saw it: full clouds all over! No open places! Nothing clear anywhere!

But it was not clouds. It was smoke from guns in battle, as when soldiers try to kill. I could see it—smoke rolling and curling around. The voice said, "Look back to your own country. Your own Wallowa."

I looked that way. A small opening formed in that smoke. Through that break I saw my Wallowa. The prairies, the mountains, the streams, the lake. The voice now told me, "Your life has escaped through where you are looking. You will not die!"

I awoke, found I was on my feet. I sat down. My mother said to me, "You were dreaming?"

I replied to my mother, "Make your heart strong. Do not get excited. We are now surrounded. Maybe in a few minutes you will hear the guns. While we have been coming slow, soldiers have been crowding us close."

Some way off, I saw strange Indian boys driving our horses. Six good horses—good horses gone. The Salish had picked our best horses. Those Salish Indians were helping the soldiers.

I now painted my hair with white earth, preparing for war. That smoke-cloud was still over me. I did not try to move from it. Nothing could now go through my body. No bullets from the enemy could hurt me. For this purpose did I paint. I understood the voice.

Mounting a horse, I hurried back over the trail. It was to try finding the six horses the Salish took. Riding a quarter mile, maybe half mile, I ran into a bunch of soldiers. Those soldiers had seen me coming. They had fixed a trap.

Some small fir trees growing there stood thick. I rode through them and, passing on a short ways, I saw a soldier sitting on a fallen tree. What was he doing there? I knew not, and did not bother him.

There were scattered pine trees, and I went around one of the biggest. I passed one soldier close. He was aiming his gun at me. It was leveled at my ear, as I could well see. That soldier was not four steps from me. That soldier was not alone. I did not see all, but four or five guns were leveled. They fired, and it was just as thunder in my ears. So close, smoke fogged all through my clothes. I could see nothing! I grew excited. Knew not anything, because of the noise. I did not know I was yelling as a drunk man. All like fire, I was out of sense. I had thought my heart right, but I lost myself.

It was just like dreaming! Twice I yelled. Third time I yelled I found myself. My *Wyakin* had come to aid me. It was as waking from sleep, from dreaming. I felt fine. I am telling you true. I was no longer afraid. I did not care how many soldiers there were. Understanding, I now knew they could not hurt me.

They could be nothing to me.

I gave the war whoop. Whirling my horse, down the steep hill, over logs I went. Soldiers were ahead of me. Blocking the way! They fired from all around. I did not stop for anything. Only changed to a little different direction.

Again I was close to the enemy. It was more of the soldiers waiting for me, and I heard shooting at the camp. I did not know which way was best to go, but I still aimed for camp. Soldiers saw me and must have thought, "Another Injun crazy."

They were not soldiers with cannon. Wearing white shirts, some soldiers, (citizens) ran toward me. They thought to kill me first. But I was not stopping for them. I did not try shooting. Only I must get away.

A soldier was ahead of me, just to one side. He was waiting to shoot as soon as I came up. As I passed that soldier, he nearly poked me with his gun. He shot my horse through the withers. I did not fall with my horse. I lit on my feet and went out from there. That soldier got no other shot at me. They were all calling, but I knew not their words.

I could see down to camp, surrounded on my side by soldiers. I did not run, could not run. Too much fallen timber. I passed other soldiers who fired at me. I dodged on down the way. Among tangled logs I thought only of getting to camp. Escaping through the fallen trees, I reached camp. Nobody there! Tabador called from where he was sheltered, then came out and said, "Brother-in-law, we are going to die. We will not run away!"

I knew Tabador a brave man, and I answered him, "All right.

We can die right here. The soldiers shall not drive us from our last blankets!"

Tabador did not give a small heart. It was like he was giving me a big heart, for I was going to die with him.

But those soldiers made no more attack.

It was sunset. I sat down just as I am now. No blanket, no saddle, no horse. We were afoot. A little way from me just across the canyon, soldiers had all our horses. I was thinking hard. Soldiers still over there, fixing to camp.

Came the dusk. We heard the soldiers chopping wood. We did not know if cutting firewood, or for trench protection from our bullets.

Full dark settled. The other Indians all came from safe hiding. We still heard the chopping. Henry Tabador, the half-blood Indian, called, "Why are you making trenches? Come over! We will have a war!"

They never answered. We were not mad at them. We only wanted to get back to Lapwai. But we acted right with them. We could not turn them down if they wanted to be friendly. It was near the end. We only had a little way more to travel, but all our horses were gone. Skoloom said to me, "Let us get back our horses!"

"I can hardly walk," I answered him.

"What is wrong with your leg?" he asked me.

"I dragged my leg," I told him. "Knee bone stiff."

I did not think I could go with anybody. But there were only us two, and Tabador spoke again: "I can not go alone. You must go with me."

"If you say that, I will go with you," I told him.

Skoloom told the plan to the other men, and said, "I do not want to force any of you, my friends, but if you want to go I will be glad. When there we will see how to recover our horses."

Peopeo Tholekt, Ooyekun, Tabador, and Soklahtomah, five of us would go. It must have been near middle of night, and we could hear soldiers still chopping. They had a fire, and I told the men, "We must go there and see."

We crossed the creek and came opposite the soldiers' fire. It was a big fire and soldiers were standing around in the light. Skoloom told his plans to Peopeo Tholekt, "My brother-in-law will go with me up above the soldiers' camp. You men circle the other way. If you hear us shoot, you do the same. We will try getting our horses some way."

Skoloom and I went up the hill, circling to far side of soldiers. They were moving about the fire. We crawled closer, but it was still long shooting through brush. We fired and heard the guns of the other three Indians. We all gave loud war whoops. We shot only one time. Too much woods and no soldiers now seen. They dodged down among the logs.

After we went away, the soldiers commenced shooting. We could not tell direction of their shots. We took everything they had, food and packsaddles. Their horses were tied up. We drove our own horses towards our camp, and got them all.

Next morning Tabador called across to the soldiers, "What you doing over there? You followed us a long ways. Come over if you want to have a talk!"

The soldiers never answered. We thought they were afraid. We asked the interpreter to tell them again, so he called, "Do you want trouble?"

There came no answer. Maybe they had left during the darkness. We did not go see if they were still there. We now had our horses, and nobody hurt. That was all we wanted.

Those soldiers and citizens we could not count. They appeared more than of us. They got first advantage, but they killed no Indians, got no horses. We recovered all our horses.

We saw no more of those soldiers, so we packed and left. We came to a small stream (Clear Creek) where we camped. While in this camp some Nez Perce came to us, three of General Howard's "good" men—Lawyer and two policemen. One used the bad language to us. Soklahtomah got up and said, "I will get my whip and whip that man."

He then took his quirt and whipped him. One of our men stopped him from striking more. Soklahtomah said to this whipped man, "You are the *religious* man! Why do you use the bad language? You are one of *Christian* men helping Agent Monteith and General Howard! All you Christian people joined to make the war! You caused the trouble! You made a *thief* treaty! Chiefs have been killed! Good men have been killed! Good women and little children have been killed! Babies too small to walk, crippled and killed! All this because of you Christians! Many of our people taken prisoners will never see this country again.

"Many good white people did not want war, but could not help themselves. They got killed because you Christian people helped Agent Monteith and old General Howard. I could kill you right now!"

"Do not kill us! Do not kill us!" begged General Howard's good men.

Soklahtomah was mad. All the Indians were mad. During this time one of Lawyer's policemen, Kipkip Elwhekin said to Wottolen, "You come with me to the Agency!"

"No! I will not go with you to the Agency!" replied Wottolen.

Kip again said, "Yes, you are coming to the Agency. You will not be hurt."

Wottolen, more mad, answered: "No! Kip, you are not headman! You do not know what they can do to me. Not headman, you could not help me. You would not help me if you could. I am doing no harm. I do not steal anything. Only traveling around to find some of my own property, my own cache."

Kip was silent for short moments. Then he said, "You are going with me and have a talk with the Agent! You hear me?"

Wottolen was now full mad. He was standing, his rifle on the ground. Partly lifting it, he told Kip, "I hear what you say. Kip, you better go! I am telling you three times, I am not going with you! Kip, you better go now. Go before you get in trouble! If any women want to go with you, take them. Any not wanting to go will stay with me. Go, Kip! Be quick with your going!"

Kip answered, "Yes, I will go right now!"

I, Yellow Wolf, made no council with those Christian Nez Perce. I did not want any talk with them. My heart felt poor. Everything was against us. I considered, and then said to my mother:

"You and the other women better go with these, General Howard's men. For me, I will stay in the prairie like a coyote. I have no home!"

My mother did not cry. She spoke to some women, then made answer to me: "Yes, we will go with General Howard's men." A few of the women and my mother then went with Kip and his Christian policemen.

Our party now separated. Wottolen, leader of those from White Bird's band, had talked strong to the men from the Agency who came to us. His heart was heavy, but he would not surrender. Wottolen and most of the others headed for old camping grounds in the White Bird country. Going over a mountain, there was no timber, no way to hide themselves from being seen. Police from the Agency were watching everywhere.

Wottolen, an *inatsinpun* (prophet), said, "Do not be afraid! Something will help us!" Soon the sun was covered over. It grew dark. Wottolen declared, "This is what I was telling you would happen for us! No enemy can now see us passing through the open land! I asked for this!"

They all reached the Salmon River without being seen. The women with Wottolen afterwards surrendered. Some of the men also surrendered.

A Voluntary Surrender

WE STARTED and reached Lapwai, which is now Spalding, about noon. We stopped at the store. An Indian policeman took me to the Agency. The Agent instructed this policeman, "Sit around until one o'clock. I will see him and talk to him then."

While waiting, three men came and shook hands with me.

One was Charles Monteith, brother to the Agent. Many Indians gathered around me. They were saying to me, "If you make any mistake, they will hang you. Tell nothing but the truth, the facts."

They kept telling that to me. Told it many times. I got mad when they talked that so much, and I spoke the order, "Shut up! Say no more! If the old Agent makes his mind to hang me, I will take it. It is all right. He will get fat off me when he hangs me. That is reason I come to this Reservation!"

They said no more. They did not want me to get hanged or killed. The Indian policeman came and told me, "About noon, about half an hour, the Agent will see you and talk to you."

I never answered. Then the policeman asked me, "Do you hear?"

That policeman was one of the Christian Indians.

I replied, "I do not want to listen to anyone. If I belonged here, you could talk. If I was raising anything, whatever stock I might raise, then I would come and see the Agent, who might help me. When the Agent comes will be time if I want to talk. I am one of the warriors! I never belonged here. I am a stranger! You will all know if the Agent hangs me, without saying anything. If he hangs me, that will be good. I no longer have a home!"

That Indian policeman said no more to me.

I stayed a long time in the office, waiting. Finally the policeman came to me again and said, "I am just letting you know that the Agent will see you in short minutes."

"Mr. Monteith is still the Agent?" I asked him.

"Yes, he is the Agent," he told me.

"Do not tell me anything about him. If some of the good men come to me, I will listen."

That is all the reply I made to the Indian policeman. I did not want to know when the Agent was coming. Then I heard his steps in the other room. I knew those steps! He opened the door and came in. I did not look around, but I knew who it was. The same man! I felt him—as with a needle he pierced the hearts of our chiefs—our chiefs killed! He stood looking at me. I did not look at him. I did not want to see his face. I just turned to one side. Then the Agent spoke, through an interpreter.

"Look at me!"

No, I did not look at him at all! He spoke again, "I know you. You are a very good boy. I would not bother you!"

He walked up to me and shook hands with me. I thought not to touch his hand, but I did. He said, commandingly, "You must tell what you know. You were fighting General Howard. Four days ago you had a battle with the soldiers. They killed six Indians of you, and captured two women."

That was what the Agent said to me. I answered, "No!" I thought, "Why is the old Agent asking me?"

"You are a pretty good boy."

When the Agent said that, I replied, "No! I do not want to speak about such things as that. Everything is over! The war is quit! I do not want it brought back as new. I do not want to talk, for everything is quit. Look at me (standing in demonstration, both arms lifted)! I have no weapons about me! I do not want to speak about war any more. It is gone! It is like you taking gun and shooting me again, the way you are speaking."

Eeikish Pah: The Hot Place

The Agent showed some mad. He walked around a little. But before he could make answer, whatever was his mind, a noise outside came fast. The door opened, and there came in an officer, a sergeant, and a few soldiers. The officer made request, "Where is that Indian who came and wanted interpreter?"

"There he is," and they pointed to me.

Those soldiers shook hands with me. They told me to stand up and come with them. I went as they said. They put me in the jail (guard house). They did not stay there fifteen or twenty minutes, but went right away.

In a short while I heard steps outside. Then the door opened, and quickly entered Lieutenant or Captain, named, I think, Fellis. He shook hands with me, and asked, "Who is your chief?"

"My chief was Joseph," I told him.

Of course we talked through an army interpreter. When I said, "Chief Joseph," that officer replied, "Yes, I understand. That is why I sent the lieutenant and sergeant. I sent them because I know the Agent. He will never help you. The white men are mad about you Indians, and if they found you on the Reservation, they would kill you. The Agent can do nothing. He would do nothing. The white men will not bother you, so long as you are in here. Our soldiers will protect you. But do not think you are prisoner. We put you here just to be away from the whites."

That was what the captain told me all the way through. Then he began asking questions. He said, "I am glad you came to your home country. You tell us the story true what you did as you came. Swear to it. If you lie, the Government will punish you."

I gave him the answer, "Yes, I thought you a good man. I came over to see you, if all right. I can not swear anything (i.e., the Christian oath)!"

That captain looked strong at me. Then he spoke, "I am going to ask you. Did you take a horse, kill a cow, or something? I want you to tell all."

"Yes, I replied. "I am glad you asked me that. War was quit. Chiefs on both sides shook hands. Since I was in a strange country, and all had been settled, I thought to come back to my own country. We made no trouble as we came along. But some took shots at us. Would that make you mad? What would you think? Would you shoot, or just say, 'I am going to die?' "

"I want you to tell only truth so the Government will protect you," the officer made reply. "Anybody will shoot in self-protection. I would do that."

"Yes," I told him, "I am telling truth. When anybody takes the gun to me, I will take his horse. Will shoot him, or he may get away. They bring the gun on themselves."

The officer said, "That is so." He then took a rolled paper, and looking at it, continued speaking, "This is White Bird's country. Why were you there?"

I did not go there for trouble. We went to get cached stuff. Charley Wood took a shot at us, and of course we took his horse."

"Report is you took Charley Wood's horse?"

"Yes. He took a shot at me. I made my mind to take his horse and did so. Not for nothing did we take that horse. We saw another man's brand on the buckskin. Wood did not own him. Must have stolen him."

"You are telling truth?"

"Yes."

"You had no right taking that horse. You should have witness. You might get in prison three or fours years."

That would be all right if they wanted to send me there. The officer looked at more papers, then spoke again, "You tell the truth. In the mountains you found a horse with saddle on?"

"Yes."

"Good horse? Did you take it?"

"I do not deny it."

"You had a fight with soldiers. Those soldiers killed six men and captured two women from you."

"Yes," I said, "it was about two suns before the real fight. The soldiers fired on some of us when we went to get beef. That made us mad, and we had a little fight. I took one soldier's horse which got away from us. We found one horse saddled and took it. Afterwards came the fight, but nobody was killed, nobody wounded. No women captured."

"Is horse you got with saddle here?" the officer asked.

"No, I gave that horse to Skoloom," I answered.

"Yes, you are the party soldiers took women, children, and horses from."

"No! We got all our horses back. No women, no children captured."

"You are telling lies?"

"No! They killed none of us."

"You are telling truth?"

It was three times this officer asked that question. I answered him. "Yes, I am telling true. If that had happened, any killed, any captured, I would not deny it."

The officer made no more questions. He now said, "I am glad you tell the truth. If Skoloom will bring in that horse, and the man (owner) comes along within a year, we will give it to him. Since you left Canada, and killed some people on the trail, somebody will trail you here. For this reason you must stay with soldiers for protection. You were making a new war, but other parties, whites, started it first. I am glad you told everything. If they trail you here and make complaint, we will have this, your story, as evidence for you. We will also take good care of other Indians coming from Canada."

Then he asked, "Who is this with you?"

"My cousin. I slept in his house last night. He brought me to the Agent this noon," I told him.

When I answered him that, he wrote on a paper that I was from Canada and turned me over to the sergeant of the soldier guards, with instructions to keep me from trouble. He then shook hands with me, and told me I was to go to that place (Indian Territory). Said he was glad I was now back from Canada, and advised, "Do no wrong, and all will be well for you."

That was what the captain told me all the way through. After that I was treated right while prisoner there. I had no more trouble with anyone. From that time, I have come through safe to this night (May, 1935).

I went with the sergeant. When the soldiers saw us coming, they waited for us. They took me to a building, their room. Then we went to the next room. They asked, "You starving?" They divided crackers with all.

After four or five suns, Tabador came of his own will. A few nights after, we heard a calling to soldiers, wanting to "leave somebody in jail." Then soon I heard horses running up the road. Whoever did that calling to leave somebody in jail, escaped from the soldier guards. Whites had come to kill us but they did not fool the soldiers. After that we were watched carefully. No white men could pass who did not look good.

A band of eleven men and one woman of White Bird's band had come through from the Sioux camp to the Salmon River about fifteen days ahead of us. The leader, Tahmiteahkun, was a brave warrior. The woman with them was his wife. This band never was captured.

A few days after Tabador came, five more came and surrendered of their own mind. The Agent was glad to see them, but he must take them to the soldiers. He told the soldier captain how they had escaped from Canada. That they must be protected from whites mad at them. Must stay close around and sleep in jail nights. The Indians were told not to go too far away in daytime. Whites might kill them. They were kept around there, but were not made to work. Never were sent to the Territory, but remained on the Nez Perce Reservation.

Tahmiteahkun, his wife, and the other four men stayed in the mountains for some time. Never were captured.

There were four others at this jail, all running loose. Four women, among them my mother. They came in with the Kamiah Indians, Lawyer, and the policemen after we parted. Chief Joseph's daughter was among them. But she was not brought to the jail, was not sent to the Indian Territory.

I was not permitted liberty, but kept locked inside. Another man in the Spokane jail was under lock all the time he was there. We were never fed heavy, but did not go hungry.

I was sent to the Territory with these people—nine others—of Chief Joseph's band. There we united with our old friends and relations—those left of them.

The horse and saddle I rode to the Agency, I took from an unfriendly white man (Charley Wood). The Government got them. Government kept all horses and saddles that General Miles got from us at the last battle. We lost everything. Many horses, many cattle on Snake and Salmon rivers. Only the few clothes I had on and my blanket were left me.

My war club which I had carried all through the war, I held onto. Keeping it concealed in my legging, I had it while in prison. I carried it when being taken to bondage. Kept it all the snows, the same club I gave you.

We were not badly treated in captivity. We were free so long as we did not come this way, towards Idaho and Wallowa. We had schools, only the climate killed many of us. All the newborn babies died, and many of the old people too. It was the climate. Everything so different from our old homes. No mountains, no springs, no clear running rivers. We called where we were held Eeikish Pah (Hot Place). All the time, night and day, we suffered from the climate. For the first year, they kept us all where many got shaking sickness, chills, hot fever.

We were always lonely for our old-time homes.

Chapman was there during entire years of our captivity as interpreter. He lived with a Modoc woman as his wife, but left her there when he came back with us in 1885. Of course Chapman was Government employed. Andy Davenport was also interpreter, but Chapman was the main one. James Rueben sometimes did interpreting.

When finally released from bondage (1885), brought back to this country, religion had to do with where they placed us. We believed in our own Hunyewat (God, or Deity). We had our own Ahkunkenekoo (Land Above). Hunyewat gives us food, clothing, everything. Because we respected our religion, we were not allowed to go on the Nez Perce Reservation. When we reached Wallula, the interpreter asked us, "Where you want to go? Lapwai and be Christian, or Colville and just be yourself?"

No other question was asked us. That same had been said to us in our bondage after knowing we were to be returned from there. We answered to go to Colville Reservation.

Chief Joseph was not given choice where to go. But he had the promise that as soon as the Government got Wallowa straightened out, he could go there with his band. That was never to be.

On the Colville we found wild game aplenty. Fish, berries, and all kinds of roots. Everything so fine many wanted to remain there, after learning that Wallowa was not to be returned to us. Chief Moses advised Joseph to stay. The Indians were good to us. Gave us horses, and other useful property and goods. Deer everywhere, and good salmon at Keller. It was better than Idaho, where all Christian Nez Perce and whites were against us.

I have two sons, but have never told them of my warday fighting. I want them to see this story, all that I have given you. It is a true story, all as I have told you. It is a true history, what I have seen and done.

This is all for me to tell of the war, and of our after hardships. The story will be for people who come after us. For them to see, to know what was done here. Reasons for the war, never before told. Nobody to help us tell our side—the whites told only one side. Told it to please themselves. Told much that is not true. Only his own best deeds, only the worst deeds of the Indians, has the white man told.

INDEX

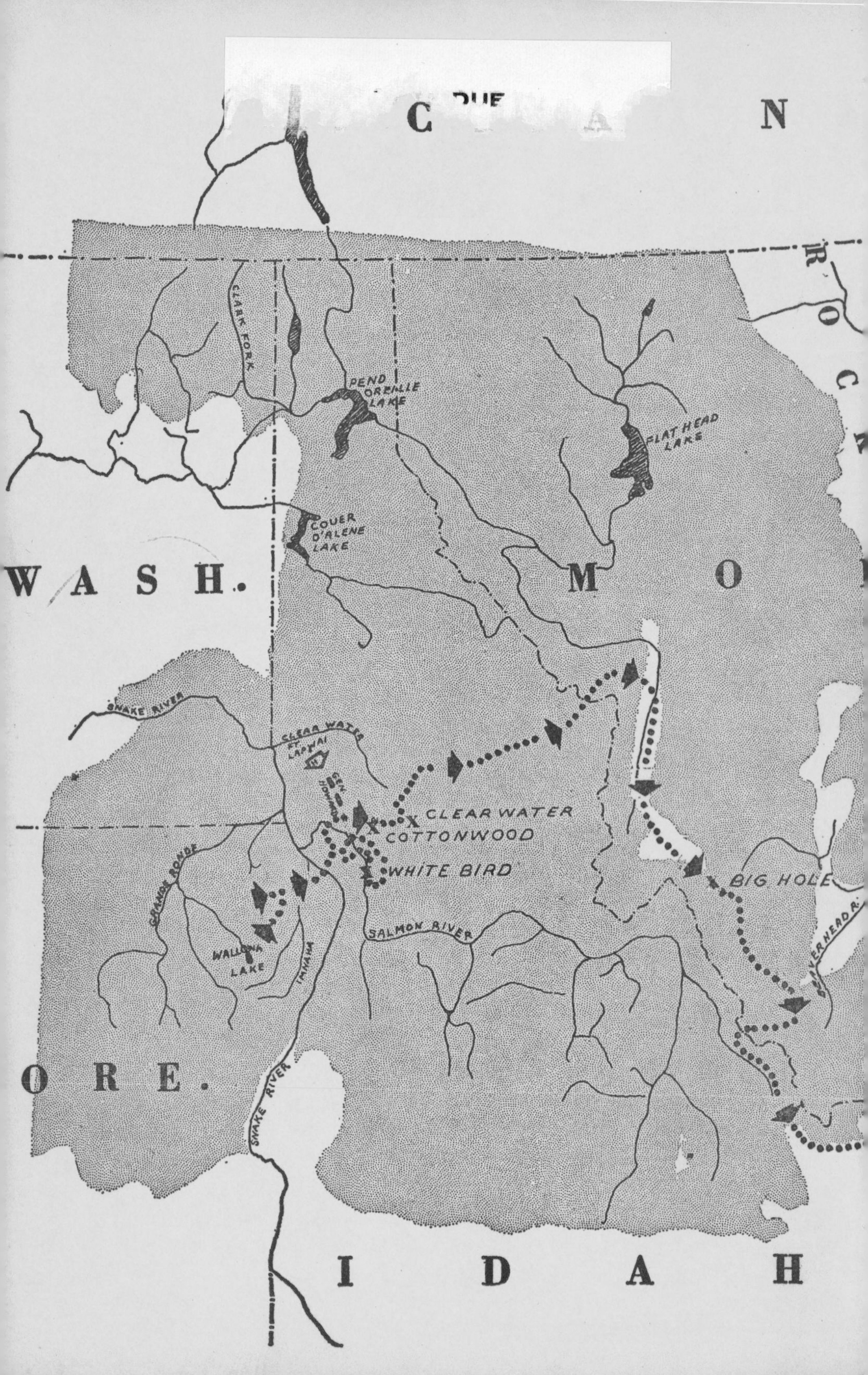
C
N
R
O
C
WASH.
M
O
ORE.
I D A H
CLARK FORK
PEND OREILLE LAKE
FLATHEAD LAKE
COUER D'ALENE LAKE
SNAKE RIVER
CLEAR WATER
FT. LAPWAI
GEN. HOWARD
CLEAR WATER
COTTONWOOD
WHITE BIRD
GRANDE RONDE
WALLOWA LAKE
IMNAHA
SALMON RIVER
BIG HOLE
SNAKE RIVER